THE RENAISSANCE IN POLAND

Photographs

Zbigniew Kamykowski

Edmund Kupiecki

Helena and Stefan Kozakiewiczowie

THE RENAISSANCE IN POLAND

Arkady Publishers · Warsaw

Art editor

Henryk Białoskórski

Translated by

Doreen Heaton Potworowska

Verified by

Edward Rothert

Original title: Renesans w Polsce

Copyright by Arkady Publishers • Warsaw 1976

Printed in Poland

by "Dom Słowa Polskiego", Warsaw

Contents

Authors' Preface

*The following album covers not only works of art executed in Poland
but also a few examples of artistic imports from other countries,
closely connected with Polish culture and commissioned by Polish
patrons. For we consider that without the latter, mainly "object d'art",
the picture of Renaissance art in Poland woult be incomplete.
Much of Poland's Renaissance architecture was, especially in Gdańsk
and western Poland, almost totally destroyed during the last war and
its present state is little less than a complete reconstruction. This is
also the case with certain buildings which were destroyed earlier and
have now also been restored to their original appearance. A number
of these are included in this album. We fully realize that what we are
presenting to the reader are works of art that are not always
entirely authentic, but where this is so, every one of them is, in
accordance with the principles of the Polish contemporary school
of conservation, not only a faithful replica, but also comprises
whatever may have been rescued, often very little, of the original
décor. Thus the style of these buildings has been reproduced unaltered
and this, we think, justifies our displaying them here; in any case the
pertinent explanation is given in the commentaries.
Thanks to the excellent photographs, taken specially for this album,
the works of art of the Polish Renaissance are in many cases revealed
to us anew, in composition that bring out frequently overlooked values.
That was exactly what we hoped: that the efflorescence of art in
Poland during Renaissance would thereby be made more vivid and
illustrated more fully and more comprehensively than ever before.*

BEGINNINGS AND EARLY DEVELOPMENT

OF THE RENAISSANCE IN POLAND, 1500—1545

In its beginnings and early period of development—the first decades of the 16th century—Renaissance art in Poland presentsus with a dual aspect. On the one hand, highly skilled Tuscan artists and craftsmen, reached who Poland mainly through Hungary, brought Italian architecture and sculpture in a relatively pure version to Cracow (Kraków), then the Polish capital, from which it emanated sporadically to certain, sometimes distant parts of the powerful realm of the Jagiellonian dynasty. And on the other, the new artistic concepts and approaches to form, gradually infiltrated the Gothic tradition in Polish art, often via Central European centres; this was reflected not only in architecture and sculpture, but also in painting, design and handicrafts. In both cases the hub of these new ideas was Cracow, a vigorous centre of late-Gothic art evolving into the principal base of its Renaissance succession. The patronage of the royal and episcopal courts encouraged the Italian trend; burgesses and guilds proved favourable soil for the second. But this division should not be treated too rigorously. For a medley of styles occurred at the meeting-point of these currents and imported works of art played an important role in both.

It is impossible to consider the art of the Polish Renaissance in itself alone without setting it against the general European background; the artists active here were too gifted, their works too accomplished, their genetic connections with other centres too strong and their later development too independent. In its pure version the new style surfaced in Cracow and there, too, arose its first centre, evidence that before the Italian Renaissance branched out northwards or westwards, it had carved out a passage to the mid-Danube and thence towards countries farther east. It was still only taking root in Italy outside Tuscany when, about 1450, a large and important stronghold grew up in Hungary around the royal court in Buda; and long before it had swept the whole of Italy, it had, about 1470, reached Moscow, through North-Italian artists, where however, it was short-lived, being crushed into the bedrock of local tradition and shortly all but absorbed by it.

In the meantime, Poland had already appeared on the artistic map of the spreading Renaissance. Its art first arrived just after 1500 from Hungary with which she had dynastic ties, the way having been paved and then secured in both countries by Humanism. The Renaissance blossomed vigorously in Poland as it continued to do in Hungary throughout the first quarter of the 16th century. In both cases the chief influence came from Tuscan artists. But following Hungary's occupation by the Turks after the Battle of Mohàcs in 1526, it was left to Poland, seconded by Bohemia, to become the new art's champion east of Germany in the European lists; at a time when north and west of the Alps the new style was being entrenched in national centres by artists from various parts of Italy, Poland alone upheld the primacy of the Tuscans.

Humanism reached Poland about the mid-15th century when it already had its Polish representatives. The new outlook was propagated by Callimachus (Filippo Buonaccorsi), tutor to the sons of King Casimir the Jagiellon, from 1472. Its current gathered force at the turn of the 15th-16th centuries, lent momentum by the inflow of Italian scholars and to an even greater extent, by the journeys made to Italy by Poles, mainly churchmen, nobles and the wealthier gentry. Although they were drawn there not so much by interests in culture and art as by a desire for practical knowledge—legal, economic and political—or else for purposes of diplomacy or commerce, they too served to bring the message of Humanism to Poland, where it spread during the reigns not only of John Albert (1492—1501) and Alexander (1501—1506), but also in the first years of that of Sigismund I the Old (1505—1548), Casimir the Jagiellon's three sons.

Sigismund the Old was the principal patron of Renaissance art in Poland. While still a prince he had come into contact with the intellectually and artistically highly developed court circles of Buda where during the reign of his brother King Ladislaus II the Jagiellon of Hungary

I.   KRAKÓW

Noua Turris.

Palacia S.R.M.tis

S. Stanislai.

...tificis.

Stabula S.R.M.tis

Lataranea

and Moravia, the tradition of Italian Renaissance planted in the times of Matthias Corvinus was kept up. These bonds largely explain the genesis of the Italian Renaissance trend in Polish art and many of the features of the first phase of its development. Sigismund was solicitous of the cultural standards of his Cracow court and supported the Italians and their art, especially in architecture and sculpture, in which he had decided and modern tastes.

Similar patronage was exercised by the lords spiritual and temporal either the king or of their own accord, the greatest credit for giving the first period of the Polish Renaissance its Italian complexion belonging to Jan Łaski, the Primate of Poland, the patron who acted most independently of the court; Piotr Tomicki, Bishop of Cracow and the ruler's closest confidant who followed his example and employed the same Italian artists, Jan Tarnowski, later Grand Crown Hetman, and Mikołaj and Krzysztof Szydłowiecki.

It all began with a great flourish, even if these first steps were limited in area and made hardly any difference to the external appearance of the royal residence on Wawel Hill, let alone the town itself. Round about 1500 a group of architects and sculptors, mainly Florentines, arrived from Hungary on the invitation of the royal court and set up an atelier at the foot of Wawel, the eminence which with a magnificent Gothic cathedral and palace towered high above the town, the river Vistula and the environs. It was headed by an artist known as Francis the Florentine (Franciszek Florentczyk) and after his death in 1516 considerably enlarged, mainly by Tuscan artists following in the footsteps of their predecessors. There were also craftsmen of other nationalities. Francis was succeeded by Bartolomeo Berrecci from Pontassieve near Florence who carried on until his death in 1537. Each of them, like so many of their fellow-Italians in that age of versality, was both an architect and a sculptor, and outstandingly gifted themselves, brought into their service artists and craftsmen of great ability and discernment. Having been made the court's premier artists, they secured authority and recognition and gave their atelier's products, the most important of which they designed themselves and supervised a uniform style. It was they who, coming one after another, lent that Italian stamp to Renaissance art in Poland already so often referred to.

Shortly after his arrival—and the partial destruction of the royal castle by fire about 1500—Francis went to work on the restoration of the so-called Queen's House, the west wing of the front. What remains are the window framings and a second-floor bay window, which merge into a stylistic whole, completed in 1505, with the magnificent late-Gothic frame of the sarcophagus of King John Albert in the chapel of Wawel Cathedral. Francis was certainly the designer and possibly also the executor of the better parts of the architecture of these works, the first harbingers in Poland of the new style. In composition and ornament, they have close affinities with the Florentine art of the late Quattrocento, so justifying their author's cognomen. There is no trace to be found here of the artist's odyssey from the city of his birth; even if it lasted several years, his various foreign ports of call failed to rub off on him. The style is Italian, pure and untainted, while the execution is a little cold.

From then, throughout the next three decades, the atelier at the foot of Wawel Hill delivered a steady stream of sandstones and limestones, cut and chiselled, to the castle and cathedral situated on the summit. There, these valuable "building blocks" were assembled into walls and arcades, recesses and niches, columns and pilasters, capitals and entablatures, vaultings and finials, tombs and sarcophagi, and set off by figurative sculptures of red Hungarian marble. More and more clearly and magnificently, the new style was materializing within the precincts of the royal residence and the Cathedral.

The two principal works from the Francis and Berrecci atelier on Wawel Hill are the arcaded galleries encircling the spacious castle courtyard, the most important part of the Italians' conversion, and the mausoleum chapel of King Sigismund I. The building of the first was begun in 1507 and was continued, to Francis designs, by Berrecci and, after his death, by his assistants. In this way the largest and most beautiful Renaissance courtyard in the whole of Central Europe was created. The arcaded galleries, which form the edifice's main means of access, served both state and social purposes enabling the court to attend ceremonies and tournaments. Mounted three storeys high on the walls of the castle wings, with arcades on the two lower ones, they frame and embellish the courtyard. With them the utilitarian and aesthetic principles which the theorists and architects of the Italian Renaissance sought to fuse together were transplanted to Polish soil. The Wawel courtyard measures up perfectly to the categories of that great ancient writer on architecture Vitruvius, whose ideas strongly influenced Italian Quattrocento building: *ordinatio, dispositio, eurythmia, symmetria* and *decor,* meaning functionalism combined with a delicate balancing of proportions and the harmonious merging of each part into an elegant and artistically faultless whole. The Wawel cloister garth derives genetically from the Florentine urban *cortile.* But though Italian in both spirit and form, there are certain concessions to the local environment and climate. In keeping with the customs prevailing in Central Europe, the state chambers are on the uppermost floor and not, as in Italy, on the first. Their height was such that, instead of arcades, the architects left only a row of columns, their upward thrust tempered by the rings binding the shafts, while the capitals support the eaves of a high roof of a kind unknown in Italy. These bows to local requirements introduce certain non-Italian accents in the upper part of Wawel's architecture. The work of Francis the Florentine and Berrecci won acclaim not only in Poland but also in neighbouring countries and was frequently imitated.

Between 1517 and 1533 Berrecci, helped by the whole of his atelier, built a burial chapel for Sigismund I, a few dozen paces from the entrance to the castle courtyard and resting against the south aisle of the Cathedral. In it, he bodied forth that "theme" of a central architectural structure so beloved of the builders and theorists of the Italian Renaissance. In the Sigismund Chapel the influence of the environment in which it stood is barely discernable; Berrecci and

1. Cracow, bird's eye view of the Cathedral and Castle on Wawel Hill. 1—Castle; 2—Sigismund Chapel; 3— Padniewski Chapel

his associates, sculptors, decorators and stonemasons, formed, as it were, a closed artistic clan, a branch of Italian art in Poland in which the principles espoused in their distant native land were cultivated and treated as all but a monastic rule. As a result one can safely include Berrecci's building within the mainstream of Italian art and range it among the series of chapels erected by Brunellesco in Florence and later by his successors in other towns in Tuscany, Rome, Naples and, finally, Hungary.

Once it is placed within these geographically distant but artistically close affinities, the Sigismund Chapel can no longer be called an imitation; it is relatively independent in concept and a tribute to the originality of its creator. Its lay-out, the composition of the walls and the decoration are chiefly reminiscent of the Tuscan style, but there are also traces of the artistic influence of the early 16th-century Rome school which had just come into the legacy of the Florentine Quattrocento and built on it to become the principal centre of Italian art. Consequently Berrecci represents a more advanced strain of the Italian Renaissance in Poland than his predecessor.

The comparatively plain exterior of the chapel is in striking contrast with the wealth of ornamentation and statuary in its interior. Bas-reliefs cover every inch of the walls and dome without, however, swamping the discipline of the architectural composition; they embrace on the whole the typical Tuscan repertoire of motifs, partly drawn from antiquity, and were probably mainly the work of Giovanni Cini from Sienna. No doubt Berrecci, the building's designer, was also responsible for some of the sculptures and certainly for the tomb of Sigismund I with the king's recumbent figure on the sarcophagus in a state of partial activity, which became the model for other such Polish Renaissance monuments. These embodied the idea of depicting the dead man deep in slumber, developed in Rome by the Florentine artists, who had arrived during the first years of the century, in accordance with their neo-Platonic philosophy. Not only the monarch's figure and the saints in the niches but also the bas-relief medallions with the prophets and the Evangelists, executed by Berrecci and his fellow-artists, among whom Bernardino De Gianotis stands out, are notable for a monumental Renaissance realism seeking the utmost plasticity of modelling and softened by a certain idealisation of portraiture; a far cry from the principles of late-Gothic sculpture, though a hint of its sharpness in the drapings of the robes has managed to penetrate this Renaissance world of form in certain of the medallions.

The Sigismund Chapel is a mature work not only by reason of its artistry but also because of its ideological programme in the formulation of which some of the humanist churchmen in Sigismund's entourage no doubt took part. Its selection of saints and prophets and the particular place in which they were stood was allusive, as though girdling the king with a wreath of ideas to accompany him in his eternal rest. All is dominated by the dome, a symbol of Heaven on which Berrecci, an artist emancipated by the Renaissance, has prominently inscribed his copyright in the words: BARTHOLO FLORENTINO OPIFICE.

The Chapel looks substantially the same as when it was built, which makes it all the easier to see what Essenwein, a 19th-century German art historian meant when he called it "a pearl of the Italian Renaissance north of the Alps". It is indeed the most beautiful work of Renaissance architecture outside Italy. Its original appearance has not been spoiled by subsequent alterations or additions, since those which have been made, like the sarcophagus of Sigismund Augustus, Sigismund I's son, and the tomb of Anna Jagiellonka, his daughter, still fall within the age and style of the Renaissance. This is also the case with the grille in the entrance to the nave, the silver altar and the candlesticks, ordered by the king in Nuremburg.

Although Berrecci and his atelier were absorbed during the second and third decades of the 16th century by their work on Wawel Hill for the king, they did occasionally execute commissions, on the side either for Sigismund himself or for other patrons. Thus before the arcaded courtyard and the Sigismund Chapel revealed the Italians' style in all its glory, glimpses of what was coming were provided by certain minor works of architecture and sculpture, notably the carved stone canopy over the Gothic tomb of King Ladislaus the Jagiellon, an example of Cini's precise ornamentation, and the tomb of Jan Konarski, Bishop of Cracow. For the first time, in Wawel Cathedral too, the pure Italian Renaissance style descended Wawel Hill and came to the city itself in the oratory and presbytery of the Church of St Mary, the principal place of worship of the Cracow burghers where, scarcely a quarter-century previously, Wit Stwosz had completed his magnificent late-Gothic altar-piece. For a town in which the Gothic tradition still reigned supreme, here were the first intimations that the rule of red brick walls, high roofs with tiles, sharp and fractioned mullions and ogived openings was coming to an end. Down the Vistula to distant Warsaw (Warszawa), was ferried the tombs of Janusz and Stanisław, the last of the Mazovian princes, which, like Konarski's, represented a type basically of Gothic provenance, but pure Renaissance in its external features, whether in the treatment of the human figure or the rich ornamentation.

During the last years of his life, Berrecci created a number of monuments which, along with the figure of Sigismund I, set the Polish Renaissance tomb evolving along a path of its own. In the sepulchral chapel, a simple central structure adjoining Wawel Cathedral, which he erected for Piotr Tomicki about 1530, the bishop's monument, one of the most beautiful Renaissance works in the Italian mode in Poland stands against the wall. Its basic pattern of an architectural and sculptural framework with socle, finial and recess in which the figure of the dead man lies in slumber on the sarcophagus in a peaceful not quite static pose is the taproot of almost the whole of the later development of the Renaissance tomb in Poland. The type is genetically Italian, the interpretation similar to the early 16th-century Roman version. Right up to the 17th century it remained the matrix in various forms of Polish tomb sculpture—as in Italy, but unlike the neighbouring countries where an entirely different type of composition prevailed.

It was also Berrecci's atelier which produced the author of the tomb of Barbara Tarnowska, the wife of Jan, Grand Crown Hetman, in Tarnów Cathedral. The figure on the sarcophagus is one of the loveliest female statues in the whole of European Renaissance sculpture, pure in its line and mass, exquisite in its composition and delicate in its detail. In both these the heads, like those of Sigismund I and of Primate Krzycki in Gniezno Cathedral, are outstanding examples of the sculpted portrait in Renaissance Poland which has survived solely on tombstones.

Thus Berrecci was, as his works testify, the foremost representative of the Italian trend in Polish Renaissance art, which he pioneered in Poland both as architect and sculptor and to which he lent his own individual stamp. His style was derived from the Florentine Quattrocento tradition but its numerous echoes of early 16th-century Roman art are evidence that he spent some time there before he came, by way of Hungary, to Poland. The direction he broached was to be continued in the 1530s by some of his associates.

The tomb of the Mazovian princes in Warsaw was not the first outcrop of the Italian Renaissance style in what were then the Polish provinces. As early as 1523 a sepulchral chapel for Jan Łaski, Primate of Poland, had been completed in Gniezno Cathedral, hierarchically Poland's chief place of worship. No longer extant, its architecture represented a central composition akin to the theories being unfolded by Leonardo da Vinci and Bramanti in Rome in the early 16th century and was probably designed by Berrecci, presumably yet another reflection of his sojourn in the Eternal City. Łaski ordered a further six plaques in memory of persons closely associated with him to be placed in the Chapel interior; imported from Hungary, these were executed by Joannes Florentinus, an artist from that very same circle to which Francis the Florentine and Berrecci probably belonged in their Buda period.

The artistic landscape of Poland in the 1530s can be likened to a broad countryside over which the Gothic Autumn was slowly fading, with new shoots shyly peeping up among the traditional nature shrubbery and at its heart a now stoutly grown and once unknown Renaissance tree whose seeds sometimes carried far afield.

While the Italian ateliers in Cracow concentrated on architecture and sculpture, there was a second native trend, which embraced all the fields of art, gradually evolving from Gothic to Renaissance. The artists behind it were never Italians, but Poles, or Slovaks and Germans, either from families already settled in Poland or recent newcomers, working on commissions from the court, with which the Tuscans were unable to keep up, even in the spheres of architecture and sculpture, and from the nobles, wealthier gentry and burgesses. In Cracow, and also partly in the provinces, their art was very much in tune with the urban culture of the day. Close to this current, which spread more and more widely during the first decades of the 16th century, stood the late-Gothic ateliers and workshops increasingly banished towards the small towns and villages, but still flourishing there beyond the mid-16th century.

In all fields of art, certain 15th-century late-Gothic paved the way to the passage of Renaissance, although not over much importance should be attached to this. In architecture it was the search for simpler forms, more symmetrical and planning, greater freedom in interior layout, accentuation of smooth wall surfaces and concentration of decoration around the openings. At the beginning of the 16th century, the influence of both the style of the Italians working in Cracow and the dissemination of models with Renaissance motifs led to the subordination taken even further, with pointed arches giving way to semicircular ones and architectural ornamentation more and more often going back to classical elements. The castle in Drzewica (1527—1535) is one example of this transitional style.

The main representative of this Gothic-Renaissance trend in architecture is thought to be a royal architect named Benedict, probably a native of one of the neighbouring countries, engaged for the work in Wawel Castle, who was also active in other places outside Cracow, mainly in Little Poland. The most typical example of the transitional style is a set of several dozen portals and window frames in Wawel Castle, executed in 1524-1529 and copied in many Polish buildings of this period. Here, a late-Gothic pattern of flutings running along geometrized lines mingled with Renaissance bands of ornamentation without the slightest attempt at integration. It seems likely that the Wawel atelier in which these portals and frames were made, had too few Italian stonemasons to undertake the whole of the ornamental work, so occupied were they by the construction of the arcaded galleries and Sigismund Chapel. Consequently, part of it was assigned to the Polish and Slovak craftsmen also employed by the atelier.

Thus these two styles of the early Renaissance in Poland had already come together in the period's principal secular building—the castle on Wawel Hill—even though its construction was directed by Italians who represented the first current alone. To some measure this was connected with Benedykt's work in the royal residence and the services of non-Italian artists. Even the composition of the courtyard galleries was, as we have seen, invaded by local factors. The remainder of the great edifice, both its exterior and its interior decoration, together with the set of portals just mentioned, belong to the native trend with its roots in established Gothic tastes. Hence, the Wawel residence combines in the most comprehensive way the imported and local elements in Poland.

In the sculpture too, in the first third of the 16th century, whatever seems at variance with the uniform Florentine-Roman style of the Francis and Berrecci atelier is a compound of artistic outgrowth very diverse in character, technique and material and only loosely linked by the common Renaissance nature of what was gradually emerging from the Gothic tradition of Central Europe. Once again there is no lack of evidence of both these strands entwinning, though the interface was a narrow one. There is the sharpness of the Gothic-draped garments derived from the Stwosz tradition so potent in Poland at the turn of the 15th-16th centuries, which crept into the medallions in the Sigismund Chapel. For all the fully Italian-Renaissance treatment of the figurative and ornamental parts, the tombs of Konarski and the Mazovian Princes are of a type whose antecedent is Stwosz's wall monument for Bishop Piotr of Bnin in the Cathedral in Włocławek built barely a few years before Francis arrival in Poland.

Quite another problem is brought to our notice by the Polish imports from the renowned Vischer casting shop in Nuremburg, although these also illustrate the gradual transmutation of late-Gothic to Renaissance. In vogue in Poland during the barren period between Wit Stwosz's departure in 1496 and the appearance of the first tombstones of high quality from Berrecci's Cracow atelier, these imports brought increasing portions of Renaissance ornamentation, Italian in origin but overlaid by the German interpretation of the design models to which the Vischer atelier worked. This is particularly apparent in the plaques, adapted to Polish ideas, executed by Hans Vischer for the Voivode of Cracow, Piotr Kmita (d. 1505), in Cracow Cathedral, Piotr Salomon (d. before 1516), in the Cracow church of St Mary and even more so in the later works in this group, the plaques of Seweryn Boner and Zofia, his wife, in this same church (1538).

In wooden-carving the Gothic traditions remained exceedingly strong in the first decades of the 16th century and the new style had great difficulty in breaking through. In the Pławno triptych (c. 1517), the panels of which were painted by Hans Suess of Kulmbach, the anonymous sculptor partly did away with the traditional architectural trimmings rounding off the central part with a hemispherical arch, displaying a new sense of space in his treatment of the scenes and introducing Renaissance accessories. Between 1531 and 1535 the coffered ceiling of the Deputies' Hall in Wawel Castle was decorated with 194 wooden heads carved by Sebastian Tauerbach from Wrocław, with the help of Jan Janda, a woodcarver. Thirty of these have survived, and can be seen in the restored ceiling. The sculpting of the wood and the cast of the grotesque features are still Gothic: the new element comes in the "Wawel heads"—their allegorical significance, secular character and a plastic form with none of that Gothic overabundance of detail.

We know of no Italian painter coming to and working in Poland in the first forty years of the 16th century, which is the main reason why the polarizing influence of the Italian Renaissance in architecture and sculpture is not to be found in painting. This makes it a field in which it is easiest to trace that slow transformation of Gothic into Renaissance so typical of Central Europe, since here it ran its course without the sudden intervention of artists from the land of the new art, working itself out within the native milieu, especially in Cracow, an exceptionally important centre of late-Gothic painting. The process of change owed virtually nothing to the work of the Francis the Florentine and Berrecci's atelier had practically no bearing on this approaching transformation; the spur to painters came rather from the pictorial models which were spreading a novel visual awareness and discussion among themselves of the wave of innovation and also from artists from Germany who had come into more direct contact with the Renaissance in Italian and Netherlands painting.

The way to the new artistic conventions was paved by the realism in the treatment of architectural or landscape backgrounds and the portrayal of figures in the case of panels which, derived from Netherlands models, appeared with a notable impact, especially in Cracow painting, during the second half of the 15th century. Nevertheless, the road was a very uphill one, particularly in panel painting. Among the obstacles was a deeply entrenched attachment to certain medieval types of altar, more intractable still, the traditional method of tempera painting on wood which suffered hardly a dent until the mid-16th century and on a realistic manner of drapery sanctified by the authority of Wit Stwosz whose decorative values were particularly difficult for the artist to abandon.

Mural and miniature painting were the least burdened by the pressure of tradition. A Cracow school of miniature painting had blossomed in the late-medieval period and entered the new age equipped with high standards of execution. The changes in style succeeding one another were mirrored in the illuminated books produced in Cracow during the first third of the 16th century which makes them the most representative part of the Gothic-Renaissance trend to set against the architectural and sculptural one sponsored by the Italians.

During the first decade of the 16th century the leading Cracow miniaturist studio issued the *Codex of Baltazar Behem*, and the *Gradual of John Albert*, by a number of artists, the first intended for the town and the second for the King. There is much that is still Gothic in the form and composition of these miniatures: the approach to the human figure, the quality of realism and scenery, the intuitive, unscientific accentuation of the space, the ornamental borders. Yet, simultaneously, the *Behem Codex* is so forceful an affirmation of thoroughly unmedieval secular concepts that it would be difficult to find its equal in the Italian or Netherlands painting of the Renaissance. Shorn of all religious overtones the miniatures of the *Codex* picture with a power of acute observation that in itself reflected a new attitude to the world, Cracow craftsmen plying their trades and genre scenes brimming with life and spontaneity. In the somewhat later *Pontifical of Erazm Ciołek*, Bishop of Płock, a nameless master from the studio strikes a more elegant and delicate note, indicating a feeling for the new harmony in the composition of the figures in group scenes, seeking a fuller unity of expression, unfolding distant landscapes as backgrounds and revealing an instinct for colour and lighting effects.

It was from among such miniature artists that there came Stanisław Samostrzelnik, the greatest Polish painter of the Renaissance, whose works appeared from the second to the fourth decades of the 16th century. A Cistercian from the monastery at Mogiła, he worked over a long period for Chancellor Krzysztof Szydłowiecki. His main province was the miniature, and he was the author of illuminations in prayer books furnished for the royal family and for Bishop Tomicki and in other manuscripts. He was also commissioned by his principal patron to decorate a *Liber geneseos* of the Szydłowiecki family. His work marks the stage immediately following that of the Cracow studios in the first years of the century in which Gothic influences were firmly overtaken by the new mode of perception and sense of form, the Renaissance feeling for rhythm and harmony of linear and colour compositions and the switch to ornamentation in the new style and its specific patterns. He was probably also an easel, and certainly a mural painter, author of polychromes in his parent monastery. A large portrait of Piotr Tomicki, which is attributed to him reveals a far-reaching similarity of style with the full-length figures typical of his miniatures; in both cases the ability to emphasize the model's individual traits, a sign of the new times, is evident. The likeness of Piotr Tomicki and certain of the miniatures can be seen to reflect a Renaissance concept of portraiture to more or less the same extent as the plaques, whether executed in the Wawel atelier of the Italians or imported from the Nuremburg workshop of the Vischers. In the former as in the latter we have the learned humanist cleric or the self-assured, lusty knight, depicted full-length with all their individual characteristics, in poses suggesting that what matters in the new age is personal energy. Lustre and dignity are added by framing the figures with coils of Renaissance arabesques and trophies that form a sort of wreath of glory.

Although the miniature was the branch of painting which evolved most consistently towards the Renaissance, its signifinance petered out in the latter half of the 16th century. This left the field to easel and mural painting.

In the first half of the century, both, although belonging in their entirety to the trend in which the Gothic was gradually leavened by the new mode of perception, have muffled echos of that division into two currents which marked the whole of early Renaissance art in Poland. On the one hand, foreign artists, not Italians but mainly Germans and Silesians, brought with them a more Renaissance-like version of art, chiefly of a German stamp; their principal base was Cracow. On the other, the sprawling reaches of guild painting, not only in Cracow but also in the towns of Little Poland and Great Poland, were slowly transformed by the innovations just managing to seep through the Gothic tradition. In both cases the influence of German engraving, especially of Dürer and Cranach was strongly in evidence.

About 1514 Hans Suess of Kulmbach, a leading representative of German early-Renaissance painting, came to Cracow to execute commissions for the burghers. These were works for the church of St Mary and included a polyptych with the legend of St Catherine of Alexandria. He was also the author, as previously mentioned, of the triptych in Pławno. These paintings show a fairly mature style, trading skillfully on the lessons of Italian art at the turn of the 15th-16th centuries, soft in their modelling and uniform in their colour composition, which was a departure from the Gothic's decorative extravagance. Another German Michel Lentz of Kitzingen, worked for Bishop Konarski during the early 1520s, presented a less mature version of the attainments of Renaissance painting in his religious pictures. All these visitors introduced Poland to a new range of subject matter: historical, as represented by the popular *Battle of Orsza*, painted about 1515 by an anonymous German artist for the Franciscan Monastery in Cracow, and mythological and allegorical, examples of which are the friezes by Hans Dürer and Antoni of Wrocław, artists engaged by Sigismund I, in the Royal Bedchamber and the Deputies' and Tournament Halls in Wawel Castle. Here too we have the moralizing *Story of Man* based the theory of the Greek philosopher, Cebes, and reviews of troops and jousting scenes. But, apart from Hans Suess, these were on the whole mediocre artists and their significance is mainly the historical one of importing the new subjects and methods characteristic of Renaissance art.

Cracow panel painting, which had reached a peak during the late-Gothic period, continued to reveal in the first years of the 16th century the imprint of certain outstanding artists and a grand style in pictures showing incipient Renaissance influences: the clearest instances are the polyptych of St John the Almoner (1504) and the Bodzentyn Altar by Marcin Czarny (1508). Nevertheless, with almost everything about so deeply rooted in the medieval tradition they can hardly be regarded as manifestations of the new style. Although Gothicism predominated in many Polish guild paintings right up to the mid-16th century, we can also find some which crossed the Renaissance boundary at a fairly early date. The most convincing examples are, in the case of Little Poland (where this occurred soonest), a painting in Szczyrzyc of the Man of Sorrows and attendants (c. 1515) and a triptych in Kobylin (probably from a Cracow atelier, c. 1518) and, of Great Poland —a triptych at Mądre near Środa (1529) and a *Virgin and Child* in Gostyń (1540). The new appeared in these paintings in a variety of ways without any common factor: in a more portrait—and genre-like treatment of people and scenes, in the realistic depiction of the background, in a new sense of space, in contours with the flowing lines, in more plastic forms, in tighter composition and sometimes in an accumulation of ornamental detail in the new style.

However, it is the portrait, as it emerged, during Sigismund I's reign as an independent kind of painting, which must be regarded as the chief expression and achievement of the new style. In the aforementioned likeness of Bishop Piotr Tomicki, attributed to Samostrzelnik, one can see not only a new subject matter but also a painterly outlook beginning to take root.

Surprising as it may seem, there is more of the Renaissance to be found in the mural decoration of the wooden village churches where its pattern of coffering appeared in the third decade of the 16th century, ornamental motifs typical of the new style were propagated and secular

themes expressed, for all that, this kind of art was also firmly bound up with the Gothic tradition. The most beautiful of the early polychromes (1520—1530) is to be seen in a church at Grębień near Wieluń. It includes the figures uncovered and written up after the last war, of a court and village musician enveloped in a lyrical atmosphere.

Against the general background of the evolution of Gothic into Renaissance which was proceeding at a varying pace, in the Thirties and Forties in painting and in the more traditional areas of sculpture, the works of the Italians, remaining in or visiting Poland, constituted a continuation of that Renaissance trend initiated by Francis the Florentine and so splendidly developed by Berrecci.

Even during Berrecci's lifetime, some of his associates had formed partnership, run on the profit-sharing principle of a modern business, which udertook assignments in both architecture and sculptures. The most important of these was the one founded by Bernardino De Gianotis and Giovanni Cini in 1531 which operated until the former's death in 1541. Soon afterwards his place was taken by Giovanni Maria Padovano, a leading artist from Padua who had arrived in Poland about 1532.

Although work of Berecci's successors was concentrated in Cracow, still as ever the foremost art centre in Poland, it was also beginning to spread to other parts of the country. The architecture and sculpture produced continued to be of a high standard, if short of the chief achievements of the first phase, and to represent the Italian style cultivated to date by their circle and revitalized by travels (Cini, for example, visited Italy in 1530), or the arrival of new artists like Padovano. But the pressure of the local environment and the nascent new habits of mind were making themselves felt ever more strongly: after all, these artists had now been active in Poland for a long time. The first, more determined step was taken to make a wider circle of Polish patrons interested in works in the Renaissance style, and it began to penetrate beyond the court and the humanist sections of the nobility and the Cracow patriciates, to the wealthier gentry. Simultaneously, there was a movement closer to the native trend of Polish art of the early Renaissance, towards a symbiosis which was to become the feature of the next period.

In 1532—1534, commissioned by Andrzej Krzycki, Bishop of Płock, a distinguished humanist and Tomicki's nephew, De Ganotis and Cini built in his see a new cathedral. Submerged by later alterations, its architecture was an outstanding example of an elongated, domed church in the new style and still represented the pure Italian trend. Although once again the remnants are scant, it is possible that the projects carried out by De Gianotis and, later, Cini out in remote Vilna, the second capital of the united monarchy, were of a similar character. Sometimes the Italians were obliged to enter into artistic affiliation with local tradition. In the mighty castle at Ogrodzieniec near Cracow, erected in 1530-1545 for a wealthy patrician named Boner, they executed the arcaded galleries and other parts of the architectural and scupltural decoration.

But the Italians' most important work, particularly in the light of what has survived, was in the field of sepulchral sculpture. This was a tune in which this men's desire to perpetuate their own and their family's fame, so characteristic of the culture and mores of the Renaissance, was spreading among the gentry who, following the example of the king and the magnates, were ordering, often during their lifetimes, tombs in the new style although for many of them humanism was still an alien culture. The result was this aspiration, the appearance via the tombstone of the new style in small towns and villages, at first in a sporadic trickle from Cracow where the main ateliers were, and then from Płock and Vilno where the artists in question made a longer stay.

In their tombstones, De Gianotis and Cini, the former probably responsible for the figures, the latter for the ornamental parts, continued the type developed in Berrecci's atelier, with

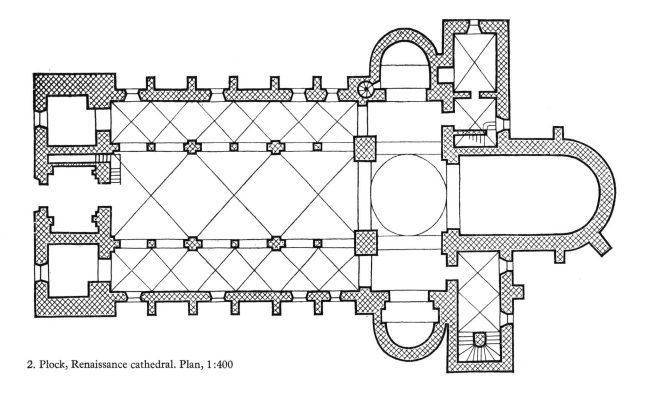

2. Płock, Renaissance cathedral. Plan, 1 :400

an inclined plaque and a bas-relief representation of the dead man in an ornamental setting to which other artists may also have completed earlier. At the turn of the 1630s such monuments were built for Canon Wapowski in Cracow Cathedral, Wojciech Gasztołd in Vilna Cathedral, Anna Szydłowiecka in the Opatów collegiate church and Stanisław Łasocki in the church at Brzeziny; only the plaques have been preserved. From the records we know that De Gianotis was the author of the last of those, revealing a supreme command of rich, vivid form and a mastery of vigorous and pithy characterization, obvious Renaissance qualities. In the same period came the magnificent tomb of Chancellor Krzysztof Szydłowiecki, the work of both artists, which can be regarded a sign of the development of the Polish Renaissance monument striking out on its own, cutting loose of Italian models and expressing a separate version of Italianism. The old design was enriched by lateral niches while the plaque became decidedly less slanted and was blended into the rectangular framing of the recess, as though the lay-out of the Tomicki tomb was starting to exert en influence, leading to a more organic fusion of the plaque with architectural setting.

The Szydłowiecki plaque and certain parts of the decoration were cast, no doubt in a Cracow workshop, in bronze, the material which was so very highly thought of the Renaissance. The figure of the knight, firmly modelled with sharply etched features, is reminiscent of the likenesses Italian *condottieri*; the standard of execution is high and the ornamental detail probably Cini's work, shows a purity of Italian style not inferior to the decorative parts of the Sigismund Chapel.

A frieze, also cast in bronze, was mounted under the plaque with the Chancellor's figure in his Opatów tomb; it dates to the 1630s and is popularly called the *Opatów Lamentation.*This is a fairly enigmatic work, not only as to subject but also as to style. The large gathering of Poles and foreigners are presumably mourning the Chancellor's death, although other interpretations have been put forward. The awkwardness in the treatment of the figures is, apart from the heads which are vividly and incisively portrayed, so awkward that the *Lamentation* seems a long way from the uniform, purely Italian style of the other bronze parts of this monument; on the other hand, it has a striking sincerity of expression, spontaneity of gesture and variety of degree of projection—in short, it bears the stamp of an outstandingly individual artist, though his name is unknown. Most certainly he was neither De Gianotis nor Cini, but someone who was more a medallist, no doubt from Cracow and connected, at least partly, with the native current in the early Polish Renaissance.

By this time Giovanni Maria Padovano had arrived in Cracow as a sculptor of small forms. In 1532 he made some fine-wrought medals of Sigismund I and Bona, and Sigismund Augustus and Izabela and carved a ciborium for the Tomicki Chapel. Little is known of his other work in this period, although he undoubtedly gave up his original speciality, an unfashionable one in Poland, and turned his hand to shaping the development of the Renaissance tomb. In due course he was responsible for the codification of the formulas used so far and, above all, for the incorporation into the monument of the deceased figure in a ruffled pose on the lines of Berrecci's statue of Sigismund I in his chapel. This kind of arrangement, rejected by De Gianotis, was at that time rare, one example being in Mikołaj Szydłowiecki's plaque from 1532 in the church in Szydłowiec.

In the Twenties a new factor began to affect the picture of the Renaissance in Poland, following the arrival of Italian artists from Como and Ticino. Since the Middle Ages, a wave of specialized architects and stone-masons had been pouring out of these poverty-stricken Italian-Swiss borderlands all over Europe and it swelled during the Renaissance. Unlike Tuscans, they were on the whole modest pioneers of the new forms in their popular Lombardian-Venetian version, tempering the artistic innovations they picked up outside Italy in the countries where they worked to the requirements of their patrons, to which they were specially sensitive. Hence, they did not represent so pure an Italian trend as the artists who came from Florence and Rome; on the other hand, they felt no attachment to the Gothic tradition. They entered Poland from two directions, encircling, as it were, the artistic bastion of the Tuscans with its centre in Cracow: from Germany and from Bohemia, to which it was they in contrast to what had happened, who had brought the new style. Appearing simultaneously in both Wrocław and Lvov, they worked on religious and secular building, carving Renaissance details in stone. But it was only the next stage of the Renaissance in Poland that their influence grew, as more and more of them arrived and dispersed over other parts of the country.

Commentaries to the Illustrations

1—3 In the first years of the 16th century a chapel with the tomb of King John Albert (d. 1501) was built in the Cathedral on Wawel Hill in Cracow. They were endowed by Elizabeth of Hapsburg, his mother (d. 1503) and the wife of Casimir the Jagiellon, and Sigismund, his brother, from 1506, King of Poland. Here can be seen a watershed between two periods which had a significance reaching beyond Wawel Hill and Cracow. The chapel and the tomb itself with a bas-relief of the king, probably the work of the Cracow atelier of Stanisław Stwosz, Wit's son, are still Gothic, but the tomb's magnificent architectural setting, which is likely to have been the idea of Sigismund, the principal patron of the Renaissance in Poland, makes the new style the keynote of the interior. The work of Francis the Florentine and completed about 1505, at the same time as the window framing and bay window in the west wing of Wawel Castle (ill. 5, 6), it marks the first manifestation of the Renaissance in Poland, which he transplanted to

Cracow in the pure forms of the late Florentine Quattrocento. He was, however, forced to adjust his design to what was already there before he set about his task. The dark, cramped chapel and the large dimensions of the tomb led him to accentuate, more vigorously than tradition required, the architectural side of the Florentine archetype of an arcaded wall monument; thus he deepened the niches, doubled the number of pilasters and topped off the whole with a prominent arch. From Tuscany he also brought a rich repertoire of ornament derived from antiquity: pilasters with Corinthian capitals, candelabrum patterns on the recess panels and inner pilasters, trophies on the outer pilasters and, in the coffers of the niche vaulting, a frieze with a palmette on the entablature and festoons of fruit on the socle; all was carved in stone with impeccable precision. Between the blazons of the House of Hapsburg and the Grand Duchy of Lithuania the Polish coat of arms was placed in a salient place; its motif of an eagle, familiar already in the ancient world, was well suited to the Renaissance crown.

4—6 In 1502—1507 Francis the Florentine, at the request of Sigismund, heir to the throne, converted the west wing of Wawel Castle into a residence (called the Queen's House) for Elizabeth, his mother. This was the first stage of Renaissance alterations, and it survives in the splendid bas-relief frames of the courtyard windows on the second floor, one of which also decorates a bay window. The ornamental motifs belong to that same Quattrocento world of form used for the Albert tomb (ill. 2, 3). Over the bay window, on the frieze entablature, the Polish eagle was placed between the blazons of the Hapsburgs and Lithuania; the decoration of the socles is an 18th-century addition.

7—9 The three-storey arcaded galleries on the courtyard side of the west, north and east wings (see figures 4, 5) are the most important Renaissance element of Wawel Castle. They date to the major conversion of the castle carried in the years 1507—1536, under Francis the Florentine up to 1516 and Bartolomeo Berrecci from 1530 to 1536, Niccolo Castiglione and Matthew the Italian in 1536—1549. The original plans were Francis' and his successors stuck to them. These are the most beautiful Renaissance galleries in Central Europe. This design, which stems from the spirit of the late Tuscan Quattrocento, exerted a notable influence on residential architecture in Poland. Two of the tiers fully catch the Renaissance quest for harmon-

3. Cracow, Castle on Wawel Hill. Architectural frame of the west wing bay window, 1:50

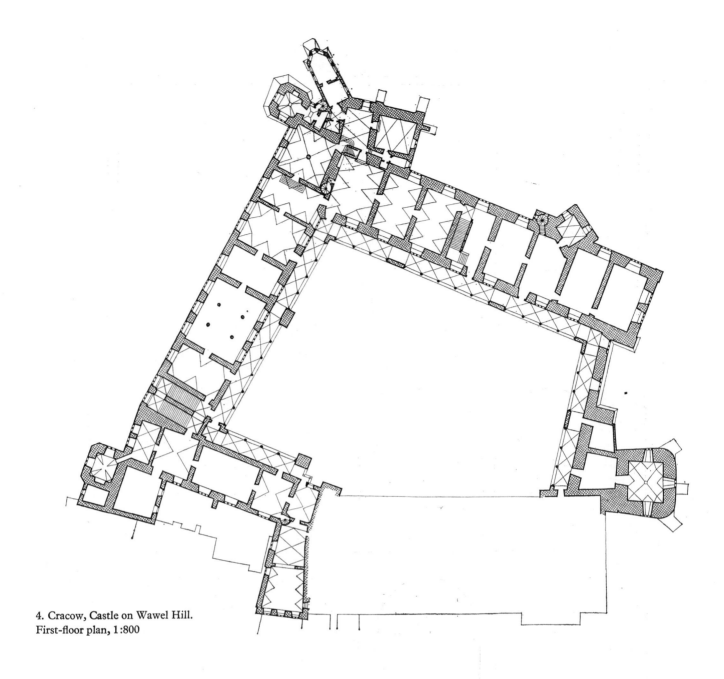

4. Cracow, Castle on Wawel Hill.
First-floor plan, 1:800

ious and rhythmical composition with alternating
patches of light and shadow shaped in the gentle forms
of the new style. The uppermost tier, on the other hand,
made concessions to the Polish climate and customs.
Here the gallery runs alongside the castle's state apartments, these being higher-ceilinged than the rooms
on the lower tiers (in contrast to Italy, where the main
storey—or *piano nobile*—was at ground level) and to
support the eaves of the steep roof required by the
Polish climate. Instead of an arcade, which would
have been out of proportion with the lower tiers, the
architect decided on a row of extremely slender columns,
girding the shafts half-way with rings to lessen their
upward thrust and placing on the capitals decorative
butts (or "jugs"), optically supporting the eaves. It
is this arrangement, which also differs in the details
mentioned from the Italian pattern, that gives the
Wawel arcaded galleries a distinctive native identity.

10—12 During the conversion of Wawel Castle, the
openings of the passages into the galleries and between
the chambers were adorned, with elaborately carved
stone portals. The two examples selected from among
the twenty most ornamental ones—dating mainly to
1527—1530—give a good idea of the look of the
whole set, which was of a piece as regards the composition and its elements but differed in its details, especially
in the lintels. As in the whole of Wawel Castle, two
style co-exist. The Gothic world is represented by the
traditional form of the door-frame, by the flutings
rising in clusters from a crystal base and tracing on
the lintels intricate linear geometrical patterns and by
sharply chiselled openwork branch and cordon motifs;
the pure Renaissance decorative repertoire—by the
classical ornamental bands in the cornices made up of
bull's-eyes, chaplets, dentils, acanthuses, and by the
rosettes, cherub's heads, cornucopia and other motifs
profusely scattered over the surface of the lintels; some
of the flutings outline a hemispherical shape typical of
the new style. The Gothic-Renaissance Wawel portals
are generally associated with Benedykt of Sandomierz,

25

5. Cracow, Castle on Wawel Hill. Section of the north wing gallery, 1:125

one of the king's architects and an advocate of the local tradition recast in the Renaissance mould. Nevertheless the credit for the door-frames, so compact and strikingly original, seems more likely to belong to Berecci, who supervised their execution in his Wawel atelier. The introduction of the Gothic forms would have suited the four stonemasons called Gallus, Mathis, Franciscus and Laurentius, either Poles or from neighbouring countries, specially engaged for

the task, who were accustomed to decoration of a traditional character.

13—15 The Deputies' Hall was the largest of the state apartments on the second floor of the east wing of Wawel castle on Wawel Hill completed in the 1530s and served the king as an audience chamber. In the course of the castle's alternating fortunes all of them suffered damage and disrepair, losing their original, typically Renaissance entablature and coffered ceilings.

During restoration work, carried out under Adolf Szyszko-Bohusz in the years 1916—1939, the chambers recovered something like their old appearance, repairs being undertaken of what was left of their decoration, which in the Deputies' Hall included the painted frieze (ill.16) and the carved heads in the coffered ceiling (ill. 13, 14). Nevertheless today the interiors are only a pale reflection of the dazzling effect once created by the distinctively native blend of polychromes, brilliantly-coloured friezes, tapestries, tiled stoves (the present ones come from the 18th century) and red carpets.

In 1531—1535 the Deputies' Hall was roofed with a magnificent ceiling, and 194 wooden heads, life-size, and complete, were placed in its richly sculpted, polychromed coffering. Their author was the court cabinet-maker, Sebastian Tauerbach from Lusatia, aided by Hanusz, a goldsmith and woodcarver. The idea of such an, as it were, overhead portrait gallery, was an absolutely original one and has no counterpart among Renaissance ceilings in any other country. Represented were men and women of various estate and age: sovereigns in crowns, poets in laurel wreaths, warriors, ladies-in-waiting, townswomen. Only a few of these heads, thirty in all, have been preserved (they are again to be seen in the reconstructed ceiling) and so it is impossible to decipher the iconographic or historical programme which must have been their unifying factor. They display a fierce portrait-like candour, often with a strong streak of humour, satire or grotesquerie. Executed with much care and technical skill, they are a far cry from late-Gothic naturalism. These distinctive traits make, the Wawel Heads one of the great achievements of Polish Renaissance art.

16 Painted friezes skirted the walls immediately beneath the ceilings of the state apartments in Wawel Castle. In the Deputies' Hall they were painted in 1532 by Hans Dürer, the brother of the famous Albrecht, who worked for the royal court. Its subject was taken from a then popular tract, *Tabula Cebetis*, by Cebes, a Greek moralist, about the course of human life. Over the years, the frieze suffered considerable damage and depletion; in 1926 it was restored and made complete by Leonard Pękalski. The better preserved of the original parts include a scene of young ladies and gallants enjoying a carefree banquet to the strains of music. Decorative festoons run along the bottom of the frieze. Through its secular subject drawing on ancient literature, Hans Dürer's work reflects the humanist aspirations of the Cracow community. In Wawel Castle it represents the current born of the reception of Renaissance art in Central Europe and cultivated by Polish and German artists which developed alongside the Renaissance work of the Italian architects and stone-masons. The standard of the painting's execution is average but it is not without certain decorative and colouristic values.

17, 18 The names of most of the Wawel Castle state apartments are derived from the themes of the painted friezes below their ceilings. The frieze in the Tournament Hall was begun by Hans Dürer in 1534 and, after his death, completed in 1535 by Antoni of Wrocław, another painter working on the decoration of the castle interiors and the author of a frieze depicting a military parade in the Tournament Hall's antechamber. The frieze in the Tournament Hall shows knights competing in equestrian contests to the music of two orchestras and, along the bottom, is embellished with garlands. The favourite Renaissance subject of chivalry has here been present in its stock Central European version in the new style.

The walls of the royal chambers and other rooms are hung with Netherlands tapestries from the collection purchased by Sigismund Augustus (Pl.V, VI). These are all that remain of the original furnishings of the interiors which have been lost through looting, chiefly during the Austrian occupation. As now decorated the rooms have the character of a museum. The historical exhibits include, besides the tapestries, paintings by Polish and foreign artists, furniture, including a magnificent collection of Italian Renaissance and Baroque pieces, and other *objects d'art*.

19—21 "An Italian was here with the model of a chapel which he will erect for Us and with which We are well content", wrote King Sigismund the Old from Vilna to Jan Boner, Burgrave of Cracow Castle in 1517. This Italian was Bartolomeo Berrecci, a Tuscan who had arrived in Poland a year earlier. The king had conceived the idea of building a chapel after the death of Barbara Zapolya, his first wife, in 1515; and it was also to be his own mausoleum. The foundations were laid in 1519 off the south nave of Wawel Cathedral, a Gothic chapel being torn down to make way for them; by 1533 the building was completed. Over a hundred years ago, Essenwein, a German scholar, called it "a pearl of the Renaissance north of the Alps", and it is indeed the most beautiful structure in the Italian Renaissance style outside Italy. Its heritage value is all the greater in that it has retained entirely its original appearance, without any later alterations or additions. The lower, fundamental part is in the form of a hexagon, emphasized by a geometrical arrangement of panels brought into relation by fluted Tuscan pilasters; above there is an octagonal, richly decorated tympanum, pierced by large round windows and supporting a dome and lantern. A central plan, as represented by the Chapel, was the fullest embodiment, the builders and theorists of Renaissance art believed, of the ideal of architectural beauty to which they aspired; traditionally, it was also considered the most appropriate one for a place of worship and internment, which is precisely what the Sigismund Chapel was. Although built far from Italy, its design sprang from the currents stimulating the Italian artistic world during the Renaissance. It is also in Italy, especially in 15th-century Florence and in Rome during the first years of the 16th-century, that we find the closest approximations to its organization of space and architectural composition. It is, however, a tribute to the originality of the creator of the Chapel that nowhere are there any exact counterparts. The nearest is a central structure to be seen in one of Leonardo da Vinci's drawings. At the time that the Sigismund Chapel rose beside the medieval Cathedral it was full-fledged manifestation of the new style. Against the background of the Gothic building with its steep ridge roofs, its red bricks and tiles and ogival windows, the Chapel presents an arresting contrast of restrained and regular proportion—this partly conditioned by the height of the Cathedral aisle—the yellowish-grey colour of its masonry, the differentiation of its mass in which spherical forms appear and the wealth of its architectural division and decoration with their echoes of antiquity.

The dome of the Sigismund Chapel was ready by the close of 1526. To this same year dates the kneeling cherub (or "putto") holding up a crown topped by a cross which rounds off the lantern. The whole was cast in bronze, a task undertaken by Berrecci himself since the putto and its accessories were to be cast by a wax process technique of which the Italians were the chief masters. Berrecci was assisted by Arnolf of Racibórz, a bell-founder. The putto was very carefully executed from a single mould, wings and all, apart from the arms. To enhance the visual effect, it was given to Stanisław, a goldsmith, for gilding; his first effort did not meet with the approval of the king who was satisfied only after a second attempt. As a type, the angel recalls the winged figures of children used to enliven Italian altars, pulpits and tombstones made popular by the early Renaissance Florentine art of the 15th century.

22—24 Against the west wall of the Sigismund Chapel interior to the right of the entrance, stands the founder's tomb (ill.35) raised to a higher position in 1574—1575 to make room for the monument of Sigismund Augustus, his son. In these same years a commemorative plaque to Anna Jagiellonka, Sigismund the Old's daughter, was mounted on the parapet of the throne compartment by the south wall (ill. 173). Thus, the Chapel eventually became, despite the initial idea, the mausoleum of the last of the Jagiellons. The east wall was assigned to the altar (ill. 22). It is the Chapel

7. Cracow, Wawel, Sigismund Chapel. Vertical section with view of wall tomb, 1:125

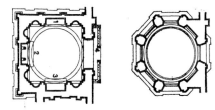

6. Cracow, Wawel, Sigismund Chapel. Plan and horizontal section at the height of the drum of the dome, 1:400

interior which brings out most fully its ideological programme, rooted in the outlooks of the Renaissance. Very likely its authors were humanist clerics from the court, but there can be no doubt that the monarch himself influenced it. The king is represented sleeping on the tomb with saints and figures from the Old Testament attending him in his eternal rest; their sculpted images are in the niches and medallions on

III.

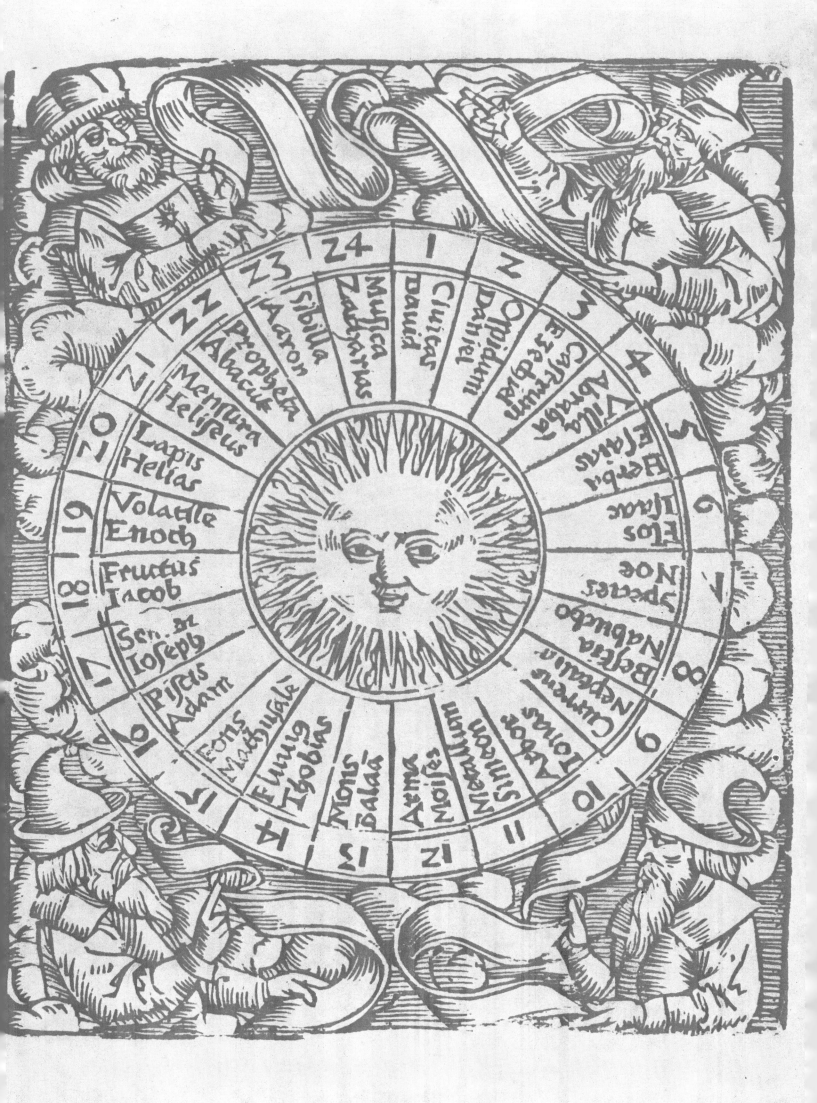

the lateral parts of the three main walls. Hence, the lower section is not only devoted to the sepulchral ideas connected with the founder but could also be used for services. An atmosphere of awe and solemnity reigns in the interior, helped by the lucidity of the layout and the wealth of sculpture decoration, which remind us that the creator of the Chapel was, like many Renaissance artists, both architect and sculptor. In the lower zone, Berrecci had, by means of the pilaster division, given predominance to vertical lines checked by the corniced entablature. Into his intricate and varied play of forms, he has introduced semicircles and circles and blended them in typical Renaissance fashion into harmonious chords of increasing power as the eye climbs upwards towards the upper zone of the Chapel, where they form the underpinning of the spherical forms of the dome framework (ill. 27). The light, falling from above through the lantern and the drum window, models the rich relief of the walls, animated by its colour accents; the figurative sculpture, tomb framing and compartments are in red Hungarian marble and the other parts, in greyish-green sandstone.

Berrecci used the formula of the triumphal arch, drawn from Roman antiquity and popular in Renaissance art, in the composition of each wall of the Sigismund Chapel; the pilasters, rising to the height of the socles and supporting the entablatures with prominent cornices, divide the walls into a central bay and narrower lateral ones. The deep round-topped recesses, serving different purposes on each wall, are flanked on the three main ones by niches, holding statues of saints and by bas-relief medallions with the busts of the Evangelists and Salomon and David. Above the cornice, the shields have been placed near the pendentives supporting the drum whose sides define the shape of the segmental arch surmounting it. All the panels of the walls are densely covered with bas-relief decoration (ill. 28—33) subordinated, for all its wealth, to the discipline of the basic composition. In the architecture and ornament of the Chapel, its creator tapped the art of Florence and Rome at the turn of the 15th—16th centuries and transferred it to Polish soil unalloyed. But he also preserved a certain independence—when, for example, without any Italian precedent, he placed secondary cornices in the central and lateral parts at varying heights. On the west wall the original sarcophagus of Sigismund the Old was replaced by a lower one when his monument was raised in 1574—1575 and an additional arcade introduced in order to set apart a recess for the sarcophagus and statue of Sigismund Augustus (ill. 171). In the adjoining niches stand figures of St. Florian and St Wenceslaus, patron-saints of the Polish State, in the medallions above the Evangelists Luke and Mark (ill. 36, 37). St Sigismund, the patron-saint of the founder (ill.42) and Solomon, the personification of kingly wisdom (ill. 38), are to be seen in a niche and medallion on the lateral axis of the south wall adjoining that of the tombs.

Sigismund the Old ordered the most important parts of the decoration of his Chapel in Nuremburg, whose workshops had a high reputation for quality, especially in metalware. This was the source of the altar placed in the east wall recess (ill. 90, 93). In its niches stand statues of St Peter and St Paul, Christ's vicars on earth, in the medallions, busts of the Evangelists, John and Matthew.

The programme composition of the north wall of the Chapel, which contains the entrance, has been simplified in relation to those its other interior elevations. The lateral bays are bereft of niches and medallions and have been greatly narrowed making possible a wider, arcaded entrance from the Cathedral nave. The bronze grille on the nave side, was cast by Hans Vischer in Nuremburg in 1530—1532 (ill. 89) and rounded off in 1545.

25—27 Perhaps to an even greater extent than the basic part of the structure, the dome of the Sigismund Chapel is the quintessence of the mature Italian Renaissance, and that not only from its technical but also from its artistic aspect. The voussoirs of the vaulting from which the dome is formed were executed in the Wawel atelier of the Italians together with their bas-relief decoration—like all the other architectural features of the Chapel for that matter—and, as a special kind of prefabricate, were assembled into a precisely mounted whole without the use of mortar. This was an exceptionally difficult operation which required the highest level of technical knowledge of the day, for which the Italian architects were famous. In the composition of this dome, together with its drum Berrecci accentuated the form of a circle, and naturally so in view of the characteristic shape of the framework. To it he led the externally octagonal drum, piercing it with a crowning of circular windows and on its upperplate, repeated several times the concentric circle motif in the arrangement of the panels. The effects of the lighting are sophisticated. The light falls into the interior from below through the windows in the drum (the two on the nave side were walled up during the 18th century) and from above, through the lantern; it winds its way with varying intensity through the bas-reliefs of the upper plate of the framework. Separately crossing the concentric circles of the transverse arrangement of the panels, it helps to create with them the characteristic coffering of the new style; these panels run like rays from a luminous globe at the base of the lantern. This play of forms is furthered by the symbolism of the dome towering high above all that is earthly. On the lantern vaulting and in the sphere of the most intense light, Berrecci signed this superb work: *Bartholo Florentino Opifice* (Bartolomeo the Florentine was the creator).

28—33 The bas-relief ornament of the Sigismund Chapel does not leave an empty space on the walls.

Composed of rectangular panels, it covers the socles, pilasters and the framing of the central recesses and lateral niches, and, in irregular five-panel arrangements, fills the shield walls. Above it passes by way of the pilasters and the arches of the drum windows, onto the soffit of the dome framework. Its singularity lies in the mythological figurative scenes in the shield walls (ill. 31). The motifs, mainly drawn from the repertoire of antique ornamentation, are very varied. Entangled in, and lending a grotesque to, the stylized plant-like coils of arabesques, which form candelabra patterns in the vertical panels, are the heads of winged angles, bunches of fruit, weapons, birds and sphinxes; often the dolphin makes an appearance, a symbol of the immortality of the soul. The individualized capitals of the pilasters are free travesties of Corinthian capitals. The decoration has been chiselled in the stone precisely but with verve. It is among the most beautiful produced by Italian Renaissance art. Its origin, apart from the scenes on the shield walls, is eminently Tuscan. Related and similarly executed ornament can be found in Florence and Sienna at the turn of the 15th—16th centuries. There is a particular close resemblance with the bas-relief carved in 1513 by the group of Tuscan artists engaged by Michelangelo to decorate the famous tomb of Julius II in St Pietro in Vincoli in Rome and directed by Antonio of Pontassieve—the home-town of the creator of the Sigismund Chapel. The ornamental parts of the Cracow edifice date chiefly to 1525—1528. The design must have been Berrecci's; in its execution it is possible to distinguish several of his associates, including Giovanni Cini of Sienna.

The decoration on the shield walls of the Chapel, enriched with figures and mythological scenes drawn from the ancient world, has a truly astounding iconographic programme. The principal theme are sea gods, nereifs and tritons, at play. Scenes such as these were common subjects for the bas-reliefs on Roman sarcophagi and furniture; they were adopted by Italian Renaissance art and made popular through engravings. The striking similarity between one of the scenes—a nereif in the arms of a triton—and Raphael's fresco *The Triumph of Galatea* in the Villa Farnesina painted in 1516—1517 indicates extremely close contacts between the authors of the Sigismund Chapel decoration and the artistic environment of Rome during the early years of the 16th century. The introduction of mythological subjects and high-spirited, naked figures into an interior steeped in religious gravity is eloquent testimony not only of Berrecci's love of antiquity but also of his secular autlook.

34, 35 Under an agreement signed on 6 February, 1529, Bartolomeo Berrecci undertook to carve the statues for the Sigismund Chapel, which were to include the figure of the King in armour, crown and cloak on the now completed sarcophagus. This he duly did, the monarch holding an orb and sceptre being sculpted in red Hungarian marble (the sceptre is no longer there, and the original sarcophagus was replaced in 1574—1575 by a lower one when Sigismund Augustus' tombstone was placed in the wall recess). The royal accounts indicate that the sculpture was ready before 31 March, 1531. It is not only an outstanding work in artistic terms, but also had a far-reaching impact on the development of the sepulchral figure in Polish Renaissance sculpture. For it both marks the birth both of a novel composition of the figure in the tomb and represents the new idea of showing the deceased as though he were not so much dead as asleep, lying on one side with his head supported on his arm or hand and with flexed legs. This idea, a decided contrast to medieval usage, was a bow to the neo-Platonic philosophy which was a feature of the high Renaissance and influenced Italian sepulchral sculpture in the early years of the 16th century. It come out in the tombstones carved by Andrea Sansovino, a Florentine sculptor, in 1505—1507, for cardinals Girolamo Basso and Ascanio Sforza in the church of St Maria del Popolo in Rome. Henceforth, the depiction, not necessarily with deliberate philosophical intent, of a sleeping figure in a self-determined pose spread throughout Italy and was brought to Poland by Berrecci. However, the figure of Sigismund I is lent an original touch by the theme of waking and rising denoted by the movements of the head, torse and legs. Its impact on Polish Renaissance sculpture was considerable, this type of recumbent figure remaining standard right up to the second quarter of the 17th century; outside Poland and Italy, it only occurred sporadically. In the statue of Sigismund I, it is worth emphasizing the true-to-life portraiture of the face, the anatomical accuracy of the body and the decorative stylisation of the armour and the folds of the drapery.

36, 37 From the agreement signed on 6 February 1529 between Seweryn Boner, Governor of Cracow and Bartolomeo Berrecci, it appears that the medallions with the Evangelists in the Sigismund Chapel were ready earlier. "The likenesses of the four Evangelists for the aforesaid chapel [...] were conceived and sculpted by Berrecci himself", states the agreement which must be credited, though the words do not exclude the participation of his assistants. The four tondi, carved in red marble, reveal a personal style, expressed in the abrupt twists and gestures of the figures, while the dishevelled folds of the garments give them a dynamic force and graphicness not to be found in the other statues in the chapel. A hint of the Gothic still lingers in the sharpness of the draping. This feature of their style sets the four medallions apart from the other sculptures in the interior and is evidence that Berrecci's art also owed something to the Gothic-leaning strain in Italian Quattrocento and its accent on restless forms. Matthew, Mark, Luke and John are shown, knee-length, seated almost frontwise to the viewer but with their faces in profile. Each of them is a wholly different figure, the features individualized to such an extent that we may presume that living people were portrayed and perhaps, among them, the sculptor himself.

38, 39 Under the aforementioned agreement of 6 February, 1529, Berrecci contracted besides the statues of the saints for the niches, the carving of two tondi in red marble representing Solomon and David, in the same way as the four Evangelists (ill. 36, 37). Like the rest of the items specified in this agreement, they too were ready by 1531. David was placed above the niche statue of St John the Baptist; Solomon, endowed with Sigismund I's features, over that of St. Sigismund, whose name he bore. Both these biblical kings were universally regarded as the patron saints of rulers and there were frequent references to each in the Polish 15th-century coronation ritual. They were depicted in a monumental attitude of great solemnity and aplomb ideally harmonized with the roundness of the medallions from which they slightly protrude. The style differs from that of the Evangelists, which may testify to the hand of one of Berrecci's associates. Solomon holds a sceptre in his right hand and an unfurled scroll of parchment in his left; David's left hand grips a harp and a similarly unrolled codex but the fingers of his right hand are strumming the harp. In this way David is symbolized as the "Psalmist" and musician, Solomon as the wise ruler and legendary author of the *Song of Songs*. Both images form essential elements of the thematic programme of the Jagiellon mausoleum.

40—42 The six saints' statues, commissioned in February, 1529 for the niches of the Sigismund Chapel, show a stylistic dissimilarity testifying to the fact that they must have been the work of various sculptors from Berrecci's atelier. Its master had cast the way for the models in 1526, the red Hungarian marble arrived at the turn of 1527/1528 and the statues were completed by 1530. The figures of the Apostles Peter and Paul and St John the Baptist were presented in the conventional garments, those of Sts Florian, Wenceslaus and Sigismund, in armour, the latter two clad in the fluted Renaissance armour made popular in Poland, St Florian in the armour of a Roman legionary. The statue of St Sigismund displays the highest artistic standard. It is the best free-standing Renaissance sculpture in Poland and in no way inferior to anything achieved in this period in Italy. The superb mastery of material, the plastic rendering of the hardness of the fluted metal armour and coupled simultaneously to the absolute lightness of the etching of the cloak, the unforced, contraposto attitude of the figure, and the individualization of facial features, all bear witness to the high artistic qualifications of its author who almost certainly was Berrecci himself. The statue of St Wenceslaus is meant to compete with St Sigismund, but there is an element of hardness in its design, and the ponderous composition of the figure points to a less gifted author. Yet he has revealed a psychological ability to characterize and aptly deliver the disturbed and impetous emotions agitating this saint. Together with the treatment of the features as in a portrait, these traits indicate that the artist made use of a live model.

43, 44 In 1520 a Renaissance porch-cum-gallery at the top of the right aisle of the church of St Mary in Cracow was either built or completed. Endowed by wealthy patrician Kaufman family, it was linked by a picturesquely situated passage with their family chapel. The porch has the design of an elongated balcony and balustrade supported by consoles; it is richly adorned and on its lower part can be seen a burgher's cachet on a shield. The proportions and forms of the pillars, balusters and consoles and the exquisitely carved decoration are in the pure Florentine-Roman Renaissance style of the close of the 15th century. The porch bears a very close resemblance to the choir erected during the last quarter of the 15th century by the Florentine artists working under Mino da Fiesole in the Sistine Chapel in Rome; an affinity which can be explained by the ties between the Berrecci atelier in Cracow and the Florentine-Roman school. The former was also undoubtedly the source of the architecture and sculpture, this feature of the church of St Mary, as is indicated by the many similarities between the decoration and its techniques and other works from Berrecci's atelier, especially the tomb of Bishop Jan Konarski (ill. 49) and the Sigismund Chapel. This is the first work known to have been executed by this atelier outside Wawel and dates to the preliminary work on the Jagiellonian Chapel. Placed in the murky aisle of the late-Gothic church it marked the first manifestation of the new style among the townsmen community of the then Polish capital.

45—47 A Renaissance canopy in stone was commissioned by Sigismund I from the Berrecci atelier to replace the original, damaged covering of the Gothic tomb of Ladislaus the Jagiellon from 1435 in Cracow Cathedral. Work of the canopy, in which the sculptor Giovanni Cini of Sienna took part, was under way in 1519 and finished by 1524. It is a masterly example of architecture and sculpture in the new style. On to the capitals crowning the shafts of the old Gothic columns fall the arches of an arcade fastened by keys and above them rises an entablature with prominent cornices. The soffit of the canopy has ten coffers with, apart from the crest of Poland (a white eagle) and Lithuania (horse and rider brandishing a sword), tritons, mounted youths, and arms and trophies. The facettes and capitals are decorated with stylised plants and weapons, masks and fantastic human and animal forms. This ornamental repertoire with its Florentine, Siennese and Roman character and the style of execution have close affinities with the decoration of the Sigismund Chapel.

48 In 1525 there died the one-year-old first son, Ludwik Mikołaj, of Krzysztof Szydłowiecki, Chancellor of Poland, Castellan and Voivode of Cracow, heir-apparent to the vast wealth and glory of his family. That same year, the heartbroken father erected in red marble "to my son, who blossomed like a little flower to gladden the heart of his most noble house and withered a year later," as the Latin inscription on the plaque has it. It initiated a type of monument —the child's tomb—which was to enjoy a flourishing development all its own in Renaissance Poland, but took root nowhere else, Italy included. Its author was either Berrecci or someone from his atelier then engaged on the architectural and sculptural decoration of the Sigismund Chapel. Although the form and mood of the tomb derive from Florentine art of the close of the 15th century, its general design is fairly individual and has no other counterparts in Poland. The monument in there parts, is suspended against the wall with the infant's figure lying on the sarcophagus in the uppermost part and the Szydłowiecki-Odrowąż blazon in the central part. The figure of the child is especially interesting as it does the sleeping cherubs of Andrea Verrochio, the famous Forentine artist. It should be emphasized that the child's pose—asleep, with his head resting on his folded arms and one leg thrust in front of the other, anticipated by five years the design of the statue of Sigismund I on his tomb in the Sigismund Chapel, which was to become characteristic of the recumbent figures on Polish Renaissance monuments.

49 The tomb of Jan Konarski, Bishop of Cracow, in Wawel Cathedral, built in 1521 while he was still alive, was the work of one Berrecci's chief assistants, but his identity is not entirely certain. It came unquestionably from the Wawel atelier of the Italians then principally occupied with the construction and decoration of the Sigismund Chapel. It is the earliest work of sepulchral sculpture from this atelier known to us. The author of the monument, partly at the founder's wish, let himself be influenced by a type of tombstone—popularly called a "show-case"—unknown in Italy which derives from the Central European Gothic tradition and was brought to Poland by Stwosz; an example is his monument of Bishop Piotr of Bnin in the Cathedral in Włocławek. Konarski's tomb consists of two parts: a high socle, an echo of the Gothic sarcophagus but reduced in width, and a slab lying obliquely across it with the bas-relief figure of the deceased. The decorative repertoire is pure Italian Renaissance and comes from the realm of the motifs used in the Jagiellonian Chapel; to it belong the garlands and eagles in the socle, the ornamental volutes on the sides of the slab and the cornice with bands of classical ornaments. The bishop's figure, although related in posture to the late-Gothic figures of the Stwosz tombs, is Renaissance in form, the draping of the garments mould following the

tectonics of the body. The combination of vestiges of the Gothic tomb and forms belonging to the new style created an entirely novel effect. Konarski's tomb represents a first version of the wall-monument typical of Polish Renaissance sculpture. It was later taken up in other tombs built by the Berrecci school whereas the Italian's ateliers developed more elaborate but compositionally more compact versions.

50 The tombstone of Stanisław (d. 1524) and Janusz (d. 1526), the last of the Mazovian princes, in Warsaw Cathedral, then a collegiate church, constitutes the first representation in Polish sepulchral sculpture of knights in a fully Renaissance form. Originally it had a rich architectural frame of the kind we can see on Bishop Jan Konarski's tomb from 1521 in Cracow Cathedral (ill. 49). The passage of time took a heavy toll, and the slab itself was seriously damaged during the Warsaw Rising in 1944. The monument was endowed by the princes' sister, Anna. Commissioned from the Cracow atelier of the Italian working on the Sigismund Chapel, it was executed in 1526—1528 by Bernardino De Gianotis, Berrecci's close associate. De Gianotis liked to sign himself "Romanus", not by reason of his birth for he was a Tuscan, but on account of the many years he had lived and worked in Rome. In keeping with the specialization that was a feature of the Berrecci atelier, De Gianotis seems to have devoted himself mainly to figurative sculpture. In the Warsaw monument he proved himself a master of rendering not only the physical, but also the psychological attributes of both princes. Their faces, carved with the fidelity of a portrait, reveal how skilfully the Italian observed and caught their specific, unmistakably Slav features, a gift, for that matter, displayed in his other sculptures. He was able to suggest a strong sense of brotherly ties by posing the princes with their arms around each other's necks and slightly turned towards one another.

51, 52 Simultaneously with the Sigismund Chapel, Berrecci completed the St Thomas Chapel in Wawel Cathedral, commissioned by Piotr Tomicki, Bishop of Cracow and Deputy Chancellor, which he had commenced in 1524. A friend of the king, a humanist and scholar (he had studied Medicine and Law at Bologna), a bibliophile and authority on art, the Bishop had this chapel built as a mausoleum with his tomb. Completed in 1533, it was a wall-monument with a central rectangular niche, a socle and a finial, notable for its extreme decorativeness. The niche is flanked by columns covered with coiling plants in delicate bas-relief, and through a frame of rosettes can be seen the sarcophagus with the bishop's recumbent figure (ill. 51) against a bas-relief background depicting St Peter recommending him to the Madonna (ill. 53). The designer of the tomb must certainly have been the builder of the chapel, i.e. Berrecci who no doubt also, with the help of two or three sculptors from his atelier, carved it. This would be consistent with the custom prevailing ni Italy where one artist generally worked on the figurative sculpture, a second on the decoration and a third on the bas-reliefs. Today the tomb of Bishop Tomicki, who personally supervised both the architecture and decoration of the chapel, is recognised as an outstanding work; in 1545, Queen Bona commissioned Gianmaria Mosca, known also as Padovano, another Italian sculptor in Poland, to carve a similar tomb for Piotr Gamrat, Bishop of Cracow and Archbishop of Gniezno, in Wawel Cathedral. Tomicki's tomb initiated a new type of sepulchral monument in Poland: one, supported against the wall, with a rectangular niche for the sarcophagus bearing the deceased's recumbent figure. This kind of recess is characteristic of Roman Renaissance sepulchral architecture. We may conjecture that Tomicki's visit to Rome in 1500 was spent not only improving his legal training in the Curia but also soaking up the beauty of its art. It was a time when the monument of Pope Paul II in the basilica of St Peter for which its authors, Mino da Fiesole and Giovanni Dalmata, invented the design of a rectangular niche bordered by columns. It exerted a considerable influence on the new Roman school in which almost certainly the Tuscan Berrecci served an apprenticeship.

The figure of Bishop Tomicki carved in red Hungarian marble, rests on a sarcophagus decorated with the beloved Florentine motif of hovering cherubs, who bear aloft his coat of arms. Deep in a peaceful slumber stressed by the hand supporting his head and the relaxed attitude of his body, it recalls, even more than figure of Sigismund I in his tomb in the Sigismund Chapel (ill. 35), the aforementioned figurative convention employed by Andrea Sansovino in some of his Roman tombs. Tomicki's face has been modelled true to life: boney, wide-nosed, with wrinkles running from nostrils to chin; it exactly matches the portrait painted about 1530 to be seen in the gallery of the Franciscan Church in Cracow (ill. 76).

53 The bas-relief, enclosed in a picture-like frame, carved on the back of the niche of the Tomicki tomb, represents a Madonna with a halo of angels' heads and the Bishop and St Peter, his patron-saint, kneeling before her. The Madonna's head is turned towards the face of the deceased, recumbent on his sarcophagus. The Child, however, has his arms stretched out towards the genuflecting figure of the Bishop in the bas-relief. This is the only example in Polish Renaissance sepulchral sculpture of a multi-figure background (apart from the 1545 tomb of Archbishop Gamrat which, after all, is a copy of the Tomicki monument). It is, however, characteristic of turn-of-the-century Roman tombs which almost always had religious scenes, frequently of great detail, as background. The Tomicki bas-relief is remarkable for its superb execution, splendid modelling, mastery of material, the gentle passage from the shallower to the more convex parts of the relief and the subtle variations in the expressions of the faces—

from St Peter's extreme dignity and austerity, to the gravity and compassion of the Madonna and the mischievous and glee of the Child and the angels. The modelling of the Madonna's garments recalls the draping of the Evangelists' robes in the medallions of the Sigismund Chapel.

54—56 The monument of Barbara, wife of Hetman Jan Tarnowski, in Tarnów Cathedral is outstanding among Polish tombs for its artistry and the figure of the dead noble woman is one of the most beautiful female statues in Renaissance sculpture as a whole. For years its date and authorship have been a matter of dispute. Barbara Tarnowska died when she was 31, either in 1521 (as given by Paprocki in *Polish Heraldry*) or in 1527 (according to Starowolski in *Monumenta Sarmatarum*). The last date would seem more likely for we can hardly imagine the Hetman, endowed as he was with a small son, living as a widower for all of ten years: we know that in 1530 he remarried his bride being Zofia, the daughter of Chancellor Krzysztof Szydłowiecki. It can, however, be assumed that he built his first wife's tomb shortly after her death and before his second marriage. Hence, the period between 1527—1530 would seem the most probable, which means we must seek the author only Italian workshop of its kind at this time in Poland; it seems very likely that it was Berrecci himself, with assistance who was the author. At one time it was attributed to Gianmaria Mosca (Padovano), who came to Poland after 1532, and its execution to the 1540s. The main reason for such an assumption is the present framing of the monument with its affinities with Venetian sculpture and the work in Poland of Padovano. But the present appearance of the tomb is not its original one. Initially placed by the presbytery, it had to make way for the massive multi-tiered monument of the Hetman and his son, Jan Krzysztof built by Padovano in 1561—1567 and was moved to a none too prominent site on the west wall of the right aisle, high above the window. The orginal architecture of the tomb, which may have echoed Bishop Tomicki's tomb in Wawel Cathedral (ill. 51) was too bulky for this narrow wall. Padovano, therefore, left the deceased's figure on the sarcophagus and some of the features as, for example, the tondo with a Madonna, identical to the one at the back of Tomicki's tomb (ill. 53), and furnished it with a new setting reminiscent of classical forms. At the same time the inscription was changed (Jan Tarnowski now being referred to as Castellan of Cracow; a title was conferred on him in 1536). Certain mistakes were made in the re-mounting of the tomb: for example, far too little space was left above the figure and, worse still, the positioning of the tondo, ignored the formal and ideological relationship between Madonna and Child, and the figure lying on the sarcophagus, which is so important in the Tomicki tomb. Despite these faults, the harmonious blending of the architecture with the tranquility of the recumbent figure of the young woman make the Barbara Tarnowska monument one of the peak achievements of the two Italian ateliers in Poland: Berrecci's Florentine and Gianmaria's Venetian-Paduan one. The design of the figure, associated with Berrecci's atelier, derives from the Florentine-Roman school and has a classical and contemporary Renaissance pedigree. In composition, it is close to the female figures on Roman sarcophagi which, together with other relics of antiquity, inspired the creative imaginations of sculptors around 1500. Transplanted to Polish soil, the result was a woman's figure of exceptional beauty, far from lifeless but steeped in a serenity and harmony conjured up by an interplay between smooth surfaces or folds and skilfully shaded chiaroscuro which delicately and lyrically sets the mood. A supreme command of sculptural skills and sense of shape are also apparent in the subtle passage from the sumptuously ornamented body of the sarcophagus to the quiet forms of the figure itself achieved by separating them with the wide smooth surface of the slab, on which the hem of the dress lightly falls. The slight raising of one knee and the cushioning of the head on a hand banish all thoughts of death and suggest a dreaming of slumber.

57, 58 The tomb of Primate Andrzej Krzycki in Gniezno Cathedral was built after his death in April 1537. Of the original monument there remains the slab with the high-relief figure of the Archbishop; the original frame was destroyed when the tomb was transferred to another site in the 18th century. Unquestionably a wall tomb with the deceased's figure lying on a sarcophagus, it was modelled on the Wawel tomb of Piotr Tomicki (ill. 51) whose nephew Krzycki was and for whom he had composed its inscription. Krzycki, a bland courtier who, with his uncle's assistance, climbed the rungs of the court and ecclesiastical ladder to the highest church office in Poland, a scholar, humanist and poet, was a fervent advocate of Renaissance art in Mazovia where, as Bishop of Płock, he had presided over the construction in 1531—1535 of a Renaissance cathedral in his diocesan capital, the first big church in Poland in the new style; it was built by Berrecci's closest assosiates: Giovanni Cini of Sienna and Bernardino De Gianotis. The Gniezno tomb was put up in Krzycki's memory by his friends. Its author is unknown, but it seems probable that the designer was Bartolomeo Berrecci and the sculptor another artist from his atelier, possibly Antonio da Fiesole who had close contacts with Florentine art (Berrecci met his death in July 1537, murdered at the hands of a compatriot). The Krzycki's tombstone is of notable artistic quality. The Archbishop lies in a deep slumber, the upper part of his body resting lightly on cushions, his hands loosely arranged, his feet crossed. The face is remarkably life-like, strongly modelled with a feel for the sculptural possibilities of red marble. In treatment it strongly recalls the portrayal of Bishop Piotr Tomicki (ill. 52) and Mikołaj Szydłowiecki,

Crown Treasurer, and the Chancellor's brother, on the tomb in the church in Szydłowiec. The ornate pontifical vestments and cushions have been treated with a decorative freedom, the surfaces being given varied textures and their polished and matt parts contrasted. Such mastery of the sculptor's art and such markedly individual portraiture of the head bringing out the powerful inner emotions and mental activity of a man steeped in slumber could only in the 1530s have come from Berrecci's atelier.

59 There are in Gniezno Cathedral four identical tombstones in the form of an upright rectangle with a principal motif of a crest enclosed in a wreath and an inscription in the lower part; a fifth slab of this type is to be found in Włocławek Cathedral and a sixth was once in Cracow Cathedral, but is now lost. All were endowed by Jan Łaski, Grand Crown Chancellor and Primate of Poland (1455—1532). A politician, jurist (author of the famous Łaski Statutes) and royal envoy to various courts, among them the Vatican where he served over a longer period of time, he decided to build himself a funeral chapel in Gniezno near the Cathedral,: it was finished in 1523, several years before the work on the Jagiellonian Chapel was completed. The designer of this building, which has long since disappeared, was no doubt Berrecci since it was probably Łaski who brought him to Poland from Hungary and recommended him to Sigismund I. He ordered four slabs to be placed in the Chapel in memory of his predecessors and benefactors: two for archbishops Jan Gruszczyński and Andrzej Boryszewski, a third for his gifted brother Andrzej, Canon of Gniezno, on the brink of a brilliant career, and the fourth for himself, the fifth for Krzesław of Kurozwęki, Bishop of Włocławek, went to its cathedral, while the sixth commemorated a Cracow bishop of the 14th century named Radlica. The five surviving slabs are identical in design but have various crests in the wreaths. Though related in style to some of the work of the Florentines in Poland, they differ in their lack of figurative elements and their heraldic accents. They represent a type of Renaissance tombstone imported from Hungary where it appeared in the early years of the 16th century. Returning to Poland from Rome in 1516 with his friend Tomas Bakócs, Primate of Hungary, Łaski halted at Esztergom where a mausoleum for the former had just been completed. Introduced to the Florentine artists working for the Cardinal, he ordered his six tombstones from a sculptor named Joannes Florentinus. They were modelled on the classical pillar type of monument known as the cippus, a number of which has been excavated in Hungary and placed in the royal collections. These too, have as their principal adornment a wreath, for that matter a favourite motif of the ancients adopted by the art of the Renaissance; the inscription is in the lower part. However, the main emphasis in Joannes' Renaissance tombstones is on the armorial motif; the centrepiece of Łaski's tombstone is chis crest set in a thick floral wreath with flowing ribbons the smooth surface of the epitaph at the bottom of the slab serving to accentuate still more the decorativeness and importance of the bearings.

60 A source-attested work by Bernardino De Gianotis is the tombstone of Stanisław Lasocki in the parish church in Brzeziny. It was commissioned in 1535 by the executor of his will. On the evidence of this tombstone it has been possible to draw up a list of other works that can be attributed to this sculptor, Berrecci's senior assistant on the Sigismund Chapel. They include the tombs of the Mazovian Princes in Warsaw Cathedral (ill. 50), Wojciech Gasztołd in Vilna and Chancellor Krzysztof Szydłowiecki (ill. 64) and his daughter Anna (ill. 61) in the collegiate church in Opatów. Through them we have a clearer picture of the style of Bernardino De Gianotis who was chiefly a figurative sculptor skilled in the forms of the High Renaissance. The common features are the face-on attitude of the figure and the outstandingly realistic portrayal of the features together with accurate depiction of details (armour, jewelry and adornaments, etc.). In spite of its posture, Lasocki's figure is prevented from looking rigid by the movements of his hands which hold a banner and a sword at his side. The forceful face with its prominent lips, characteristic square-chin and strongly accentuated ears, is far from idealised and gives the impression of a study made from life. At the same time, it is one of the many examples of portraiture inherent in the sepulchral sculpture of the Polish Renaissance.

61 The Opatów collegiate church contains one other valuable work of Polish Renaissance sculpture: the tombstone of Anna, Chancellor Krzysztof Szydłowiecki's daughter who died when she was fourteen in 1536. The lovely figure of the young girl, her head resting on a cushion, suggests the idea of serene slumber rather than of death. Gently curled hair falls loosely from beneath a chaplet of flowers encircling the pure oval of a face sunk in tranquil dreams. She is clothed in a typical dress of the period with parallel hanging folds crossed by three girdles with a Renaissance leaf pattern and bedecked with jewellery and a gold chain; the tips of a pair of slippers protrude from under the folds of her dress. It adds up to a portrait of a young lady of the court of great grace and charm. The monument was the work of Bernardino De Gianotis, who had carved the figure on her father's tomb (ill. 64)

62—66 The tomb of Krzysztof Szydłowiecki, Grand Crown Chancellor and Voivode of Cracow, in the collegiate church in Opatów was commissioned before his death on December 31, 1532 and built in 1533—1536. It is the principal work of the partnership set up in Cracow by Berrecci's closest associates—Giovanni Cini of Sienna and Bernardino De Gianotis called Romanus—to carry out orders for architecture and sculpture after the work on the Sigismund Chapel had been completed. Its present appearance is not the original one; alterations having been made when it was moved from the presbytery to where it now stands in the arm of the transept during conversion of the church in the 18th century. The marble epitaph was removed (and placed under the tombstone of Anna, the Chancellor's daughter) the armorial cartouche in the finial was replaced with an earlier bronze plaque of Zygmunt, the Chancellor's son who died in 1525, and the central part of the tomb with the slab bearing the Chancellors' figure (ill. 64) in its upper part, and a bas-relief depicting the mourning after his death (ill. 64, 65) in the lower was moved forward. As a result the sides consisting of the niches with the statues of St Christopher and St Sigismund and below them plaquettes with representations of arms (ill. 66) seem recessed. All these alterations spoiled the original architectonic cohesion of a monument which represents an important stage in the evolution of the Polish Renaissance tomb. By enlarging the lateral parts and adding niches, Cini and De Gianotis created a new tri-axial scheme that was later to be developed by the sculptors of the third quarter of the 16th century.

The centrepiece of the Szydłowiecki tomb is the slab on which the Chancellor lies clad in a magnificent suit of Renaissance fluted armour, its moulding and burnished surfaces made all the more realistic by being cast in bronze. A lover of luxury and splendour, he cannot—since the tomb was commisioned during his lifetime—have omitted to give his sculptor instructions on the emblems that were to commemorate his authority and might for posterity. But it is the face which is the most memorable, not only by reason of the striking beauty of the features but also for the look of haughty, imperious assurance of his own greatness (ill. 62). The figure was carved after Szydłowiecki's death and the sculptor must have worked from a death mask, judging by the realism with which the deep eye sockets with closed lids under heavily emphasized brows, frowning slightly as though in pain, have been depicted. A jutting jaw intimates a man of iron will, which the Chancellor had indeed shown himself to be in his ruthless pursuit of the highest offices of state. The arresting realism of the face is heightened by the smoothness of the forehead beneath the arch of his cap from which protrude the lobes of his ears. The author is Bernardino De Gianotis, expert observer and master of psychological portraiture that he was.

The cherubs gambolling on dolphins which appear in the finial of the Szydłowiecki tomb echo the angel on the lantern (ill. 20) and the putti in the decoration of the Sigismund Chapel. Their superbly delineated naked bodies effortlessly seated on the slippery backs of the dolphins, a symbol of eternal life-lend the Opatów tomb that same touch of lightness given to the Jagiellonian Chapel by the frolics of the sea gods. The dolphins themselves are shown in motion and their supple forms are full of vitality and abandon. The author of these decorative motifs, so purely Tuscan in style—this type of winged and frisky putto is derived from Donatello—was probably Giovanni Cini.

The two square plaques in bronze (ill. 66) placed under the niches flanking Krzysztof Szydłowiecki's tomb in the Opatów collegiate church, are remarkable for the magnificent artistry of both their draughtsmanship and carving. They represent the panoply of a knight comprising two superimposed shields, one oval, the other hexagonal, and an ancient helmet, with sword hilts, arrows axes and maces protruding from beneath the shields: the date 1536 under the sword hilt on the left side records the year which the plaques were executed. Their author has revealed a great gift composition: the foreground, formed by the shields and helmet, is in extremely high relief, while the assortment of weapons is much lower and forms a background. He has also skilfully contrasted the strongly projecting parts by covering the lower shield with a beautifully engraved plant pattern which makes the smooth upper shield, accentuate all the more the decorativeness of the Roman helmet on top of it. The similarity between the arm motif on the Szydłowiecki tomb and on the canopy of Ladislaus the Jagiellon's tomb in Cracow Cathedral (ill. 45) indicates that the author of these plaques was Giovanni Cini.

The *Opatów Lamentation*, as it is termed, is an exceptional work in many respects. Mounted in the form of a frieze under the slab of the Szydłowiecki tomb, it represents an unusual theme for Polish sculpture: a scene of mass grief and mourning. It is connected either with the Chancellor's death or with some tragic historical event. The composition is that of a triptych, the central panel consisting of a long table with people seated at, or standing behind it and the sides of two rows of individual figures, standing face-on, of various age, class and race. They are dressed in quasi-classical, Renaissance or 15th-century Italian costume, with Italian berets or eastern calpacs on their heads. The common feature is a stark expression of anguish. The group seated at the table, in which Hetman Jan Tarnowski, the Chancellor's son-in-law, is easily recognisable, undoubtedly represents humanists connected with the royal court, although the central figure cannot be said to be the king since all the others seem to be real-life portraits and he resembles Sigismund I neither in appearance nor dress. The Szydłowiecki' family's *Liber geneseos* (ill. 75) refers to the affection in which the Chancellor was held not only by the monarchs but also by entire states and nations, like Spain, Britain, Portugal, Italy, Germany, Turkey or the Scythians and Muscovites. It may therefore be concluded that the mourners are not only the Chancellor's friends but also men from various eastern and western countries. The *Lamentation* probably dates to 1533—1536, and its author was either a Pole or an Italian familiar with Polish realities;

though difficult to attribute with any certainty, it was indubitably cast (in bronze) in Cracow. The sculptor, obviously a superb physiognomist skilled in expressing a wide range of emotion from melancholy to prostation and in addition, organizing a multi-figure composition. His artistry extended to his worksmanship which deftly blended all the degrees of relief from the almost fully sculptural faces to a Donatelloesque *schiacciato* in which there was only the barest projection from the background. He may have been a medallionist commissioned to do a larger-scale project. This is suggested by the busts and especially the heads, being far better executed than the lower parts of the bodies which betray a certain crudeness in the proportions and arrangement of the legs.

67—70 Towards the end of his life, King Sigismund the Old endowed a main altar for Wawel Cathedral. With the onset of the Baroque age, its style fell out with the artistic tastes and, though it escaped being torn down, it was twice moved to churches of diminishing stature: in the 17th century to Kielce Cathedral and in the 18th century to the parish church in Bodzentyn, where it is still to be seen. Fortunately, it suffered little damage in the process. Built in 1545—1548, it is a rare Polish example and an outstanding sculpture in wood by any standards of Renaissance fretwork. It betrays numerous affinities with the Sigismund Chapel: the same design of a Roman triumphal arch with niches and statues in the lateral axes, the same subordination of elaborate decoration to the basic architectural pattern and the far-reaching similarity of the grotesque motifs, chiefly composed in panels, to the ornamentation of the Jagiellonian mausoleum. The artistry of the statues (of Sts Stanislaus and Wenceslaus—the patron saints of Wawel Cathedral, in the niches) and of the decoration have ensured the Wawel altar an important place in the Italian-Renaissance trend transplanted to Cracow in the early 16th century by Francis the Florentine and then enriched and spread by the works of Bartolomeo Berrecci and his associates. It is among them that the author of the altar should be sought; the most likely candidate is Giovanni Cini, one of the chief artists involved in the Sigismund Chapel, since it was in the 1540s and early 50s that his volume of work reached its peak, most of it commissioned for the royal court, among them the altar for the Vilna Cathedral in 1533. Although the artists of Berrecci's circle specialized in sculpture in stone, the possibility that Cini and his assistants embarked upon the execution of an altar in wood cannot be excluded, for it was by no means an alien material to the artists of the Italian Renaissance.

71 One of the earliest Renaissance works in Silesia is a 1517 portal framing the doorway from the presbytery to the sacristy of Wrocław Cathedral. Unlike the architectonic and sculptural works of the Florentines in Cracow during this same period which, though also extremely decorative, respected the Italian Renais-

IV.

GRĘBIEŃ

sance's adherence to the principles of tectonics and harmonious composition, its design reveals the author's spiritedly unconstrained attitude to such rules: it is ui fact one that is general feature of the art of the Silesian Renaissance. Embellished with offsets, the doorposts have been tapered to a degree and the pilasters adorning them truncated unconventionally so that they might almost be super-imposed plaquettes narrowed both at top and bottom by extravagantly elaborate socles and capitals. The entablature has been extended to no obvious functional purpose. Above it there is a tympanum with a horseshoe arch and a representation of the beheading of St John the Baptist, the patron saint of the Wrocław Diocese, and the figure of Jan V Turzon, its bishop at the time, who endowed the portal; he is kneeling on one side of the scene which is framed at the edges of the tympanum by the genii bearing torches and the arms and insignia of the Bishop. The medieval tradition is all but imperceptible, though a faint echo may perhaps be detected in the actual idea with a commemorative tympanum and that love of ornament and unrestrained fantasy proper to the late-Gothic Silesian School of art. However, the forms themselves and the decorative features belong entirely to the new style, especially the very plastic and compressed shape of the figurative sculpture on the tympanum. The early dates of the portal and its many Renaissance features suggest its author was one of the émigré artists from Como who propagated a popular and decorative version of the Italian Renaissance in Europe and were highly susceptible to the influence of the environments in which they worked; they had come to Wrocław precisely at this time.

72 The gateway of the castle in Legnica is a comparatively early example of Renaissance architecture and decorative sculpture in Silesia. Completed in 1533, it is the work of Georg of Amberg who was engaged in the conversion of the castle carried out at this time by the Legnica line of the Piasts. Designed along the lines—so popular in the Renaissance—of a Roman triumphal arch, this gateway is remarkable for its rich and precisely stone-carved sculptural decoration. It consists of figurative bas-reliefs set in the panels and medallions and a sumptuous array of ornamental motifs in the new style on the columns, entablature and consoles. The decoration does not conform to the architectural divisions which are in any case treated with licence that basically disregards the classical canons observed as a rule in Renaissance art. Such decorative interpretation of architecture is fairly typical of the German artists who were working during the 16 century in Silesia.

73, 74 The tomb of Jan V Turzon, Bishop of Wrocław, a leading humanist and patron of the fine arts who died in 1520, was erected in 1537 in Wrocław Cathedral and endowed by the brother. All that has remained in the slab with the recumbent figure of the deceased. Ths magnificent, decorative architectonic structure was destroyed in the early years of the 18th century. Jn consisted of a canopy supported by the five columns and crowned by two conchal niches with inscriptive plaques and four putti on little plinths. This wall structure was the work of Andrea Walter I, Wrocław master-builder, while the Bishop himself was probably carved by a Silesian sculptor trained in Cracow. The representation of the figure sleeping peacefully in the manner so characteristic of Polish Renaissance sculpture was deliberately chosen by the founder to stress the ties between the Hungarian-born Turzon family and Cracow in which the Bishop was born and studied. It exerted a strong influence on the type of figure found in Renaissance sepulchral sculpture in Silesia.

I p. 9. *The Bell Foundry* is one of the most characteristic scenes in the miniatures which adorn the renowned *Codex of Baltazar Behem*. In the yard of the workshop the master is shown presenting bells to a clergyman accompanied by a city worthy; a journeyman is busy by the furnace; other products cast in the foundry are littered in the ground. The *Codex* contains altogether twenty similar miniatures depicting Cracow craftsmen at work and guild cachets. Behem was a town scribe and notary; in 1505 he offered the Council the Codex named after him in which he had drawn up a list of privileges and laws of Cracow, the statutes of its guilds and had it illustrated with full-page illuminations. In 1825 it was acquired by the Jagiellonian Library. It is clear that a number of artists collaborated in these miniatures; these must have been representatives of the Cracow school of miniatures which flourished during the transition from Gothic to Renaissance. The miniatures of the *Codex* are the quintessence of the art and culture of the Cracow burghers on the threshold of the 16th century, a token of their interests, aspirations and ambitions. A particulary revealing feature is their fully secular content; it testifies to the spread of humanist ideas not only through the court, but also among the Cracow townsmen and especially its university. In this respect the miniatures of the *Behem Codex* excel many other artistic achievements of the age, being the most splendid set of illuminations to be found anywhere in Europe north of the Alps in which all trace of religious matters has been completely eliminated. They are also the most important pictorial record in the art of their time of the life and occupations of the urban commons. At the same time, the *Codex* represents the high water mark in the interest in man at work burgeoned in European miniature painting in the Middle Ages, a counterpart of the pictures of husbandsmen in different months of the year which graced the 15th-century French prayer-books. The docummentary value of the *Behem Codex* is immense. The accuracy with which the miniatures depict people and things makes them a unique source of information about the Cracow crafts in the early years of the 16th century, the appearance of workshops and market stalls, methods and tools, guild products and the costume of the various sections of society. It is indeed remarkable how sharply the artists observed the world and life around them. The figures have individual features graphically and perceptively drawn, a realism which extends to whole scenes visibly caught and placed in recognizable settings, whether townscapes, as in *The Bell Foundry,* or in interiors. These traits, typical of the artistic outlook of the new era, are not wholly realized in the technical execution of the miniatures. There are still faults of perspective in the rendering of architecture and scenery and of anatomy in human figures. Though the artistic value of the miniatures is considerable, allowance must be made for the passage from one style to another. The contours, though imbued with individual verve, are none too fluent; the colours, though pure and fresh and boldly matched with a feeling for their values, lack the harmonious coalescence of composition typical of Renaissance painting. The architectonic backgrounds, striking in their relationship of tone and draughtsmanship, are nevertheless idealized in contrast to the scenes themselves, having been modelled on prints not always true to Cracow realities. The ornamental parts are fairly traditional. The grotesque and satirical touches added for seasoning have a similarly pre-Renaissance provenance.

II p; 19. The *Pontifical of Erazm Ciołek,* now in the Czartoryski Collection of the National Museum in Cracow, is one of the most splendid illuminated codexes of the early 16th-century Cracow School. A Pontifical is a book containing the offices and rites performed by a bishop. Ciołek, for whom it was produced, was Bishop of Płock from 1503, a leading Polish humanist, a generous patron of the arts and a passionate bibliophile. One of the scenes shown in the *Pontifical* is the *Building of a Church;* the wealthy patron and several of his retinue are watching bricklayers and masons at work on the building with a sprawling landscape and castle in the background. In its genre character and narrative manner, this miniature has close affinities with those in the *Behem Codex* and it has been conjectured that it and several other illuminations in the *Ciołek Pontifical* are by the same hand. Against this, the style of this miniature seems definitely different. At all events it corresponds to a somewhat later stage—c. 1510—in the development of the Cracow miniature and is more essentially of the Renaissance than the *Behem Codex.* Furthermore, in the composition of the scene, in the treatment of the landscape and in many details, it bears the impress of Netherlands painting which, together with Italian then led the way in Europe. Gothic echoes have all but disappeared and the miniature is given a new stylistic stamp by the blending of people and surroundings fluency of contours, comparatively three-dimensional portrayal of the figures and colourful composition bearing traces of the influence of Renaissance easel painting. Not without significance

in the general stylistic expression of the illumination is the costume of the people in the main group of figures.

75 About 1530 Stanisław Samostrzelnik illustrated the Szydłowiecki family history—*Liber geneseos illustris familiae Schidloviciae* with twelve full-page miniatures on parchment. Of these eleven have been preserved and are now in the Kórnik Library. The other illumination and the text of the book exist in later copies. The series opens with *The Conferring of the Odrowąż Crest on the Progenitor of the Line;* the rest portray the members of the family. The miniatures were Samostrzelnik's way of paying homage to Krzysztof Szydłowiecki, Grand Crown Chancellor (his tomb—ill. 62-66), and a patron and protector whom he served as chaplain and court painter for some twenty years. The portrait of Anna Tęczyńska, the wife of the Chancellor's brother Mikołaj, Grand Crown Treasurer, follows the same scheme as the other miniatures. She is shown in full-figure with a medallion of her patron saint opposite her head and framed by an ornamental border in which is enclosed the Tęczyński blazon, an axe. The most striking thing about the miniature is the decorativeness characteristic of Samostrzelnik's art. It takes the form of vivid colours in which the painter used fairly pure pigments revealing a fondness for reds, liberal application of gilt and of accentuating the linear values and the purely ornamental parts. An alumunus of the Cracow school of miniature of the first years of the century, his face was firmly turned towards the Renaissance as is apparent in the formal conception, in the search for individualization of features and in the repertoire of decorative motifs. On the other hand, he still betrays a certain clumsiness in the rendering of background and of the figure itself. The likenesses in the Szydłowiecki family history are among the earliest examples in Polish art of the independent portrait; in them can be detected the influence of the Italian Renaissance miniature and European graphic art, while the placing, in the illumination reproduced here, of a draped curtain in the background suggests the inspiration of the Renaissance tombstones from the Vischer's Nuremburg workshop, examples of which he had come across in Cracow; in them a similar motif appears.

III p. 29. The miniature on the title page of the codex *The Lives of the Gniezno Archbishops* (once in the Zamoyski Library collections, now in the National Library in Warsaw), illustrated by Stanisław Samostrzelnik, belongs to his best works. These illuminations were painted in the early 1530s. They were commissioned by Piotr Tomicki, Bishop of Cracow and one of the leading Polish humanists who held a high opinion of the artist, once remarking that "he paints better and more beautifully than any other artist". The title-page miniature shows a blessing being given by St Stanislaus the Bishop, the patron saint of Poland, whose figure symbollically presides over a group of contemporary notables, among them King Sigismund,

Tomicki and Krzysztof and Mikołaj Szydłowiecki (on the right, their heads in a row). In this picture we can see the quintessence of Samostrzelnik's style and hardly notice the slight faults in the representation of the figures which have been drawn with eminently individual features true to his penchant for portrait-like realism. Even more striking is his typically superb and Renaissance treatment of ornament. It comes out in the colours with their predominance of reds and golds, the rich material of the garments, the vegetal arabesques in the borders and the heraldic motifs of which he was so fond. Among them are the eagle of King Sigismund and the crest of the Tomickis, but it is the Polish coat of arms on a banner, the shaft of which is held alongside the patron saint by one of the two angels attending him, which arrests the eye. Thus figuratively the White Eagle dominates the scene, a sign for all to see the hardening sense of national and state identity that spread through Poland during the Renaissance.

76 During the Renaissance with its glorification of the great and the illustrious, the custom of creating portrait galleries spread through Europe. One of the most interesting in Poland is a collection of likenesses of bishops of Cracow in the Franciscan Monastery in that town, which began to be assembled in the 16th century. Pride of place among the Renaissance portraits belongs to the full length larger-than life figure of Bishop Piotr Tomicki with whom so many of the works of art of the first developmental stage of the Polish Renaissance are connected. Dating to the second quarter of the 16th century and painted in the traditional tempera on wood technique, it is one of the first independent portraits in Polish easel-painting and of a fairly high artistic standard. Its author has shown a portraitist's gift in the rendering of the face, successfully negotiated the problems of the relatively complicated arrangement of the hands and revealed a feeling for varied texture and the material of the garments and props, ect.,—all features of a fairly advanced stage of Renaissance realism in which there are few survivals of the Gothic idiom left. The most original thing in the Tomicki portrait is its extremely decorative style, a departure from the prevalent canons of portraiture. It is manifested in the emphasis on the elaborate patterns of the clothes and their jewelled adornments, the treatment of the props and the setting of the figure in a Renaissance arcade with richly detailed and decorated columns with motifs drawn from contemporary German models. The closest analogy is to be found in Samostrzelnik's miniatures (ill. 75, III), so that the name of this artist-monk who also dabbled in murals and seems, according to the sources, to have accepted orders for easel-painting as well has been advanced as a possible author.

77, 78 In many respects the triptych from the church at Pławno near Radomsko, now in the National Museum in Warsaw, occupies a leading place among the art works of the early Polish Renaissance. Made of lime wood, it consists of a central panel with a semicircular top and two folding side panels. When open, it discloses six polychromed and gilt bas-reliefs with scenes from the life of St Stanislaus, Bishop of Cracow. On the back of the side panels there is a painting of Christ, wearing a gold crown and Mary, also crowned, to whom he is turned in a gesture of benediction. On account of its style and quality, it is ascribed to Hans Suess, a painter from Kulmbach who worked in Cracow in 1514—1518. These also must be the date of the triptych's origin. The author of the bas-reliefs, undoubtedly a Cracow sculptor, is however nameless, though his work is in both form and content of a high standard. Though the altar-piece is still basically medieval in character, it no longer has a Gothic architectonic setting and conforms to the Renaissance principle of a unity of plastic value in both the side and the central panels which is not, as with Gothic altars, distinguished by three-dimensional sculptures. The story of the legend begins in the left lower compartment with the Bishop purchasing his village from Piotrowin. Above comes the scene, in which the chief character is Boleslaus the Bold, of the testimony of Piotrowin. On the right side the lower compartment shows the removal of St Stanislaus's body, the upper one the preparations for the Bishop's canonization. The climax of the drama is shown in the central panel: above, the killing of the Bishop by the king, below, his quartering by courtiers (ill. 77). A remarkable feature of this triptych is the absence of any reference to the miracles in which this legend abounded, this secularism which permeates all the scenes was consistent with the ideology of the new style, long ago suggested to scholars that the author was no religionist. We should also emphasize his objective portrayal of the king who is shown as a representative of the law and the lack of idealization in the treatment of the Bishop. The authenticity of the details of daily life in the early 16th century and the depiction of Polish customs and types also lend the triptych from Pławno considerable documentary value.

79—81 A painting of the Man of Sorrows attended by the Virgin Mary, St John the Baptist, St John the Evangelist and St Andrew, in a monastery museum at Szczyrzyc near Limanowa, basically adds to our knowledge of the evolution of the Renaissance outlook in Polish panel painting in the first decades of the 16th century. In the foreground, shown in keeping with medieval tradition in miniature, kneel the founders of the painting: a cleric and a knight of the "Ogończyk" blazon (possibly Andrzej Kościelecki, Grand Crown Treasurer and Castellan of Wojnice who died in 1515). The image of Christ as the Man of Sorrows seated deep in thought with his head on his hand is rare in panel painting; it appeared in late-Gothic art but was more characteristic of sculpture. The painter, probably one with an atelier in Cracow, has made a very individual attempt to cast off late-medieval methods and habits and given vent to what were new departures in Poland, but also betrayed certain crudities of craftsmanship. The use of three scales for the human figure is conservative: Christ much larger than the persons beside him and the tiny founders. Nor is the artist fully in command of anatomical accuracy. Nevertheless his evident sense of the plasticity of form is in the spirit of Renaissance painting. Another novelty for Polish panel painting at the turn of the age is the cohesion and monumentalism of the composition, achieved not only through the harmonious relationship of parts to each other and to the whole, but also through the restrained gestures and concentrated expressions of the figures which produce a second linking element. In all of this we can detect the influence of the *Santa conversazione* compositions which became popular in the 15th century in Italian painting; a central Madonna is flanked by saints intent in their mute attendance and positioned according to Renaissance categories. The Szczyrzyc painting, except for the Virgin, yielding precedence to Christ, is precisely this type of "holy conversation", though in in a more modern vein which is a far cry from the turmoil and over-emphasis of the late-Gothic group scene. Equally striking are the innovations in the portrayal of the two Johns: the Baptist, youthful and human without any trace of sternness and austerity and, even more so perhaps, the Evangelist with his expressive countenance suggestive of a young humanist absorbed in philosphical musings over human suffering. Christ grieving over the fate of mankind is reminiscent of some large folk art sculpture carved out of wood with smooth surfaces and a characteristic texture which gives the painting a very Polish flavour. It dates to about 1515.

82, 83 *The Battle of Orsha* (in the National Museum in Warsaw) was painted to extol Poland's prowess in battle. It was no doubt inspired by court circles and reflected the Renaissance realization that art could be harnessed to the glorification of the successes of the State, dynasties and generals. Such a programme matured in Poland during the first quarter of the 16th century and gave rise to many works of painting of an exclusively secular character and an interesting variety of themes. To match this novel purpose of art there were devised equally novel formal conventions though these still showed that strong streak of medieval tradition typical of the emergent period of the new style. For example, the anonymous author of this painting had not yet mastered the correct, that is perspective from one point, depiction of mass in space and relied on the rule-of-thumb methods which West-European painting had been seeking to perfect since the third quarter of the 15th century. Though he respected the unity of place, he disregarded in contrast to the new art, unity of time lumping together what were in fact succeeding phases of the battle: the Polish commander, Konstanty Ostrogski, can be seen at three different stages of the battle. Nevertheless there are numerous Renaissance features as well, partly due to the artist's

realistic observation which stemmed both from his predispositions as a painter and the nature of his commission. He was concerned with the accuracy of his representation of topography, scenery and tactics and sought to produce life-like portraits of the more important figures and, above all, a faithful rendering of costume and arms which give this painting the value of plastical and historical evidence. Its qualities only become apparent on close inspection. Viewed from a distance, it looks more like a colourful tapestry composed of hundreds of separate little strands which only after a moment knit themselves into a picture of the tumult of battle. The masses of soldiery are, however, fairly ordered and controlled by Renaissance rhythms. Here we are dealing with a work in the new style but it still falls short of the clear and harmonious compositions of the contemporary Italian compositions of the Renaissance. It represents its popular Central European version, adapted to the artist's task of reporting an event involving a host of figures and has particularly close affinities with German painting of the day, especially with the work of Lucas Cranach; similar battle scenes were also painted by Jörg Breu and Albrecht Altdörfer and can be found in German engravings as well. The author was no doubt a German representing an average standard of craftsmanship, but already proficient in the use of oils and not without individual characteristics. The authenticity of the whole scene and its countless details suggests that he may have himself been at Orsha, like the painter mentioned by Sarnicki in his *Books of the Hetmans* from 1578: "when armies pass through unknown parts to paint the *situm loci* of that country" and "to sketch the persons of the King and Hetman." Working from drawings made on the spot and studies of reality, the artist did the actual painting later in his studio, either shortly after the battle or several years later. There is a striking resemblance between the cannons-royal, appearing in the right foreground, and the subject Albrecht's Dürer's 1518 engraving *The Big Cannon*; similar pieces of ordnance which were not produced as single items were, as it happens, then used by the Polish-Lithuanian army.

84 The large triptych from about 1518 in the parish church at Kobylin near Krotoszyn, endowed by Jan Konarski, Bishop of Cracow, depicts in its central panel and the four compartments of its side panels scenes from the legend of St Stanislaus, popular in Poland in the 16th century. It was probably commissioned in a studio in Cracow, since this was where Bishop Konarski, a leading humanist and patron of the arts, generally placed his orders; in any case its style has much in common with the art of Cracow. For all its naivety, it shows its nameless guild painter to have been an artist of some individuality who, by daring introduction of Renaissance innovations, broke out of the traditional medieval conventions which had a particularly strong hold on panel painting of the first quarter of the 16th century. In this respect, the scene of the saint purchasing the village in the left panel is the most advanced in style. Although continuing to use gold backgrounds and showing an imperfect knowledge of perspective and anatomy, the artist is not only concerned to make the figures three-dimensional and render costume and details accuratelly, but has also under the influence of the new age presented this episode in the legend as a mundane true-to-life incident: St Stanislaus and Piotrowin are seated on either side of a table for all the world like two brokers attended by exactly the same sort of people who might be present at a sale. The artist's most distinctive trait is his fondness for portraiture. The heads in the scene are strongly individualized so much so that they must have been drawn from living models; owing to this they have a striking strenght of characterization achieved by what was for those times a modern form of modelling which forcefully and succinctly compressed shape and feature to substantiate their personal characteristics. The youth on the extreme right of the painting is no doubt the author himself; certainly he is one of the most characteristic figures in Polish Renaissance painting.

85 The central panel of a triptych once in the parish church at Mądre near Środa (today in the P.A.S. Library at Kórnik) dated 1529 presents two scenes from a cycle devoted to the Virgin: the Annunciation in the foreground, and behind it, in the distance in a landscape setting, the Visitation; below is the truncated figure of the founder, Łukasz Górka, Voivode of Poznań, kneeling beside a cartouche with his coat of arms. This is one of the most represenative examples of the painting of Great Poland in the first thirty years of the 16th century, the period in which it was starting to depart unmistakably from the Gothic tradition. What makes it arresting is the extremely decorative effect of the whole, thrown into relief by the strongly accentuated contours and the wealth of ornamentation and gilt. But it also has many conservative features; the simultaneous presentation of scenes which the Gospels record as taking place at different times and places, a traditional compositional scheme, a lack of atmospheric quality, and an attempt to express space by means of fore-shortenings made without a proper knowledge of perspective. However, the gentle, flowing lines delineating the figures, the portrait-like representation of the founder's face and the predominance of decorative motifs in the new style in the architectural details and utensils mark a crossing of the Renaissance border-line.

86, 87 A distinct position in Polish provincial painting in which the new was already starting to eclipse the old, is occupied by the *Madonna and Child* in the church of the Philippines in Gostyń. Signed with the monogram, S.B., of an otherwise undentified artist, it dates to 1540. It was painted for a chapel, no longer-standing, on "Holy Hill" in Gostyń: it can be seen in the left background with the town itself on the right. This first realistic townscape in Polish painting is an obvious sign of the influence of the new currents of the age and maintained in the convention of the Netherlands art. In contrast, the somewhat minute detail of the view is the representation of the main subject of the painting —the Madonna and Child, crowned by angels which shows a great sense of monumentalism and linear values. Echoes of the old still linger in the traditional technique of tempera on wood, in the clumsy treatment of the hands and the Gothic-like draping of the garments. Nevertheless, the composition of the whole is Renaissance and seems Italian in inspiration, to judge by the posing of the Madonna on a balcony against a curtained background and the strong accentuation of space from the foreground right up to the vanishing of the landscape over the distant horizon. The faces of the Madonna and Child and the arrangement of their hands also repeat Italian models of Byzantine provenance.

88, IV p. 39. On the ceiling of the nave a wooden church at Grębień near Wieluń, there can be seen amid lush coils of greenery, a village and a court musician, playing for the benefit of the Virgin Mary, Apostles and Saints who appear in the main scenes, a role reserved in medieval religious art for angels. In this painting which dates to 1520–1530, their place has been taken by more homely players. This encroachment of a non-religious legend is a new and unusual token of the ideological upheaval of the times. What is more, it has come comparatively early and not in some leading artistic centre but in the provincial environment of the guild painters either of Wieluń or in some other nearby town, of whom the author of the polychrome at Grębień must have been one. Even if in other parts of the work he has been unable to discard entirely the ballast of tradition, the figures of the two musicians show that he was alive to the innovations in both content and form, an awareness he owed not only to the circulation of popular engravings and other models from abroad but also to the heightening of his own sense of observation by the new mood of the times. In both figures, and especially that of the village musician, he is clearly seeking to catch a certain type with accent on accurate portraiture and a faithful rendering of costume and accessories. The old man playing the viola is dressed in a gaberdine with a collar and top boots and the young court minstrel, strumming a lyre, in a doublet with a long pleated basque and puffed sleeves, a typical Renaissance attire that was fashionable in about 1530. Characteristic of this painting is the folk-art interpretation of the typical features of the spreading Renaissance art. Despite a certain measure of crudity and naivety, the artist has tried to depict the figures naturally performing certain movements and gestures, a sign of the complete relaxation of the Gothic formulas. Although both figures stand detached against a plant-pattern background, there is a definite sense of space in their treatment; the same can be said of the mofifs wreathes with their distribution of light and many of the are taken direct from nature. With an awareness of the values proper to decorative painting, this anonymous artist has led the lines along fluid curves which have only occasional remnants of the Gothic's sharp angularity. The colouring of this tempera painting is lively; the vermilion of the village musician's gaberdine and the greenish-blue of the court musician's costume and his red hose stand out against the olive green background. The Grębień musicians, concealed in the plant ornamentation of a small rural church situated far off the highways were virtually discovered only after the last war and have become exceedingly popular. This is also due to the frankness, spontaneity and even charm with which the provincial guild painter has depicted them.

89 Once the architectural parts of the Sigismund Chapel were ready and its sculptural decoration drawing to a close, King Sigismund the Old made a special point of seeing that it was furnished with fixtures and ritual objects of a high artistic standard. Thus, shortly after 1530, there were installed: a bronze grille in the entrance to the Chapel from the south nave of the Cathedral, an altar with silver-wrought and painted compartments (ill. 90, 93) and silver and bronze candlesticks (ill. 95). All these precious works of art were ordered and made in Nuremburg, a famous artistic centre at this time with a special reputation for metalware, already of fully-fledged Renaissance design and exported to various parts of Europe. Great care was taken over the king's orders, the workshops being provided with exact specifications as to size and rough sketches, and some of the artists involved were invited to Cracow to acquaint themselves with what was needed on the spot. The entrance grille consists of a basic lower and a supplementary upper part which were not made at the same time. The former was cast in bronze in 1530—1532 in the famous Nuremburg workshop of the Vischers under the supervision of Hans who had visited Cracow on 1530 and signed the contract for the commission with Seweryn Boner, Governor of Cracow. The installation of the grille in the nave of the Cathedral was completed at the end of 1532. The upper bratticed part was added for reasons of safety in 1545; the plans were drawn by a Cracow woodcarver Jan Janda, and the casting done either in a local bell foundry or in Nuremburg. It certainly makes a fairly neat match with the Vischer part in which supreme workmanship and precision of detail are linked to a monumental composition of very carefully balanced horizontals and perpendiculars decoratively thickened in the centre which forms the entrance. The ornament— blazons, putti on the frieze, panels on the plinths of the columns—seem designed as an echo of corresponding bas-relief elements of the Chapel, which suggests that Hans Vischer made a personal study of the sculptural decoration of the mausoleum while he was in Cracow.

90—94 In the arcaded recess of the east wall of the Sigismund Chapel stands its most magnificent fixture, the altar, a valuable work not only of the goldsmith's art but also of painting. Like the grille in the entrance to the Chapel from the nave and the candlesticks, it was ordered in Nuremburg. In 1531, when the Chapel was all but complete, the court painter Hans Dürer made a rough sketch of the intended altarpiece sent to Nuremburg from where simultaneously came samples of the proposed silver panels; Jan, the royal woodcarver, had previously carved a model in wood indicating the desired projection of the relief. All this we know from records, but it is also thought that instructions regarding the style of the altar and, above all, its iconography, that is the content of the scenes depicted in its compartments, were supplied as well. The entire programme of the Sigismund Chapel had been so thoroughly conceived that it is quite impossible to suppose that any margin of freedom would have been left as regards the theme of the altarpiece that was undoubtedly meant to complement the subject matter presented by the sculptural decoration. Made in the Nuremburg workshop in 1535—1538, it is a pentaptych with a broader central panel, two pairs of side panels and a double predella. When open, the compartments of the central panel and the first pair of side panels show ten scenes from the life of the Virgin Mary to whom the Chapel was dedicated and the figures of St Adalbert and St Stanislaus; these saints, together with the statues of St Florian and St Venceslaus in the niches of the wall opposite, form a group of the four patron saints of Poland. All the compartments were of silver repoussé and partly gilded. On the predella can be seen the foundation inscription flanked by portraits of King Sigismund I (ill. 94) and King Sigismund Augustus. When closed, the backs of both pairs of wings and the second predella show fifteen scenes painted on wood connected with the legend of Christ (ill. 93). Wooden models of the bas-reliefs were supplied by Peter Flötner, from these brass moulds were made to be wrought in silver and chiselled by Melchior Baier; the paintings were the work of Georg Pencz. All three artists were leading representatives of Nuremburg art. They ensured this costly altar a high artistic standard and an efficient execution. Apart from the traditional shape, its style is otherwise wholly High Renaissance. Strictly built as it was to Polish specifications, this import from Nuremburg is an integral part of the artistic culture of Cracow.

Each of the silver bas-reliefs of the altar in the Sigismund Chapel can be viewed as a separate composition; their character is amply embodied in *The Adoration of the Magi*. The chiselling of Melchior Baier, the goldsmith who wrought the bas–reliefs in the brass moulds made from Peter Flötner's wooden models, has discretely and faithfully captured the effect of the originals. Although the theme itself was no doubt specified in Cracow, the treatment is Nuremburg. Flötner, who was also an excellent ornamentallist, specialized in small-scale sculpture. The Cracow altarpiece shows him to have been an artist thoroughly acquainted with the attainments of the Italian Renaissance; this is not surprising since he had visited Italy, fallen under the lasting spell of the art there and become, via his own work, its propagator in Germany. The scenes on the altar have obvious affinities with Italian bas-reliefs and paintings of the 15th and 16th centuries. The artist has made skillful use of a multi-plane composition of space defined mainly by architecture of classical form and displayed a sound knowledge of fore-shortening and perspective based on the Italian practice which Albrecht Dürer had also helped to spread in Germany on the threshold of the 16th century. However, in Flötner's hands the Italian formulas have lost their purity and become a little crabbed and cumbersome. *The Adoration of the Magi* echoes in part Dürer's woodcut on this subject in his *Life of Mary* cycle; in some of the scenes of the altarpiece these links are even more apparent. It has been conjectured that the kneeling king represents George the Bearded, Duke of Saxony and Sigismund I's brother-in-law, and the king with the chalice—Joachim II Hector, Margrave of Brandenburg and the Polish king's son-in law.

At the side of the predella of the altar in Sigismund Chapel there is a silver repoussé bust of Sigismund I in a laurel wreath adorned with palm leaves and framed by coiled ribbons. Here we have a pure Renaissance repertoire of motifs emphasizing the quasi-classical treatment of portraiture; the whole composition of the plaquette harks back for that matter to the familiar pattern of Roman reliefs. The king has been carved true to life with exactitude, perhaps with the help of a drawing sent from Cracow; the representation bears a very strong resemblance to his image on a 1533 thaler. He is shown in profile on crown and armour in the typical Renaissance heroic composition. This part of the altar is also the work of Melchior Baier, a goldsmith, while the model was no doubt again supplied by Peter Flötner.

95 The two silver candlesticks, largely repoussé and chased, on the altar of the Sigismund Chapel are inscribed on their base with a dedication from the king and the date 1536; however, they were ordered three years earlier. Elegant examples of Nuremburg goldsmith's art, they are remarkable for their variety of form and the precision of the execution of their typically Renaissance ornamentation, mainly based on stylized plant motifs. They were probably designed by Peter Flötner, a well-known Nuremburg decorative artist whose speciality was moulding and furniture, and made by Melchior Baier, a goldsmith. Both these artists were employed on the altar of the Sigismund Chapel (ill. 90—94).

96—99 The medals of Sigismund the Old and Queen Bona, together with those of Sigismund Augustus and Izabela, their children, was carved in 1532 by Giovanni Maria Padovano. They are the first works in Poland signed by this artist who had probably come from Padua to make medals, for which there was a demand during the Renaissance. By and large they served as gifts to be exchanged not only by members of ruling families but also by scholars and other luminaries. It was in Italy that medal-making stood highest and Italian artists were frequently invited to work in other countries. The Jagiellonian medals, intended as presents, among others for the D'Este family in Ferrara who were close friends of Queen Bona; the D'Este collections in Modena contain the only complete set of these medals executed in silver. They display careful draughtsmanship, realistic treatment of the face, shown in profile, and an extremely sculptural method of modelling; the figures give a clear impression of reliefs on a smooth background. Since the artist, previous to his arrival in Poland engaged mainly in small-scale sculpture, this is scarcely surprising.

100 The collection of the Wieliczka Salt Museum contains a horn once used by the local miners—a valuable relic of Renaissance handicrafts, remarkable for its fine shape and decorative framing. It served as goblet at confraternity celebrations and as guild sign. The body consists of the greenish and brown horn of an urus: the fittings and base are of silver. It is the work of a Cracow or Nuremburg worshop and dates to 1534. A silver ring encircling the horn bears the crests of Sigismund I and Queen Bona and two other blazons, probably in acknowledgement of successive owners of the Wieliczka salt mine: Andrzej Kościelecki, Grand Crown Treasurer who died in 1515 and Seweryn Boner, Governor of Cracow; there is also a cachet of the Wieliczka Mining Guild—a hummer, pickaxe and trumpet. The traceries on the brim still have Gothic traces but the decoration, repoussé and engraved in silver and consisting mainly of plant motifs, is already decidedly Renaissance, while a beautifully modelled figurine of Hercules with the countenance of a Polish nobleman has replaced the griffin or its talons on the base and distinguishes this horn from similar medieval objects.

KRAKÓW ▶

KRAKÓW

KRAKÓW

KRAKÓW

9

KRAKÓW

11

12

13

14

15

18

21

KRAKOW

26

KRAKÓW

27

29

30

28

31

32

33

38

KRAKÓW

39

KRAKÓW

KRAKÓW

45   46

47

KRAKÓW

53

KRAKÓW

54

55

56

IOANNES DE · LASKO · EX ·
CANCELLARIO · REGNI ·
ARCHIEP̄VS · GNEZNĒN ·
LEGACIONIS · NATE ·
AVCTOR · TERRAM · FIGVLI ·
EX · VRBE · ET · AB · HIEROSOLIMIS ·
INDVCIT · QVA · COMPERIV · HOC ·
CONSPERGI · ET · VINA · VCLEE ·
SVE · HOC · LOCI · PONIT · MORITVR ·
TANDEM · ANNO · D · · · · · ·

60

BRZEZINY

61

OPATÓW

63

64

65

66

70

.68

69

MDXVI

WROCŁAW

75

79

80

SZCZYRZYC

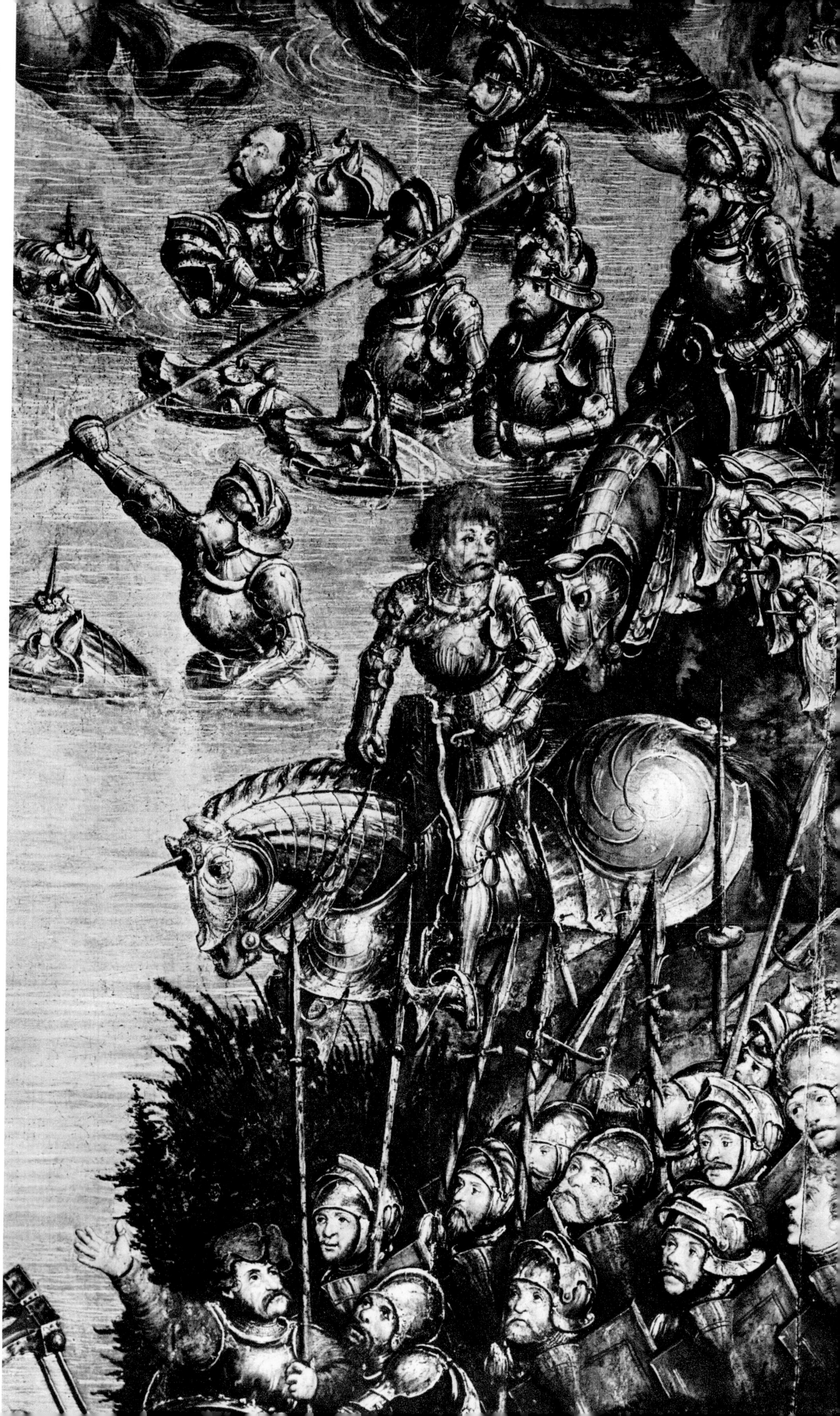

KOBYLIN

SPVS SCTVS TE D...

...VE... GRA

...PLENA

...NVNCIACIO ... EL VISITACIO

SIBILLA FRIGIA EX OLIPO EXCELSE VE...

MATER DEI
MISERERE MEI

SIBILLA SAMIA ECCE VENET DIVES ... NASCET...

...PVELLA QVE FACIE FORMOSA ... PVLCRA CAPILLIS...

85

KÓRNIK

QVE EST
ISTA QVE
ASCEDIT
PER DESER
TVM SICAN
TICORVPR·

EIIA PARES NII
VEI SALVE VIRGV
CVLA FLORIS
SALVE DVLCE DE
CVS GLORIA PRI
MA MEI

I·E·X·O

86

87

GOSTYŃ

91

KRAKÓW

92

94

95

WARSZAWA

100

WIELICZKA

CONSOLIDATION AND SELF-ASSERTION

OF THE RENAISSANCE STYLE, 1545—1575

The Renaissance style, by the close of the second and over the span of the third quarter if the 16th century, was spreading in Poland and assuming an independent standing. The main role in this process was played by architecture and sculpture; painting, of which we will speak at the conclusion of this chapter, was not nearly so important.

By now the new art had gained a more comprehensive social base. No longer was the turn towards the Renaissance matter only affecting the royal court and fairly small number of the enlightened nobles; the humanist culture, or more simply a desire to indentify with the reigning artistic fashion or to take advantage of the practical accomplishments of the new style, became more widely disseminated among the great families for whom, until quite recently, it had been alien, swept through the more prosperous gentry and reached the patricians and well-to-do inhabitants of the more important towns. Never during the modern era in Poland was there so broad a social soil for artistic development as in the period we are now discussing and the early years of the succeeding one. Obviously this was a boom not only to the evolution of art but also to its diversity.

This was also another important factor in the geographic diffusion of the Renaissance in Poland. While the patronage of the royal court was centred chiefly on the Cracow Region, Lithuania and Warsaw, the magnates were either converting or building residences in the new style on estates which were scattered over wide areas of Southern, Central and Western Poland and after the Union with Lithuania in 1569 this activity extended onto the latifundia on its borderlands. The wealthier gentry also embarked, although on a much smaller scale and less frequently, on construction of new country houses. A blossoming of Renaissance urban architecture is another characteristic of this period; town halls and other public buildings were redecorated and a fair number of Gothic mansions were modernized; at times, completely rebuilt. Thanks to this the Renaissance style entered the larger towns of Mazovia, Little Poland, Great Poland and Silesia for good, and even made an appearance in the smaller ones. It was, however, sepulchral sculpture which, even more than architecture, became the expression of the new needs; its spread during this and the next period was one of the more notable features of Polish Renaissance art. Because of the orders lodged by magnates, gentry and patricians, churches in the towns and villages of widely scattered parts of the country started to fill with tombs.

The northern areas of Poland were, however, only penetrated by the Renaissance sporadically and it secured but a tiny foothold in Gdańsk. There the Gothic endured and, though some of its new manifestations were extremely interesting, the fact remains that the North lagged behind the stylistic times.

Cracow continued to be the main centre of Renaissance art in Poland. The number of ateliers in the capital increased with the mounting flow of orders which ensured a higher standard of workmanship then anywhere else in Poland. By and large, they specialized not only in building but also in decorative and figurative sculpture, whereas the workshops opening in steadily increasing numbers in the provinces engaged mainly in architecture and less frequently in figurative sculpture. The most important were in Lvov, Lublin, Warsaw and Silesia; some moved from place to place in the wake of bigger commissions. Renowned at this time were the Cracow sepulchral sculptors who held a virtual national monopoly. "Ready-made" monuments were placed in crates and dispatched from Cracow by road or river for assembly on the spot. Competition existed among the sculptors and sometimes we can even chance upon the beginnings of advertisement. One artist gave his address on two tombs in Poznań: "The work of Hieronymus Canavesi who lives in Cracow on St Florian's Street."

The gentry made use of artists' services, though they considered the profession itself beneath them, and it was the sole preserve of townsmen, apart from a few outstanding individuals working for the royal court, who were associated in guilds. The new style in architecture and sculpture was no longer disseminated by Italians alone for they had now been joined by Netherlands and German artists. But these were few in number and it was the Poles who became the other chief propagators of the Renaissance. Their contribution helped Polish art to stand independently.

It was only now that the native strain in Polish Renaissance architecture and sculpture took root. The contrast that had previously existed between the Italian trend derived from the Florentine Quattrocento tradition, and the hybrid artistic manifestations, connected with the survival of the Gothic, faded. The Italian artists who continued to arrive in Poland formed a closed clan no longer, the new style fused more and more firmly with local tradition and building and sculpture, becoming the expression of spreading social and cultural needs, developed an independent canon followed within the boundaries of Polish art. A common stylistic seal appeared on buildings, tombs and decoration, although complete uniformity was not yet achieved.

The general character of the architecture and sculpture of this period was to a great extent determined by the bonds with Italian High and Late Renaissance art. Contact was maintained not only by the constant stream of artists from Italy, but also by the visits to Italy of artists who had settled here and art patrons among the aristocracy. No small role was played by architectural models and publications, especially by copies of Sebastiano Serlio's treatise. These same channels also brought the Italian Mannerist influences to Poland. From the middle of the century onwards, the stamp of Northern Renaissance and Mannerism made itself increasingly evident as a result to a lesser degree of the work of German and Netherlands artists, for they were few, to a much greater degree by the impact of copies of engravings. These external factors should not be allowed to distort our picture of the Polish Renaissance in its prime, which would be the case if we place too much emphasis on its ancestry. More important by far was the independent development of sculpture and architecture in Cracow, the principal centre of 16th-century Polish art. For here, in the artistic ateliers there existed a continuity of artistic transformation for which the starting-point had been the architecture and sculpture brought here by the Florentines during the first years of the century. The new arrivals from Italy also drew on this legacy, but its imprint was the strongest on the work of the Poles, especially Berrecci's, Cini's and Padovano's pupils. All of them carried on, with a far from doctrinaire latitude, the tradition of Cracow art though they too were responsive to the external influences mentioned above. Here were elaborated new blends of form, types and elements of the architecture and sculpture that met the local requirements. This art radiated to all parts of the country, especially to Central Poland, and only in the east, and the west, in Lvov, Great Poland and Silesia did the work of numerous Comoans propagating the decorative and vernacular North-Italian Renaissance version, plant different stylistic features.

In the field of architecture, the new style was characterized by the emergence of native elements with a far-reaching impact on the shape of Renaissance building in Poland; however the consequences for its evolution were still embryonic. The activity of the ateliers was too widely dispersed which, if anything, encouraged the appearance of local versions. Cracow was unable to impose a uniform countenance on the architectonic art of the country as a whole with the same force as it had in the heyday of the previous period or as it was in the field of sculpture. To a certain measure developmental continuity was hampered by the fact that only a small proportion of buildings were completely new structures, most of them being conversions from the Gothic. In the efforescence of the urban architecture, there was now crystallized a very distinctive feature of the Polish Renaissance and one of the visiting-cards of its native element, called the Polish "attic". A decorative parapet wall masking the roof, such as are to be found in various forms in Classical, Gothic, and Italian Renaissance architecture, it was in Poland given specific constructional and functional tasks and made extremely imposing and ornate. It thus developed into an entirely separate type and hence that qualifying adjective "Polish".

An attic generally ran round the whole of the building, even when this was part of a terrace, as was the case with the town houses. It isolated their roofs from one another and so prevented flames from spreading in the case of fire; a safety factor closely linked with their genesis. At the same time, it provided support for a valley roof with the slopes pitched inwards, the water collecting where they met was led off through the openings in the attic on the axis of the re-entrant. The visible parts of the parapet—the whole of it in the case of detached buildings like town halls standing in the centre of a marked square—were treated with exceptional decorativeness. The sources of ornament of the Polish attic lie in late-Gothic crenellations or the pinnacled crests typical of Venetian Renaissance buildings. But it left these sources far behind becoming an architectural feature with absolutely new qualities. It was extended upwards and given a lower tier (frieze) divided by pilasters, small columns or, more often, blind arcading and a crowning ridge indented with rhythmically repeated pinnacles, pins, socles, volutes, spheres and other ornamental Renaissance motifs.

The Polish attic first appeared on Cracow town houses before the middle of the century. The Cracow Cloth Hall (1556—1557) presents the attic in its fully shaped form and exterted a considerable influence on later Polish crowning of this type. It became, in the course of the period under discussion and the next, an indispensable element of most secular buildings, not only burghers' mansions and municipal buildings, but also the castles of the magnates and manors of the gentry. This attic crossed the Polish frontiers and, during the 16th century, entered Silesia, Moravia and Slovakia and, in the 17th, Muscovite Ruthenia.

The new or converted ex-Gothic building of Little Poland, Great Poland, Pomerania and, in part, the eastern borderlands can be regarded as representative of the stylistic phase now overtaking the Polish Renaissance in which native features were materializing. This version of Renaissance architecture appeared in its purest form in smaller buildings, for example, in the town halls in Tarnów and Sandomierz which were enlarged in about the middle of during the third quarter of the 16th century. Their mass is simple, all but cubic; the decorative parts, set specially apart in certain places and subjected to the forms of the architercture as a whole. But this subordination has an entirely different character than in the buildings designed by the Florentines during the initial phase of the Polish Renaissance. The divisions introduced by means of elements of the classical orders have gone from the main body of the building; the tradition of the first stages late-Gothic at the turn of the 15th century is still alive in the smoothness of the wall surfaces and the ordered, though not always regular, arrangement of the windows. The attic parapet walls, however, lofty and ornamental, give the buildings the unmistakable stamp of the new style; closing the mass horizontally, they are the opposite of the steep roofs of medieval buildings. The repertoire of decorative motifs of these crownings is echoed by the ornament of the framings of windows and portals. The treatment of their sculptural decoration is plastic, a little soft-looking and far from the precise carving of the artists from Berrecci's atelier, but lending the whole a touch of the popular shaping of forms. The most beautiful secular building of the third quarter of the 16th century in Poland is the Town Hall in Poznań (complete conversion of the Gothic structure, 1550–1560). Both in its lucidity and clearly delineated mass and in the introduction of the attic, it is closely associated with the style being shaped at that time in Central Poland. But the architect, Giovanni Battista Quadro, a Comoan, gave it a specific decorativeness modelled, in the layout of the arcaded loggias and the vaulting of the magnificent Aldermans Hall with its stucco decoration, on the patterns supplied by Serlio. The complicated allegorical programme of this chamber testifies to the high level of development of Poznań's humanist culture half-way through this Renaissance century. The Poznań Town Hall, like the majority of buildings from the period we are discussing, was plastered and has sgraffito decoration, the colour schemes, typical of the Renaissance style, standing in brilliant contrast to the Gothic red-brick wall surfaces with their geometrical friezes. The motif of a loggia with staircase used in the Poznań Town Hall also embellished, although in another arrangement, the Cracow Cloth Hall, the attic of which we previously mentioned.

Besides the attic, the arcaded loggias are the second characteristic architectural feature to become popular in Poland from the 1540s. The classic example which made them so, were courtyard galleries of Wawel Castle, although not all arcaded galleries referred to this model. The gallery or loggia motif bears the same native stamp as the attic but it links the second phase of Polish Renaissance architecture more strongly with Italian models, also through the medium of Wawel Castle. Arcaded galleries then appeared in the palace or statelier urban mansion, above all in the chateau.

The characteristic type of Polish Renaissance residence, for which to a certain measure, Wawel Castle served as a model, matured in the years the in 1545—1575. Very few buildings were completely new-designed; the majority of cases they were enlargements or conversions of Gothic castles. The ideal of universal aspiration was a building with a regular plan, with three or four wings and two storeys and a galleried inner courtyard; by the close of the present stylistic phase the attic appeared as an indispensable addition. The most magnificent buildings from the third quarter of the 16th century were the castles in Vilna (the lower castle, enlarged in the mid-16th century) and in Tęczyn (enlarged about 1570). The best preserved is the royal hunting-lodge in Niepołomice (1550—1571) although it lost its top floor many years ago and the galleries we now see replaced the original wooden ones in the 17th century. Apart from Wawel Castle, the most beautiful examples of Polish Renaissance residential architecture date, however, from the last quarter of the 16th century and the first years of the next one. On the other hand the type, in its developed form, is well represented by smaller gentry residences, such as the manor-houses with attics in Szymbark (after 1550) and Pabianice (1566—1571, architect Wawrzyniec Lorek), although the latter, as an urban residence, had a different assignment.

The castle building of the mature Renaissance period in Poland is characterized by the spread of more up-to-date defensive systems, especially in buildings situated on the borderlands as, for example, the castle in Brzeżany.

A group of Renaissance churches in Mazovia, remarkable for their specific constructional, spatial and decorative features, is linked with the name of Giovanni Battista of Venice. This is all the more interesting that church building receded into the background in the Polish Renaissance; this was due to the satisfying of believers' needs by the flurry of church construction in the 15th century, the strong influence of the Reformation in Poland and the secular character of the humanist culture in general.

To this group belong the churches in Brochów (converted in 1551—1561) and, in particular, in Brok and Pułtusk (both converted about 1550). Within the buttressed layout of the walls with its marked Gothic reminiscences, the architect has introduced a uniform interior which bespeaks a Renaissance concept. It is closed in a daring and original way by a barrel vault without lunettes supported by rows of arcades on the upper portions of the side walls; the soffit is decorated with a dense network of ribs in geometrical arrangements. All this was a departure from the decorative and constructional formulas practiced in Italy or elsewhere and is proof of the architect's original ability. It is interesting to note that his work was created all but on the peripheries of Renaissance Poland.

But for the general picture of the Renaissance in its middle development, it is decorative art, especially the tomb, rather than architecture, which is more important decorative plastic art in Poland. For we are able to trace in sepulchral sculpture a consistent evolution of style, see an on the whole high standard of execution and discern the creative imprint of outstanding artists. The reason for this lies to a great extent in the fact that its principal development trend was centered in Cracow and even though represented by tombs dispatched from here and to be seen all over the country. It was there that the leading artistts worked and settled; thus the rising demands from other areas were best met by the establishment of new ateliers in Cracow. This enriched the general development picture of sculpture. In the 1650s, ateliers in Lvov also started to play a role in the field of tombs.

The types of sepulchral monuments accepted during the second quarter of the century, were continued but in a more diversified and enriched form. The principal role was played by the wall tomb, commissioned by the nobility and gentry, with an architectural setting comprising socle, sides and peaked coping and a central niche in which the deceased's figure lay; an important place was allocated to the ornament. Numerous versions of this basic type emerged; the top of the niche might be flat or semicircular, the sides extended to form wings, as it were, with small niches for allegorical sculptures; the figure of the deceased either appeared as a sculpture in the round or as a bas-relief; the pose displays a degree of activity, the legs crossed on the lines of Sigismund I's monument in the Sigismund Chapel. Besides this basic type, however, there were versions with standing figures and manifold kinds of small tombstone or epitaph mounted on the walls, these mainly ordered by burghers.

Even though within the general European framework the Polish sepulchral monument of both the high and late-Renaissance is in its architectural type of a recumbent figure composition similar only to that found in Italy during the 16th century, there now emerged a series of divergences from the Italian model and inspiration, which are the proof of the Polish art-world's own individual achievements. Among these are the predominance of figure in a state of activity and with a characteristic positioning of the legs, whereas in Italy a much more quiescent composition continued to be the rule. But, above all, the Polish Renaissance tomb achieved its originality through the development of the dual figure monument, a version very rare in Italy but exceedingly popular in Poland. It is called the "tiered" tomb and has the figures of two deceased persons—father and son, two brothers or husband and wife— situated in the niches one over the other. This type of tomb took shape during the 1540s. Far-reaching departures also arose at this time in the realm of sepulchral monument decoration and in other architectonic elements like portals or window framing.

All this testifies to the native character of Polish sculpture corresponding to similar manifestations in the field of architecture. But there is also a difference: this native character in Polish sepulchral sculpture has little of a naive or folk art quality to it, deriving as it did from an extremely integral development of art in the constant contact between client and artist and as a rule associated with a fairly high standard of workmanship. It was the further activities of Giovanni Maria Padovano and his Cracow atelier that had the basic significance for the changes occurring in the development of Polish sepulchral sculpture as regards the design of the monument and the figure of the deceased. Although this artist entered some sort of partnership with Giovanni Cini who specialized chiefly in the decoration of tombs, during the Fifties he basically worked on his own with the cooperation, no doubt, of a continuously expanding atelier. He died in about 1574.

The "tiered" tomb was created in the ateliers of the Padovano circle. The first example that we know of is the monument of Tomasz Sobocki and Jakub, his father, in the church at Sobota in the Łowicz District (about 1545). An example of the fully formed type is the tomb of the Kościelecki family at Kościelec near Inowrocław from 1559 with the figures virtually sculptures in the round; the tomb of the three Tarnowskis in Tarnów Cathedral, on the other hand, although close in style, constitutes an exceedingly rare version of a "non-tiered" multi-figure group. Padovano's masterpiece from the later period is the magnificent monument, the largest in Poland, of Hetman Jan Tarnowski and Jan Krzysztof, his son, spanning the presbytery wall of the Cathedral in Tarnów (1561—1570). Commenced as a single tomb, it was enlarged during the course of its construction into a two figure variant; it contributed to the further consolidation of the "tiered" tomb type in Poland.

Padovano's style is restrained, calm and monumental. It represents the phase of the high Italian Renaissance in its impact on the Polish environment; the natual correlations are comparatively close and may well indicate Padovano's contact at this time with the artistic environment of his native land. At the same time, however, this artist played a vital part in shaping the profile of Polish sepulchral sculpture. His inspiration is to be seen mainly in the types of tomb and figure, his style subdued and leaving little space for ornamentation. The tomb of Bishop Gamrat in Wawel Cathedral (1545—1547), an authenticated work by Padovano, was commissioned by Queen Bona and, in so far as it was executed as a "copy" of Berrecci's tomb for Tomicki, does not represent this artist's style.

To a certain extent Hieronymus Canavesi (c. 1525—1582) carried on Padovano's classicizing style but gave greater scope to the ornamental motifs typical of the now succeeding phase of Renaissance decoration in which the still enduring tradition of Berrecci's atelier started to be transmuted in a less constrained direction. This artist was very fond of rustication, panels of multi-colour marble, cartouches, vases, and simplified grotesque and arabesque patterns. In the accentuation of the straight course of the compositional lines of the architectonic parts, there is evident a certain austerity and stiffness which have a counterpart in the smoothed and angular forms of his bas-relief figures in which it is possible to preceive a departure from the realistic manner of depiction, hitherto proper to Polish Renaissance sculpture, towards Mannerism. Canavesi may be regarded as a quite typical representative of this trend, which he tailored to Polish tradition. His most important tombs are the two splendid monuments of the Górka family (1574), a characteristic example of the "tiered" configuration, and of Bishop Adam Konarski (both dating 1576, or later) in Poznań Cathedral, and of Jakub Rokossowski (d. 1580) in the church in Szamotuły.

The greatest native Polish artist of the Renaissance period was Jan Michałowicz (d. after 1583), a sculptor and architect. His fluent, ornamental style departed from the classicist trend represented by Padovano and Canavesi and initiated the salient trend of late-Renaissance architectonic decoration in Poland. In figurative sculpture, on the other hand, Michałowicz adhered faithfully to the Cracow realistic tradition of Berrecci and Padovano.

This artist's main work are: the tombs of bishops Izdbieński in Poznań Cathedral (1557—1560), Zebrzydowski (1560—1565) and Padniewski (1572—1575) in Wawel Cathedral, Bishop Uchański in the Łowicz collegiate church (1580—1583) and of Urszula Leżeńska in the church in Brzeziny (third quarter of the 16th c.); even though one or two of them have undergone alterations, they still amply represent Michałowicz's art in which the development is not so important as the style itself. It appears in the Zebrzydowski tomb already fully formed and, against the background of Cracow sculpture, constitutes—at any rate in its architectonic parts—a somewhat startling phenomenon. Even by European standards, this artist's work is very individual. Both as an architectect and a sculptor, Michałowicz represents the "anti-classical trend" that started to spread through Europe in the second quarter and particularly after the middle of the century. Wherever possible the artist treated the architectonic elements as decorative motifs thus blurring the boundaries between architecture and ornamentation. In these cases he paid no attention to stressing that this element supported that, that the ordering had to follow certain pre-determined rules, that the principle of weighing of proportions mattered. He freely embellished the typical compositional schemes of the Polish tomb, crowned the niches with decoration and extended or contracted the traditional disposition of the monument against the wall as if it were a fan. He was an eminent ornamentallist and we can find in his work an exceptionally rich and personally interpreted fund of motifs.

Michałowicz made copious and unrestrained use in his ornamentation of the repertoire brought to Poland by Berrecci's atelier, amplifying it with Netherlands elements which he drew no doubt from engravings. He carved his decoration with the precision of a jeweller, and it is in this virtuosity above all that can be seen a foretaste of Mannerism. His figurative sculpture, on the other hand, is very far from decorative treatment. The heads of the figures in his tombs have enriched for all time the Polish Renaissance portrait gallery.

Michałowicz's penchant for decoration may have been engendered by the ornamental wealth of the Sigismund Chapel and Cini's later works as a decorator, with both of which he had become acquainted during his training in Cracow. Amid the tide of swelling "anti-classical" currents and Netherlands influences, Michałowicz gave his decorative style a very original stamp and contributed to the further development of Polish monumental sculpture towards that ornamental wealth so characteristic of the next phase of the Polish Renaissance.

In this coupling of ornamental interpretation of architecture with realistic treatment of the figure, it is possible to discern not only an individual but also a more general feature of Michałowicz's art binding him intrinsically with the development of Polish Renaissance art. This same contrasting juxtapositioning of the figurative with the ornamental previously characterized the portrait painting of Stanisław Samostrzelnik.

Michałowicz was also an architect. The Padniewski and Zebrzydowski chapels in Wawel Cathedral and that of Uchański in the Łowicz collegiate church which he built together with the tomb, are all examples of still rare—in the period we are discussing—continuation of the Sigismund Chapel model.

In these days Silesia constituted a separate artistic province. Here, the Renaissance had taken root before 1520, initially in the form of an original type of parapet wall with small "dove-tails," and in portals, window framings and sepulchral plaques. The main role in its propagation was played by the Comoans who established in Silesia one of their most powerful bases in Europe from which they disseminated the new style in decoration and painting; the local artists, mainly Germans, held similar artistic attitudes. One of the earliest examples of their style is the castle gateway in Legnica (1553, Georg of Amberg); interesting architectural and sculptural ideas are also to be found in the castles of Prochowice and Płakowice (before, and about 1550). The Comoans' most important Silesian atelier was directed by architects from the Pario (Parr) family. Its major work was the conversion of the castle in Brzeg into a magnificent Renaissance residence for Prince George II (1541—1560); though most of it later fell into ruin, there remains a gatehouse which is the most beautiful Renaissance work in Silesia (c. 1550—1553 by Francesco Pario, architect, Andrea Walter I and others, sculptural decoration) and displays a rich Renaissance armorial and genealogical programme in its sumptous decoration. The eldest Pario, Giacomo, was the author of the Town Hall in Brzeg (1570–1572), the best preserved Renaissance urban building in Silesia.

Both in architecture and sculpture, the Silesian Renaissance was to some extent distinct from neighbouring centres. One revealing feature was the absorption of Polish Renaissance influences. These may have been revealed in the no longer existing cloisters of Brzeg Castle but are, most certainly, apparent in the busts of the Piasts on the façade of the lodge of the Castle, which are partly modelled on the woodcuts from Maciej Miechowita's *Polish Chronicles* from 1519. The Polish influence was in Silesian sepulchral sculpture more notably pronounced imposing the composition taken from the royal tombs on Wawel Hill, of a semi-recumbent figure on a sarcophagus and a canopied architectonic framing on all the more representative monuments. Examples are the tombs of Bishops Jan V Turzon (1537) in

Wrocław Cathedral and H. Rybisch (1539) in the church of the St Elisabeth in Wrocław (both chiselled by Andrea Walter I) and of Bishop Baltazar of Promnice (d. 1562), and Kasper of Łagów (d. 1574) in the church of St James in Nysa.

In the 1570s the Pario atelier undertook the conversion of Wrocław Castle. Subsequently it was active in Mecklenburg and Sweden to which country, in particular, it brought the Polish influence in architecture.

As during the previous period, painting played a secondary role in relation to architecture and sculpture; indeed with the decline of the Cracow school of miniature, it tended to be even farther in the rear. The preserved works seem to testify to a momentary collapse of certain thematic threads which had appeared before on the wave of Renaissance innovations; gone are the earlier mythological and non-religious allegorical subjects and battle scenes, while genre and landscape motifs appear only in the backgrounds of the paintings. The altar-piece played the main role in panel painting and the portrait continued to progress; in monumental painting we can find new polychromes in the interiors of wooden country churches. Foreign artists, mainly Germans, were active in the towns; the demand for religious paintings over extensive areas of the country was in general met by local artists.

The Gothic tradition still endured in altar-piece painting and the medium continued to be tempera on wood; the influence of Netherlands Mannerism disseminated via engravings made pronounced inroads into the traditional composition; it first appeared in Great Poland (in the triptych accredited to Mateusz Kossior at Połajewo near Czarnków, 1572) and then spread to other regions. In portrait painting, on the other hand, oils on canvas became the increasingly frequent technique; the traditional conventions were on their way out and a fairly popular version of the Renaissance portrait based more on West European than Italian models became current. The portrait of Benedykt of Koźmin (c. 1550) may be selected as an example accentuating the humanist element.

In 1558 the walls and ceilings of the church at Boguszyce near Rawa Mazowiecka were adorned with a mural. Thus was created one of the most interesting Renaissance polychromes in Poland emphasizing the ornamental parts and figurative motifs in a coffered composition being typical of the new style. It is curious to note the fading of medieval tradition in this example of semi-folk art.

The period we are discussing belonged to the reign of King Sigismund Augustus whose enthusiasm lay chiefly in the artistic crafts, mainly goldsmithery and weaving. His collection of tapestries, the renowned „"Wawel Arrases", comprising 356 items (of which 130 have been preserved), was one of the most magnificent in Europe. Although these are not Polish works, having been commissioned in the Netherlands ateliers of Willem Pannemaker, Jan van Tiegen, Nicolas Leyniers and others, they have become a part of the history of Polish artistic culture testifying to the Poles' increasing fondness for beautiful and decorative hangings. From the times of Sigismund Augustus, there also come exquisite products of other art handicrafts.

Commentaries to the Illustrations

101 The Niepołomice Castle in Little Poland, erected in 1550—1571 by King Sigismund Augustus as one of his country residences, is a product of the spate of construction undertaken by the last of the Jagiellons. Despite appearances, this castle has unfortunately lost some of its main parts; about 1800 the second floor, which contained the principal suite of the richly furnished royal chambers was torn down, and of the original decoration little has survived. The galleries on three sides of the courtyard date to about 1637 and, with their pillared layout on the parterre and their colonnade on the first floor, belong to the final development phase of the Renaissance arcaded loggia in Poland; the original galleries were of timber. The external elevations are modest and, for the time when the castle was built, fairly traditional; only the portal of the entrance gate is at all remarkable (ill. 102). The significance of Niepołomice Castle in the history of Polish Renaissance architecture lies in its basic, uniform and axial design; it was the first comparatively modern residence in Poland with a regular plan, a small Gothic hunting lodge and outbuildings having been dismantled to their foundations. The four single-enfilade wings with galleries around the courtyard and the open stairways in its corners indicate a further infiltration of the Italian *palazzo* concept from the close of the Quattrocento. Since the upper part of the building, perhaps crowned with an attic, no longer exists, we do not know to what extent it underwent native additions. The Niepołomice Castle is an early example of the continuation in Poland of Renaissance residence type with courtyard and galleries initiated by Wawel Castle. The architect is not known; Tomasz Grzymała, a royal builder, whose name appears in the accounts, was probably only the superintendent.

102 With the passing of time the architecture and sculpture of the entrance gate, dating from 1552, of the Niepołomice Castle underwent alterations in which some parts disappeared. We know from inventory descriptions that it was surmounted by a carved eagle *"cum insigniis of the House of Jagiello"* and, beneath it, a black marble plaque with the inscription *"Vive, Vince, Regna"* [Live, Conquer and Rule]. However, there still remains the main part of the gateway—a deep arch with a frontal archivolt ornamented with rosettes and soffit decorated with rows of coffers containing rosettes arranged in bands with plant patterns; it is supported on imposts covered

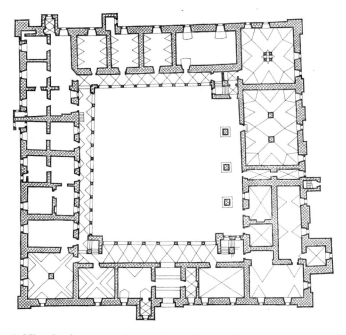

8. Niepołomice, castle. Ground floor plan, 1:800

with bas-relief traceries. The proportions and forms are pure and sedulously executed; this is unquestionably a work from one of the Cracow ateliers continuing in the domain of ornamentation the Italian decorative tradition of the Sigismund Chapel.

103 Prior to the mid-16th century Andrzej Górka, General of Great Poland, had his family palace in Poznań converted in the Renaissance style. This stately edifice with a courtyard gallery and splendidly furnished chambers was turned in the early years of the 17th century into a Benedictine monastery, losing most of its Renaissance features. The remnants of the Renaissance palace include a portal of pure and fairly mature design with bas-relief plant patterns, chiefly arabesques, representing the vernacular decorative style of the Comoans; particulars of the artists working on the conversion of the palace are lacking. The portal, adorned with the date 1548, is the most valuable relic of the new style from before the middle of the century in Poznań where it appeared in the town's architecture and decorative sculpture twenty years earlier.

104 Jan Michałowicz carved the decorative lintel of the portal of the chapter-house at No. 18 Kanonicza Street in Cracow (its jambs come from the first half of the 16th century and the heraldic cartouche from the 18th century). The lintel was executed between 1560 and 1563 and almost certainly commissioned by Marcin Izdbieński, Canon of Cracow and Archdeacon of Poznań, to whom this house belonged at the time. The ornament is carved with Michałowicz's usual precision. The repertoire of motifs is derived from the decoration of the Sigismund Chapel; the artist has added to the Italian-type ornamentation a frieze on the portal archivolt with a typical Netherlands linen pattern (rollwork). The volutes on the sides and the major part of the lintel ornamentation are found in earlier work by Michałowicz: the tomb of Bishop Benedykt Izdbieński in Poznań Cathedral (1557).

105 The brick country seat of the Gładysz family at Szymbark near Gorlice, built after the mid-16th century, is a typical example of the fortified manor-house from the middle and third quarter of the 16th century. In the past, this manor was considered a fairly isolated manifestation of building in the history of Polish Renaissance architecture; recent findings have shown its affinities with manors with similar plan—in Gołuchów from the 1560s and in Pabianice from 1566—1571—(ill. 106). Within the broad evolution of the brick-built residences of the gentry in Poland from the late-Gothic period up to the early Baroque of the first half of the 17th century, the manor-house in Szymbark clearly represents one of the new development phases. In it, perhaps for the first time—in Poland traditional—the rectangular plan with simple interior partitioning was organically combined with corner alcoves: the straighforward mass with its neat proportions is enriched on the outer walls of the alcoves by bays suspended over the machicolations, the whole being given an attic crowning. This and the framings of the windows and portals invest the buildings with an eminently Renaissance character. A part of the decoration dates to the turn of the 16th to 17th centuries. The defensive character of this manor-house is obvious: the alcoves provided a lateral field of fire and the whole building was enclosed by wood-and-earth fortifications.

106 The manor in Pabianice may well serve as an example of the Polish "attic" manor with defensive features from the second half of the 16th century. Commissioned by the Cracow Chapter and built in 1566—1571 by Wawrzyniec Lorek, a mason who also drew the plans, it was to be used to board officers carrying out inspections of Church property. Erected on a rectangular plan with two alcoves on the opposite quoins of a projection on the west axis, the manor-house in Pabianice greatly differs in the design of its exterior from related buildings of this period. The division of the elevations, apart from the alcoves and projection, by high arcaded recesses created by a rhythmical arrangement of arch-topped buttresses stresses the verticality of the building and gives it a look of massive fortification. The smooth walls of the alcoves on the quoins strongly contrast with the perpendicu-

lar buttresses with their long shadows. The perpendicular lines are subordinated to the horizontal band of the attic on whose south and north sides the compositional scheme of the lower walls is repeated: the rhythmical partitioning by means of plaster strips with blind arcades within their span, whereas the attics of the side walls have been given a scalloped contour suggesting a crowning coping. With the exception of the north elevation, the stone Renaissance window frames, made by Jerzy of Lutomiersk, have only been preserved on the first floor.

107 In 1550—1560 Giovanni Battista Quadro, a Ticino architect from Lugano, enlarged the Gothic Town Hall in Poznań into a magnificent edifice in the Renaissance style; thus, he created one of the most beautiful town halls, not only in Poland but also in the whole of Central Europe. Partly destroyed during the Second World War, its rebuilding was completed by 1954. The building's principal accent is its façade with three storeys of arcaded galleries crowned by a parapet wall. Here, the multi-tier loggia scheme, which had become an indispensable element of the Renaissance courtyard in Poland since Wawel Castle, has been used for the front of a municipal building, giving it an exceptionally characteristic stamp of the new style in a fairly advanced version. Quadro has, in his introduction of Doric orders on all the storeys, the doubling of the number of arcades on the upper storey in relation to the lower ones, the composition of the staircases and certain architectonic details, followed models drawn from the treatises of Sebastiano Serlio, the Italian theoretician of architecture. The parapet wall, one of the first of the Renaissance cycle of the so-called Polish "attics", comprises a high smooth face, containing polychrome portraits of Polish kings and crowned with a crest of palmettes, and is enhanced by three turrets. These form a bridge for the passage of the eyes from the façade up to the high upward thrust of the tower (during the last reconstruction of the Town Hall, its helmet was recreated in the classicist form given it in 1781–1783).

108 The great hall of Poznań Town Hall, one of the most beautiful Renaissance interiors in or outside Poland, runs the entire breadth of the building behind the first-floor loggia. Its magnificent decoration reflected the aspirations and pride of the prosperous, patriotic Poznań burghers, while its sumptuous iconographic programme, consisting of heraldic, symbolic and astronomical representations, typified the interests of the people of the Renaissance. This stately interior, roofed with coffered cradle vaulting with lunettes, is supported by two pillars that divide this hall into two parts. The coffers of the first contain the blazons of Poland, Lithuania, the Hapsburgs and the Sforzas (the family of Sigismund Augustus's mother and wife), the king's initials and a large coat of arms of the City of Poznań, and showing the classical heroes, Hercules and Curtius, a narrative sequence alluding to virtue

137

and fortitude, and the biblical Solomon and David. In the coffers of the other half are representations of the Sun and Moon, the planets, Jove, Saturn, Venus and Mercury, and animal exotic and fantastic figures. A pattern of plants enlivened by masks and human and animal heads meanders between the coffers which are octagonal, hexagonal or cruciform in shape. Elements of native and Italian forms, adapted to local requirements, blend into an integral whole, while the polychrome enhances the magnificence of this interior.

109–111 Next to Poznań Town Hall, the second large municipal building to be converted in the new style after the mid-16th century was the Cracow Sukiennice (Cloth Hall), a covered market with annexes housing draper's stalls, storerooms and superintendents' offices. Although the alterations, carried out in 1156–1560, were not as thorough as those of the Town Hall in Poznań, the new Renaissance exterior completely altered the building's apperance. The elongated austere Gothic mass from the 14th century with its basilica-like layout and steep roofs was given a horizontal finish to its upper parts which were covered with valley roofs and topped by decorative parapet walls. Staircases with loggias on the upper storey were added to the shorter sides of the building. Although the records contain several names of builders and masons engaged in the conversion, they do not make their individual contribution entirely clear, or at any rate, identify the chief architect. In 1875–1879 Tomasz Pryliński converted the Cloth Hall in a neo-Gothic style introducing, for example, arcades. Although this detracted from the building's authenticity, he displayed a considerable respect for its main Renaissance elements, the splendid parapet wall on the main body of the building (ill. 109, 110) and the loggias with staircases (ill. 111). Hence, the Cloth Hall has retained its Renaissance character and forms a characteristic feature of Cracow Main Market Place.

The parapet wall of the Cracow Cloth Hall is the first fully shaped "Polish attic." This so very native element of the Polish Renaissance, although based on Italianate forms, appeared in Cracow before the mid-16th century. The earliest examples known from source references have not been preserved and thus the building in the Market Place has the oldest such attic in Little Poland. The valley roof that originally shielded exists no longer. Thanks to its length, height and ornament, this attic constitutes the Cloth Hall's most striking motif. Its composition and decorative scheme were repeated in many later Polish attics; a tall face divided into blind arcades surmounted by a decorative coping formed by socles with mascarons set in flat volutes and rhythmically repeated. These mascarons are an entirely original part of Cracow Cloth Hall. They were chiselled in Pińczów stone by the stonemason Jan, probably from a model supplied in 1557 by an Italian lapidary, Santus (Santi). This may be the first known work in Poland by Santi

Gucci, an eminent sculptor and architect who worked in Poland up to 1600. But the model could only have been a master design. The eighteen that have been preserved from the original attic all represent grotesquely caricatured male heads, a motif that became widespread in Polish sculptural decoration in the second part of the 16th century.

The addition in 1558–1560 of open staircases with loggias supported on two arcades at each end of the Cloth Hall was the final stage of its Renaissance conversion. They led up to a market for miscellaneous merchandise for which room was especially made during the alterations on the floor above the main hall. The twin picturesque annexes have a typically Italian Renaissance character and are given a special stylistic expression by the first-floor loggias and arcades. The plans for the staircases were drawn by the royal architect, Johann Frankstijn. Another version was supplied in 1559 by Giovanni Maria Padovano when the work was already at an advanced stage.

112 The reconstruction and conversion carried out during the 19th and present centuries in accordance with the rules of restoration have cleared the Tarnów Town Hall of its disfiguring accretions and returned it to its appearance in the third quarter of the 16th century when it was given its Renaissance form. The body of the building dates back to the 15th century; a single-storey late-Gothic Town Hall with an angle tower, probably raised to its present height in the first years of the 16th century, was during its Renaissance conversion extended westwards, had a second-storey added up to which led a staircase located in an external annex on the south side, and was crowned with a Polish attic protecting the valley roof. In this way there appeared one of the loveliest and most characteristic buildings representing the mature Renaissance style with native overtones. A cuboid mass, basically conforming in design to Renaissance aspirations, it simultaneously reveals the survival typical of the Polish Renaissance of the severe, regular shapes proper to the late-Gothic architecture in Poland. Contrasting with this simple mass is a picturesque decorativeness drawing exclusively on motifs in the Renaissance style and thrusting upwards by way of the ornamentation of the annex to culminate in the attic together with the near-Gothic crowning of the tower. The attic of Tarnów Town Hall is a simplified echo of the Cracow Cloth Hall (see ill. 109); the similarities are so considerable that the conjecture has been advanced that they were both the work of the same author. Tarnów Town Hall illustrates how native Renaissance forms were adapted to the scale of a most prominent municipal building in a small town.

113 One of the earliest relics of urban architecture in Pomerania during the Renaissance period is the Town Hall in Chełmno built in 1567—1570 with parts of the Gothic walls preserved; the finishing work, together with the helmet crowning the tower, was concluded in 1589–1595. Standing detached in the Market Place, this fairly small cuboid mass is remarkable among other Polish town halls for its attic, one of the most beautiful and original on Polish soil. Originally it was without windows, which were put in during the 18th century, thus converting it into a second-storey wall. A broad band of rustication divides the first storey from the attic. The attic itself, partitioned by variformed columns standing on socles with recesses and placed rhythmically on the cordon, has a painterly design because, apart from other effects, the very setting itself of columns against a recessed background gives rise to a play of light and shadow. A variety of forms—ogees, pinnacles, piers—distinguishes the coping. The attic becomes a richly designed gable on the shorter sides of the elevations. A centrally placed tower with a Baroque helmet from 1721 dominates the whole. It is to be presumed that the author was a mason associated with South Polish circles.

114 The single interior of the nave and presbytery of the collegiate church in Pułtusk, completely altered by Giovanni Battista of Venice during his conversion for Andrzej Noskowski of this originally Gothic edifice is a vivid illustration of this artist's original accomplishments in religious architecture; they are one of the characteristic manifestations of the mature Renaissance phase. Battista's name is associated, either hypothetically or attestedly, with the construction or conversion around the mid-16th century, of several churches in Mazovia, in Cieksyn, Brochów, Chruślin and Brok. In them his attention was confined to the interior; the exterior, even in the case of churches rebuilt from the very foundations, retains a Gothic character. For the first time in Poland, as far as the preserved buildings are concerned, he treated a church interior according to principles of Renaissance art as regards the unity of perspective, simultaneously bringing into play certain structural and decorative elements. Rows of pillared lateral arcades, strongly emphasized, introduce rhythm into the space. In his aisless churches, they are wall arcades, whereas in the Pułtusk collegiate they open onto aisles. This rhythmical arrangement seems optically to support the strongly accentuated belt of arcaded recesses running round the entire interior and, in fact, the cradle

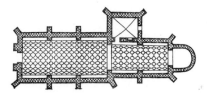

10. Brok, parish church. Plan, 1:800

vault roofing the nave with an inverted semi-cylinder. Its soffito is covered by a decorative network of geometrical ribs in a pattern of spheres joined by fillets. Although lateral arcades were a standard feature in the Renaissance as well, the placing of an arcaded frieze above them and the spreading of a full cradle with decorative ribs are a supremely original idea. The Renaissance restored the use of cradle vaulting but it was with lunettes; here, it accentuates the uninterrupted course of the perspective of the nave. This original Renaissance version of the interior was given a form that was free and soft in its linear outlines, apparently to allow for the none too precise workmanship of local craftsmen. Nevertheless it does not spoil the conception itself, adding in fact a native touch. The influences guiding Giovanni Battista were complicated. The majority of them were Italianate: e.g. the search for spatial unity of perspective and the different parts of the scheme of the interior in which the impact of certain Venetian Renaissance churches is apparent (e.g., S. Maria dei Miracoli) and also perhaps the perspective of the interiors in Italian painting of the Renaissance period: the decoration of the vaulting also seems to be derived from Italian coffering. But, irrespective of these influences, Giovanni Battista set his own original and individual stamp on his churches. At a time when the Polish early and high Renaissance were finding expression mainly in secular and sepulchral buildings, the Mazovia architectural group belongs to the rare sacral programmes of the period; this may be explained by Mazovia's special situation for, during the 16th century, the clergy retained influence over the life of the community and the Reformation made little progress.

115, 116 The church of St Roch in Brochów is the result of a complete conversion of an originally Gothic building; it was probably commissioned by Jan Brochowski, a Warsaw provincial officer, in 1551 and was completed by Giovanni Battista of Venice by 1561. The edifice was not entirely finished at this date although given its basic form; later, it underwent alterations, some in the 17th century and in 1924—1929 it was rebuilt after suffering heavy damage during the First World War. The church in Brochów with its basilica scheme occupies a separate place among the Mazovian places of worship erected by Giovanni Battista and in the whole body of Renaissance religious architecture. This was because it was furnished with fortifications which included three lofty and circular towers—two

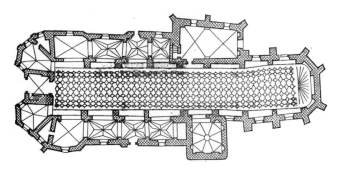

9. Pułtusk, collegiate church. Plan, 1:800

flanking the west façade, the third rising above the apse—and a covered way over the inter-nave arcading. Whereas the church exterior is virtually styless, the interiors of the nave and presbytery ending in a semicircular apse present a version of the typical Renaissance design of Giovanni Battista's Mazovian group of churches, the difference being that the row of arcaded recesses has been replaced by the embrasures of the covered way. Apart from this we have a similar system of wall arcades and cradle vaulting (reconstructed) with a network of coffered ribs with circular and rectangular motifs as in the collegiate church in Pułtusk.

117 The church in Brok, built by Giovanni Battista of Venice in 1560, belongs to those characteristic Mazovian religious edifices of the second part of the 16th century which, despite their Italian details, retained a late-Gothic mass. This church interior displays to the full a modern layout with a cradle vaulting cover decorated with coffers and supported by mighty wall arcades and a presbytery ending in a semicircular apse. On the other hand, the late-Gothic reminiscences of the façade are modified by a gable whose contours have been blunted by being segments of a circle and filling the surfaces with blind arcades between tiered pillars.

118 During the 1540s the Gothic castle in Prochowice in Silesia was enlarged by, among other additions, an east wing. The most interesting features of its architectonic and sculptural decoration are the corbels of the second-storey gallery. From the volutes which entwine each them twice, there rise either palmettes or sculpted heads with the characteristics of portraits and carved with a feeling for the grotesque; although only comprising a few sculptures, they bear a close resemblance to the heads adorning the Deputies' Hall in Wawel Castle.

119, 120 The triple wing courtyard in the mid-16th century palace in Płakowice in Silesia is framed on the parterre by arcaded cloisters with columns with Ionic capitals; on them is supported a first-floor open gallery with decorative balustrading. The faces of the pilaster emerging from the capitals and of the archivolts and piers of the balustrading are decorated with rosette motifs. The Płakowice arcaded galleries are among the earliest examples in Silesia of the use of this typically Renaissance feature in a castle or palace courtyard. They create a picturesque whole, one typical of Silesia and its Comoan architectural and sculptural ateliers of the period. In this respect the magnificent palace gateway with its rich bas-relief decoration is even more characteristic. Here, too, there reigns that picturesque style which ignores the classical principles of harmony: the gateway thrusts upwards, decidedly flouting them with double entablature whose decoration comprises heraldic cartouches in thick coils of acanthus leaves.

121, 122 The gatehouse, jutting out of the face of the south wing of the castle in Brzeg, resembled —until

it lost the belvedere helmet crowning the balcony— a large side chapel. This is not the only reason why it can be compared with the Jagiellonian Chapel, although there are of course obvious differences—of function and ideolgical content, which is purely secular. Nevertheless, the Brzeg building served basically the same purpose of attesting to the distinction of its founder and the glory of his line and used the same means of figurative and decorative sculpture, displayed, however, not in the interior, as in Cracow, but ostentatiously on its façade. The Brzeg gatehouse was erected about 1550 and adorned with sculpture in 1551—1553, although traces of earlier building may be contained within its walls. It was an important part of the Renaissance enlargement of the castle undertaken by Prince Frederick II of Legnica and Brzeg during the 1530s and continued from 1547 with a magnificent impetus to its completion in 1560 by George II, his son. Although most of the alterations, including the design of four wings with arcaded galleries enclosing a large courtyard, have been erased, the gatehouse has, apart from the demolition of its crowning part in the 18th century, survived in a relatively good state of repair together with its sculptural decoration. This outstanding work of art speaks well of the artistic endeavours of the renowned Comoan atelier which undertook the conversion of Brzeg Castle. It is likely that Francesco Pario, its most illustrious representative, was the author of both the building and its sculptural parts and that the execution was partly the work of experienced Silesian artists, including Andrea Walter I. The lower storey containing the gateway itself is composed asymmetrically and based on the popular

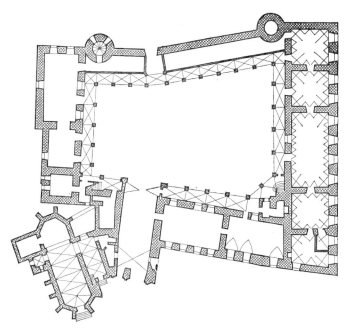

11. Brzeg, castle. Ground floor plan prior to mid–18th century, 1:800

Renaissance motif of the Roman arch of triumph; above the elevation becomes symmetrical and, in all sections of its composition, follows the principle of the "Golden Rule", so characteristic of the Renaissance feeling for harmony. Without a doubt it was the wish of George II, a prince with great aspirations and ambitions, and a lover and patron of art on the Renaissance scale, to make the sculptural decoration on apotheosis of himself, his ancestors and the past: very few works of art of the Renaissance period in Europe reflect so exuberant an individualism. These ideas—in the formulation of which a humanist from the court circle no doubt participated—are chiefly expressed by the sculptures of the friezes surmounting each storey which, in accordance for that matter with the spirit of the Renaissance style, favours the accentuation of the horizontal elements. In the frieze over the parterre are placed life–size statues of George II and his wife amidst heraldic shields held by squires, on the double frieze over the first storey are busts of the Piasts, the Polish monarchs above and the Silesian princes below (ill. 123); the frieze crowning the balustrading has in the centre a large cartouche with the Jagiellon eagle, the coat of arms of ten Polish provinces and the snake of the Sforza family (this is the only original part of the balustrading preserved today); they were probably flanked by the crests of the Hapsburgs and the Duchy of Burgundy. It is significant that George II made the emblem of Sigismund Augustus the centrepiece despite the formal dependence of Legnica and Brzeg, not on Poland, but on the Emperor; it marked in its way a heraldic coda to the Piast genealogy represented in the cycle of likenesses. The figurative decoration is supplemented by arabesque and grotesque motifs which crowd the surfaces of the architectonic elements and the divisions they introduced. In gravity of ideas, discipline and workmanship, the architectural and sculptural decoration of Brzeg Castle falls short of the corresponding parts of the Sigismund Chapel: the diffusive decorative style and the less precise chiselling reflect the tastes and talents of both the Como artists who propagated a vernacular version of Renaissance ornamentation with a North Italian source and the local craftsmen they employed. Nevertheless, the castle complex, constituting the second most important work of this type on Polish soil after the sculpture and ornamentation of the Cracow Chapel, is remarkable for the originality of its fully secular conception for which in European art we can find no direct, only related models.

The ornamentation of the façade of the Brzeg gatehouse is proliferous and wealthy albeit, as in the sculpted figurative parts, it was subjected, even though gently, to the rigours of architectonic division and its members. It ranges over the jambs, socles and pilasters, the archivolts and the adjacent panels, and the entablature friezes. The typical Renaissance motif of plant arabesques preponderate, profusely enlivened in the parterre parts by figurative and animal grotesques, though the latter are not necessarily elements of a specified thematic programme. The decoration also probably was chiselled by local stonemasons from models supplied by the Italians in charge of the atelier; many of the motifs testify to the North Italian typically Comoan provenance of the ornamentation, partially based on engravings. A comparison with that of the Sigismund Chapel in Cracow is suggested: in Cracow it is carved more carefully, precisely and shallowly, in Brzeg more lightly and plastically, thus denoting together with the blend of motifs an Italianate late-Renaissance origin.

123 The double frieze with the sculpted busts of the Piasts can be seen as a kind of "ancestral gallery" highlighting the august genealogy of the founder of the gatehouse of the castle in Brzeg and complementing, both thematically and visually, his own and his wife's statues in the frieze of the lower storey. In the top row are Polish rulers from legendary times up to the feudal disintegration of Poland, commencing with Piasts and ending with Ladislaus II; the row ends with Boleslaus the Tall who, as the first of the Silesian appanage princes, forms in a sense the head of the second row presenting the independent rulers of Silesia, from Henry the Bearded to Frederick II, the founder's father (two of these figures are reconstructions from 1865). Depicted in high relief and energetically chiselled in stone, the figures of the Piasts on ihe Brzeg gatehouse are rendered with a linear and pictoral stylization that has permitted the artist to use a fairly strong play of light and shadow. There does not seem to be the slightest doubt that Andrea Walter I was the author of these busts. By introducing, at the founder's request, and in accordance with the specified programme of the façade of the gate, a genealogical cycle of representations of rulers, he produced one of those picture sequences of eminent personalities so popular during the Renaissance period, mainly in painting and engraving. His models for these busts were also etching, especially woodcuts from the genealogical cycles illustrating Maciej Miechovita's *Chronicles of Poles* in its second edition of 1521 and Hartman Schedel's *World Chronicles* of 1493. Particular figures are accompanied by carefully chiselled explanatory inscriptions.

124 The Town Hall in Brzeg is the only Renaissance municipal building of this kind in Silesia preserved in its entirety. It was erected in 1570—1572 by Giacomo Pario (Parr), a Como architect who had previously been engaged on the "fabrication" of the castle in Brzeg for George II; the financial terms offered by the Brzeg town council were attractive enough to induce Pario to abandon the conversion of Warsaw Castle for Sigismund Augustus and return to Silesia in 1570. In the Town Hall project he consulted architects from Wrocław: the masonry details were mainly executed by craftsmen from outside Brzeg, since the large Como atelier that had worked on the castle had been disbanded. The finishing work lasted until 1577. The completed building contains Gothic sections buried in the converted walls; little remains of the Renaissance interiors but the exterior mass has retained all the alterations made by Pario. Three massive wings enclose a narrow internal courtyard that is open on the east. The front is on the opposite side bordered by two projecting towers with galleries running between them; brick arcaded loggias on the parterre and a wooden gallery on the first storey. In the contract the architect was requested to execute the gables "as well and as decoratively as possible," thus with four large ones ending the tall roof and three smaller ones in the attics of the front with subdued but decorative forms; he also enlivened the upper part of this massive building with ornamental helmets on the projections and a tower thrusting itself high above the whole. Unlike the parapet walled municipal buildings in most of the Polish provinces, the one in Brzeg presents a more traditional design topped by a saddle roof. The architect, an Italian by birth, interpreted it in accordance with the current artistic fashion accentuating wherever possible the horizontal lines and such typically Renaissance motifs as the loggia and their entire decorative repertoire.

125, 126 There are not many sculptures in bronze in Poland with such a high standard of execution as the tombstone of Tomasz Sobocki, Sigismund the Old's chancellor who died in 1548, in the small Mazovian village of Sobota. Mounted at an angle to the plinth in a recess, flanked by pilasters and modestly crowned, it is together with its architectural setting a typical example of an early 16th-century Renaissance wall tomb. A beautifully modelled high-relief figure with strongly portrayed features, a reclining composition and the delicate chiselling of the armour show that the model was supplied by an artist associated with the ateliers of Cracow, very possibly Padovano himself, and that the casting was done in a Cracow workshop.

127—130 What is now called the "ciborium" of the church of St Mary in Cracow comprises a 16th-century tall marble tabernacle with an alabaster pyx standing against the rood screen and a pier of the right aisle. In the early 17th and 18th centuries, it was enlarged and altered by the addition, on its left side, of a staircase with balustrading leading to the converted lateral wall with a receptacle for the eucharist and cartouches and vases in its coping, a Baroque cupola and coloured marble covering the tabernacle wall. Only the architectural composition of the front wall, in the form of a triumphal arch and sculptural parts, remained unaltered. On the socle cornice, with a soffit adorned with coffers with rosettes and supported on the sides by two corbels, rises the central part divided into three recesses by four pilasters. The two lateral and narrower ones are filled with bas-relief figures of the adoring angels and the central one, with a smooth wall, serves as a backing for the alabaster ciborium in the form of a rounded tempietto supported on four sides by feet formed of animal paws. Along the top runs a corniced parapet wall in the panels of which and corresponding to the width of the lower recesses are set three medallions with the Madonna and two prophets. A fourth medallion with a prophet is set on the narrower side of the parapet wall. It is likely that Giovanni Maria Padovano was the author of the marble tabernacle and alabaster ciborium. In 1551 he accepted a commission, confirmed by documents, to execute an alabaster ciborium for the church of St Mary which he completed within the short specified term of barely three months—in 1552 for a fairly low fee. However, no mention was made in the contract of the execution of so large an architectural project as a tabernacle, though Padovano built one in 1533—1536. In 1533 Piotr Tomicki, Bishop of Cracow and a great lover of art, commissioned from him a tabernacle in red marble—"*sacrarium splendidum*"—for Wawel Cathedral where it was placed in 1536. In 1605 it was dismantled and replaced by Baroque objects. Like many other treasures in Wawel Cathedral, including Sigismund the Old's magnificent altar-piece, now in Bodzentyn, it may have been moved to another church, in this case St Mary's where it was altered and adapted to the function of an altar. The St Mary's ciborium, despite alterations and disfigurations, has not lost its fine proportions, harmony and beautiful details. The superb workmanship of the sculptural parts indicates a closeness in tune with bas-reliefs executed in the basilica of St Anthony in Padua just before Padovano's arrival in Poland. Thanks to his ability to express movement and mastery of material, the adoring angels in red marble, depicted in gentle motion, full of charm and neatly composed within the narrow recesses, occupy a leading position in Polish Renaissance sculpture. Especially worthy of notice is a bas-relief of the Virgin and Child. The feeling for mood and the absoloute lyricism of the situation complements the tranquility emanating from Mary's face, which evokes the classical canons of beauty. Mary's bust, inscribed in a circle, turns her torso, shoulders and arms into a sort of second circle—a girdle in which the softly modelled living body of the Infant is enclosed.

131—133 Built by Giovanni Maria Padovano in 1561—1570, the monumental tomb of the Tarnowskis, Jan, Grand Crown Hetman (d. 1561), and Jan Krzysztof, his son (d. 1567) in Tarnów Cathedral is associated with the great late-Renaissance sepulchral compositions in Venice in which the top, in particular, is resolved in several tiers while the lateral wings, separated from the central area by columns, are extended upwards and filled with decorative and figurative sculpture. A favourite motif became the canopied draping of material over the deceased's figure. This

S.S.Trinitatis.

T.S.Nicolai.

18

14

17

19

21

tomb, initially intended for the hetman, was turned following the premature death of Jan Krzysztof, his son in 1567, into a tiered one endowed by Konstantyn Ostrogski, heir to the Tarnowski fortune. The original structure was built up by raising the already high socle in order to obtain a lower niche for the son's figure. Because of this elevation and extension of the lower parts, the monument may have forfeited some of its harmony and logical cohesion but it gained a monumental character and splendour. The realistic representations of the figures recumbent on the sarcophagi, the rich classical decorative motifs all testify to the high standard of craftsmanship of sculptor who worked for all but fifty years in Poland and influenced the development of Polish sculpture, especially its classical trend.

The faces of the Hetman and his son capture their living features. The Hetman's countenance is manly, full of spiritual strength and endurance and, despite his advanced years, robust in contrast with his son's face, a frail face of a victim of consumption: sickly, the nose elongated, the cheeks sunken. The Hetman's stalwart and stocky figure lightly clad in decorated armour, presses heavily down on the bier while the slight and somewhat mannerized body of his son suggests his physical weakness. Padovano's artistry in portraying human figures reaches its heights in the Tarnowski tomb.

134 The tombstone of little Kasia Pilecka (d. 1559) on the wall of the parish church in Pilica, belongs to a group of innumerable tombs for infants marked by an original symbolism characteristic of Polish child sepulchral sculpture of the second part of the 16th century. Its common feature is the combination of the child's usually naked body with a skull and cross-bones to signify the vanity of life. However, with the skull used as a bolster under the child's arm, this death symbol is muted and, in Polish Renaissance tombs for children, is transformed into a decorative element offsetting the cartouche containing a blazon placed in the opposite upper corner of the tombstone. It is highly likely that it came from Padovano's atelier.

135 An independent work of 16th-century Polish art is the "tiered" tomb in which the figures of the deceased were placed in a niche on top of one another in a common architectural setting. This type of tomb made its appearance before the middle of the 16th century and rapidly became popular throughout Poland among the wealthier gentry and nobility. An example with a considerable significance for the history of Polish Renaissance sculpture is the sepulchral monument (1559) of Jan and Janusz Kościelecki in the parish church at Kościelec near Inowrocław; it represents the early development phase of two-tier tomb. A work of great artistry, it is remarkable for the consistency and harmony of its architectural composition with its sparing yet varied treatment of the sculptural decoration and strong emphasis on the figurative parts. These are almost statues, the degree of the relief

designating a further step in the evolution of sepulchral sculpture. The inscription on the tombstone, which was built during the lifetime of Janusz, Voivode of Sieradz, for himself and for his father, emphasizes the faithful portraiture of the persons represented ("*imitatione naturae*"). This monument is the work of a Cracow atelier working in the tradition of the 1530s, as is apparent not only from the composition of the figures and the chivalric motifs set in the background but also from the plant ornamentation.

136—138 The monument of the three Jan Tarnowskis in Tarnów Cathedral constitutes an isolated example in Poland of a dual tomb in which the slabs with the bas-relief figures are placed, not above one an other, but in a row and topped by a common finial. The lateral and central volutes create perpendicular lines of division between the shallow niches. A small slab with a child's figure, mounted over the axis of the central volute between the inscription plaques, is more of a decorative element than a tombstone. This common tomb was founded for Jan Amor, Castellan of Cracow (d. 1500), Jan, Voivode of Sandomierz (d. 1515), and Jan Aleksander (d. 1515), Hetman Jan Tarnowski's father, brother and son. Presumably this was done during the building of the sepulchral monument of the Hetman himself in the Cathedral presbytery in 1561 when the remains of the pre-deceased Tarnowskis were removed to a side chapel. This dating of the tomb is made all the more likely by the far-reaching technical, formal and iconographic resemblances between the Tarnowskis monument and that of the Kościeleckis in Kościelec (1559). Their lucid and concise architectural compositions and figurative and ornamental parts indicate they came from the Cracow atelier. Realism in the portrayal of the face is another characteristic trait of this atelier; in the case of the Tarnowskis who were unknown to the artist, portraits were no doubt referred to. In his rendering of the adults the sculptor did not tone down the characteristic features: wrinkles, prominent noses, thick lips or protruding ears; but the child's face, like its body, is delicately modelled and, as if in contrast, is smiling; it is the tiny face of a dozing cherub.

139 Jan Michałowicz commenced work on the tomb of Bishop Benedykt Izdbieński of Poznań (d. 1553) in about 1557. At this time a trend towards a more ostentatious representation was surfacing in the development of sepulchral sculpture. The formula of a rectangular niche was embellished by making the top adding lateral habitacles for allegorical or saints' figures and enlarging the finial. There was also an increase in the painterly effects through the use of contrasting coloured stone. Jan Michałowicz became a propagator or even the initiator of these innovations filtering into the country from Italy and the Netherlands via, for example, engravings; he also reached back to the rich sources of the traditional Renaissance forms of the 1520s and 1530s. In Izdbieński's tomb in Poznań Cathedral the exposition of the sarcophagus is made particularly striking by the Bishop's figure being advanced in front of the niche, which is topped by a circular arch and the use of strong painterly effects: the red speckled marble block in which the sarcophagus and figure are executed stands out in strong relief against the white sandstones of the architecture and the tomb decoration, plant patterns which occupy every empty surface acting as a foil to the majesty and calm of the apparently dozing Bishop. Intimating in this tomb a fondness for decorativeness, Michałowicz has left the background of the niche empty to give a forcible expression to the figure's bulk. One free surface has been used for the inscription: JOHANNES MICHALOWICZ URZEDOVIEN FECIT.

140 The only known woman's tomb chiselled by Jan Michałowicz—that of Urszula (neé Maciejewska) Leżeńska in the church in Brzeziny, may plausibly be compared with the tomb of Barbara Tarnowska in Tarnów Cathedral. Its connections with the Tarnów sculpture are evident in the figure's elegant form and charm; but its realistic and livelier movement gives an impression of greater freedom and thus differentiate it from the Tarnów sculpture. The graceful, stylish figure of the noblewoman is clearly outlined against the smooth wall of a niche embellished only by a cartouche with the family crest under the arch. The architectural part is related to the form of Bishop Izdbieński's tomb in Poznań Cathedral; it is possible to suppose that it had similar lateral wings, removed during the conversion of the church. The sculptural decoration, a pattern of acanthus leaves and vines, concentrated in the upper part of the tombstone, does not divert the attention from the woman's figure in a sleeping pose supported on a softly modelled cushion. The tomb comes from the early years of the artist's work (1563—1568).

141—143 Jan Michałowicz's masterpiece is the tomb of Bishop Andrzej Zebrzydowski (d. 1560), carved in 1562—1563 and placed in a sepulchral chapel, which the artist specially converted for this purpose in Wawel Cathedral. In an individual and original departure from the conventional formula, which nevertheless still harks back to the traditional type of Polish tomb, Michałowicz has shaped an exceptionally decorative wall composition with an extended socle, a recess with a semicircular arch and flanking columns and much smaller lateral wings supported flat against the wall. The architectural and plastic effects are forceful: aerial and tracery parts intersect the massive ones. The sense of proportion and harmony proper to the Italian Renaissance are absent here; the architect ignored the classical principles and strove above all after the picturesque and the decorative in the architecture. He has also expressed them through a wealth and variety of ornament: the rustication, panels and wall parts abounding in arabesques, grotesques, lion and angel heads and other motifs taken from the

repertoire of the Sigismund Chapel, enriched, as in the Tomicki and Gamrat tombs, with plant tendrils twining the columns, Netherlands-type coils and original interpretations of other motifs. The archivolts and the entablature are pinned together by a magnificent clasp full of minute decorative details. All this chiselled precisely, a little like a jeweller, in stone. The treatment of the figure differs from the style of the architecture: it is concentrated and makes use of the sweeping surfaces of the robes; the head is a portrait, astounding in the penetration of expression; the hands are beautifully modelled with considerable technical knowledge. A high standard of craftsmanship is written all over each part of the tomb.

144, 145 In keeping with the testament of Bishop Filip Padniewski of Cracow, an erudite humanist and diplomat (d. 1572), Jan Michałowicz converted the Gothic chapel of the Różyc family in Wawel Cathedral into a Renaissance sepulchral chapel for the Bishop's tomb which he executed himself. Defaced in about 1840 when the chapel underwent classicist alterations, it lost the architectural form and richness of decoration typical of Jan Michałowicz's work. As a result for many a long year this tomb, deprived of its lateral wings with niches joined to the finial by two-tiered volutes in the form of the letter "C", gave rise to misunderstandings about Michałowicz's art and caused him in his later works to be regarded as an artist with a classicist profile. But a drawing by Lanci from the period of the chapel's conversion in 1832—1840, discovered in 1970, presents the monument in all its architectural and ornamental splendour in which male hermas, bearing the extended lateral parts, played an important role. Out of the wealth of ornamentation looms the centre-piece, covered by the first double arch in Poland and framed by original bosses, with the Bishop's figure strikingly posed on a low sarcophagus against the bare background of the niche. This part of the tomb is unaltered. Padniewski's face is treated as a portrait and constitutes one of the leading achievements in 16th-century sculpture in Poland. The artist has used alabaster for the first time in Polish figurative sculpture so as to increase the grace and softness of the outlines, since it is more easily worked than marble and lends itself to soft modelling. In the past this bright figure, harmonious and noble in composition, strongly contrasted with the fantastic wealth of decoration and colour of the tomb.

146, 147 The monument of Andrzej and Barbara Górka in Poznań Cathedral was built in 1574 by an Italian artist, Hieronymus Canavesi, long settled in Poland with an atelier in Cracow; he himself did not fail to inform everyone of this fact, inscribing on the cornice of this monument his name and address in Cracow: *Opus Hieronimi Canavexi qui manet Cracoviae in platea S. Floriani A.D. 1574.* The monument, executed in limestone and red marble, has a tri-axial composition with niches in the lateral wings accom-

146

modating statues of the bishops in the Górka family. The central recess represents the by then popular tiered design. Motifs of classical ornamentation— garlands and cartouches with furled edges—make for a varied decoration and painterly effects are evoked by inlays of coloured marble. Characteristic of Canavesi's work are his stylization of the human figure by an artificially elegant pose, the striking draping of the robes, the somewhat unnatural arrangement of the legs and arms and a realistic rendering of the features of the face and details of the dress and armour. The execution testifies to a high degree of technical skill for the figures are cleanly and sharply chiselled and this effect is further enhanced by the rays of light falling over the broad and smooth surfaces of the marble.

148 Kielce Cathedral contains the tomb with a bas-relief slab in red marble of Elżbieta (neé Krzycka) Zebrzydowska (d. 1553). Her son Andrzej, Bishop of Cracow, probably commissioned it from Padovano, famous by now in Poland as the author of the sepulchral figures of the Polish queens, Elżbieta and Barbara, the wives of Sigismund Augustus. The austere face with lightly hinted wrinkles at the corners of her eyes, a thin mouth and a strongly defined chin, is a beautiful example of a 16th-century portrait of a Polish matron.

149 The tomb of Jakub Rokossowski, Grand Trea-surer of the Crown (d. 1580), in the parish church of Szamotuły, is monumental but polished in detail. Because of the similarities of the figure and decoration with the corresponding elements of the Górka's tomb in Poznań, it is attributed to Canavesi. Executed in sandstone and red marble, its great value lies in the play of colour, the ornament being muted and concentrated mainly in the finial. The Knight's figure is treated broadly without the same elaboration of the armour as in Andrzej Górka's; in a flickering light and with highly veined marble such details would be lost and so the artist has carved the figure in shallow relief against a completely negative background, portraying only the head realistically with emphasis on the sharp wrinkles of the face.

150 During the second part of the 16th century, the content of the polychromes in the timber churches of rural Poland continued to be of a secular nature, the subjects being ordinary people, their daily lot and attitudes to the world around them. In 1558 the wooden ceiling of the church in the village of Boguszyce near Rawa Mazowiecka was covered with a polychrome comprising circular and octagonal coffers filled with rosettes of leaves, fruit and flowers and connected by parallel bands. The spaces between the coffers were filled with arabesques and masks of human and animal heads, or figures of animals playing musical instruments. The surface of the prebytery ceiling is divided into five circles with the figures of Christ and the four Evangelists inscribed in them. On the ceiling of the north aisle are allegorical figures of the Seven Deadly Sins and these are taken from foreign models, but the merry male figures with their lively gestures and realistically depicted faces and hands, set in the north nave ceiling and leaning out from behind the coffering as though out of the architecture were drawn by the artist from surrounding realities. The decoration, in subdued tones of grey, green, light yellow and pink, is delineated against a greyish-yellow background, and a little more vivid is the presbytery part. Although the authors, for there were probably several, were perhaps from various environments and drew on a medley of models, they nonetheless executed an outstanding work of ceiling painting in Poland.

151 Among the first independent Polish portraits which began to appear in the first part of the 16th century is a typically Renaissance likeness of Benedykt of Koźmin, an erudite humanist and benefactor of the Jagiellonian Library; it is by an unknown artist who painted it, judging by the sitter's age, during the forties and presented him in a standing pose, dressed in academic gown and conscious of his rank in the social hierarchy. By his side is a table on which are placed a sandglass and a vase of carnations, symbols of the passing of time and of passionate but pure love, in his case, for learning and books. In the background, a curtain hangs in the centre and, to the right of it, an opening reveals a view of mountains in a distant landscape. In 1559, when bequeathing in his testament this likeness together with his book collections in the their entirety to Cracow University Library, Bene-dykt of Koźmin wrote: "Go there, wheresoever you will, as to the most delightful gardens and blossoming meadows!" This portrait, maintained in the Central European convention of its day, has strong Italian influences. These are especiaally evident in the com-position of a curtain in the middle background with an opening to one side and the soft chiaroscuro mod-elling of the face, which is realistically depicted without a trace of idealization. The treatment of the forms in the other parts of the painting is very stiff and perhaps, here and there, somewhat clumsy but, despite these reservations, Benedykt of Koźmin's image is a fine example of the modern portrait that evolved in Poland previous to the mid-16th century.

152 *The Adoration of the Shepherds*, the central painting of a triptych from 1572 at Połajewo near Czarn-ków, is almost certainly to be attributed to Mateusz Kossior's guild atelier in Poznań because there are many similarities to an altarpiece signed by him in Kłecko. The painting in Połajewo represents the Netherlands Mannerist style which began to circulate in Poland around the mid-16th century mainly via engraved copies, and is to be found not only in the larger towns but also in guild ateliers in the provinces. There it was to co-exist right up to the close of the 16th century with the traditional technique of tempera painting on wood with a hard, somewhat clumsy feeling for form. But the composition of the Połajewo painting is entirely new, dynamic in the arrangement of the figures and firmly situated in space which embraces not only a varied fareground with figures but also a background of fantastic architecture with a vista of a distant landscape against which is set the head of the Madonna.

153, V p. 133, **VI** p. 143. The magnificent set of tapestries called the Wawel or the Sigismund Arrases were not, it is true, woven in Poland, but nevertheless they belong to the history of Polish art collecting in the Renaissance and so to the Polish culture of this period. Over the years 1553—1571, Sigismund Augustus ordered and purchased more than 350 tapestries from the then renowned ateliers of Brussels. Of these there remain, after a very tempestuous history, 142, of which 137 are in Wawel Castle, and four in the National Museum in Warsaw and one in the Rijksmuseum in Amsterdam. Among the ateliers in which they were ordered were those of Willem Pannemaker, Jan van Tiegen and Nicolas Leyniers which produced the surviving figure cycles of *The History of the First Parents, The Story of Noah,* and *The Tower of Babel* and extensive series of animals against a landscape and arrases with blazons and grotesque ornamentation. The cartoons for the figure scenes were given by Michiel Coxcie, popularly called the Flemish Raphael, and those for the landscapes with animals, possibly by Willem Tons. Although severely depleted, the Wawel Collection is still one of the largest in existence. Its value is all the greater in that the figure scenes constitute an *editio princeps*—the first tapestries woven from the cartoons; this series was repeated for other clients, whereas the landscape series with animals possesses a unique character. In both workmanship and artistry all the Sigismund Arrases represent peak achievements of European weaving of the Renaissance period. Their figurative and ornamental parts fully express the late-Renaissance style reigning in Netherlands painting and engravings, infiltrated by Mannerist elements, pronounced in the later commissions.
The figure scenes, in particular, contain numerous symbolical allusions, of a kind also found in the ornamentation with its elaborate grotesque patterns. The heraldic tapestries, including those with the coats of arms of Poland and Lithuania, were based on iconographic material supplied by the Polish court. Several tapestries have Sigismund Augustus's monogram—"S A"—prominently displayed.
These tapestries adorned the walls of Wawel and other royal residences; the monarch took the smaller ones with him on his travels using them for practical purposes like covering tables, chairs, benches and chests. In his testament of 1571, the King bequeathed his collection of tapestries to his three sisters and, after their death, to the Commonwealth. Depleted during the centuries that followed, it was removed in 1795 to Russia, whence it was returned after 1921 by the Soviet Government; during the Second World War it was taken to Canada and from there, once again came back to Poland. After careful restoration, the Wawel tapestries once more adorn the walls of the royal castle on Wawel Hill.

154 The helmet, bearing the date 1561, once in the possession of Mikołaj Radziwiłł the Black, is an example of the Polish armourer's craft which, although not of such a high technical standard as Italian or German, still produced mail of considerable practical worth. The Radziwiłł headpiece is a typical Polish burgonet without a visor comprising a fluted, lightly pointed crown, cheek-pieces, neckguard and nose-pieces. The whole is covered with a delicate pattern of plants and the rim and cheek-pieces with moulded bosses.

155 In 1565 King Sigismund Augustus presented the Archers' Company in Cracow with a silver "hen", used, as was the custom in Europe, as a drinking cup during confraternity celebrations. It is unquestionably the product of one of the guild workshops in the then Polish capital where the goldsmith's craft had attained a high level of development. In actual fact the bird is an eagle which with its crown simultaneously represents the Polish emblem. Without any of the late-Gothic angularity, its full forms and modelling with a linear stylization based on foreign motifs indicate the Renaissance style of this valuable specimen of artistic craftsmanship.

156 In 1572 a magnificent tin coffin for the body of King Sigismund Augustus was made in Gdańsk and assigned to the royal vault in the Cathedral on Wawel Hill. The bill is preserved among the royal accounts and lists, among other items, the sums payed out to "the carpenter for the moulds he carved for the casting of the figures" and "to the pewterer for the tin and his work". Their names are unknown, but they were undoubtedly leading master craftsmen of the guilds which had made Gdańsk famous for its artistic handicrafts. The aforesaid "carpenter" was the real author of the models for the coffin's bas-reliefs, the most important being the six allegorical, representations of the Soul and of the expiring Five Senses, sight, hearing, touch, taste and smell, personified by the figures of women sleeping in the foregrounds of landscapes containing animals and objects symbolizing the given sense: taste, for instance, by a basket of fruit and a monkey eating an apple beside the sleeping figure. The bas-reliefs of the Sigismund Augustus's coffin are in fact among the first allegorical representations of the Five Senses; this subject, its birth being a typical expression of the Renaissance interest in the Natural Sciences, made sporadic appearances in about 1500 but it was only in 1561 that it was given a more popular treatment in Hieronymus Cock's series of engravings from Frans Floris's drawings. They were also used by the author of the tin coffin who echoed their composition with the characteristic Netherlands Mannerist placing of an elegantly posed figure against a landscaped background.

102

POZNAŃ

104

KRAKÓW

SZYMBARK

PABIANICE

107

POZNAŃ

109

KRAKOW

112

TARNÓW

CHEŁMNO

114

BROCHÓW

BROK

117

118

PROCHOWICE

PŁAKOWICE

GEORGIVS·D·G·DVX·SILESIÆ
LIGNIC·N·&·BREGEN·DIVINA
·E·CLEMENTIA·PRIM⁹
FA·····VRAM·FIERI
HA·····RAVIT·REG·
&·ÆDI·····ANDO·REGE·
NANTE····GVSTO·MDLII
RO·SE·

124

BRZEG

KRAKÓW

KRAKÓW

134

KOŚCIELEC

136

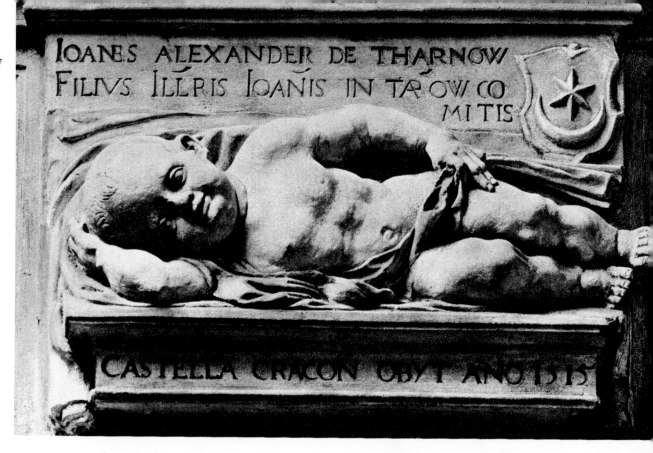

CASTELLA CRACON OBYT AÑO 1515

IOANES ALEXANDER DE THARNOW
FILIVS ILLRIS IOANIS IN TĀOW CO
MITIS

137

138

139

POZNAŃ

141

142

KRAKÓW

149

SZAMOTUŁY

151

152

153

154

HEYDAY AND DECLINE OF THE LATE STYLE, 1575—1640

From whatever angle we might look at the character and development of architecture and sculpture during the 1575—1640 period, we will get a diverse and manifold picture. To set it in order, it will be useful to introduce a date on the threshold of the 17th century dividing this period into two phases. The late-Renaissance blossoming, whose roots in the social and cultural soil of the country became even stronger, belongs to the first period; its decline, confined to architecture alone, occurred during the second phase.

By now the Renaissance, even when giving it the fullest possible scope by including the particulary numerous Mannerist manifestations at this time, no longer controlled the whole of the artistic arena. During the final quarter of the 16th century early Baroque appeared as a stylistic accompaniment to the Renaissance and Renaissance-Mannerist currents; it initially took a separate and as if independent course. But, during the second phase, its channel abruptly widened giving rise to stylistically mixed manifestations within its neighbourhood. This new style and its confines are disregarded in the present chapter since it deals solely with matters concerning the further growth and direct sequel of the already consolidated Polish Renaissance. And so we have detached from our consideration the steps taken by the Jesuit Order, the propagator of Baroque, and the patronage of the first two kings of the Vasa Dynasty: Sigismund III (1587—1632) and Ladislaus IV (1632—1648) and that of the magnates following their example. Hence, we shall not mention all that took place in art at one time; obviously, this has it shortcomings but, after all, one style does not commence where another ends and, furthermore, the subject of this book obliges us to make the necessary curtailments.

The late-Renaissance "subjects" of architecture and sculpture remained basically similar to those prevaling during the previous period. The royal court —here we are concerned with the enterprise of Stephen Báthory (1576—1586) and Anna Jagiellonka, his wife —and the magnates continued to convert or, more frequently than before, to erect palaces and castles, rural and urban, and to build, on the lines of the Sigismund Chapel, an increasing number of sepulchral chapels to enshrine with monuments the glory and memory of illustrious representatives of their families. In this period came a unique foundation: the laying out and construction of a complete fortified town, Zamość by Jan Zamoyski, the most powerful magnate of his epoch. The prosperous gentry built brick manor-houses and endowed tombs. Town architecture flourished: municipal buildings, all in the new style, were erected in the more important centres and mansions converted in all of them. The burghers also commemorated their closest relations with magnificent tombs. Many buildings were given a sumptuous sculptural decoration.

During the first phase of this period, Humanism was still spreading among the aristocrats and burghers, inspired by contacts with Italy and other European centres of progresive ideas; sometimes it was expressed in the thematic programmes of architecture and sculpture. But, simultaneously, and precisely at this time, art began to be influenced to an increasing degree by the Counter-Reformation doctrine. It revived church building and intensified the religious content in sculpture and painting. This factor played an incomparably greater role during the second phase, the first forty years of the 17th century.

It was in Baroque art that the Counter-Reformation found its chief outlet. But the force of the new ideology, propagated by monasteries, the clergy and magnates, simultaneously gaining an increasing influence on the gentry and burghers, also pulled into its orbit the capacities and artistic bents of many of the Renaissance ateliers. Thus, towards the close of the 16th century there was a wave of church building, some of it in the hitherto prevailing, though changing style. In the first forty years of the 17th century church building in the traditional artistic spirit came to occupy a prominent position. The dominant role in church decoration and furnishing was played by sculptured stonemasonry, stuccowork and wooden sculpture. The development of late-Renaissance sacral building, not particulary pure in style, but clearly different from Baroque church architecture, is a characteristic feature of the second phase of this period.

Late-Renaissance Poland was divided into two basic artistic areas with their centres in Cracow and Gdańsk. From both, art with a variegated character emanated. Cracow, its artistic significance dwindling with the rise, thanks for that matter to its inspiration, of local centres like Pinczów, Lublin or Lvov, remained nevertheless to be the principal artistic centre of the country, its own development cycle of art continuing uniterrupted. In architecture and sculpture, up to the beginning of the 17th century, an important role was played by a native tradition, which drew from Italian and Florentine sources, and was enriched with works of Padovano and Michałowicz. From the mid-16th century to its close fresh contacts with Italian centres were furthered by new arrivals from Italy, notably Santi Gucci, a Florentine. From the last quarter of the 16th century the Como ateliers began to make a greater contribution to Cracow art, for their access up to then had been obstructed by the local ateliers. Many Poles were working in the Cracow architecture and sculpture ateliers maintaining general a high standard of workmanship. They helped Cracow art to retain the native imprint it had earlier and made foreign artistic fall into line with it.

Charasteristic of the late-Renaissance period in Poland was the diffusion of art as the public demand for it increased to extensive areas of the provinces though it were moving out to meet the requirements of the steadily mounting number of clients in smaller localities. Hence, within the orbit of Cracow art were founded architecture and sculpture ateliers in the Kielce Region with Pinczów as their principal centre; their activity was especially characteristic of the turn of the 16th to 17th centuries. Fed by the local sandstone quarries, a lively output of art developed. Sculpture and stonework were "prefabricated"—portals, window framings, tombstones—for dispatch to Kielce or other parts of the country. The style of these local products was set by Santi Gucci who worked here over a long period. These ateliers employed not only Polish, but also foreign stonemasons and sculptors. Their works of art were very Polish in character but their technical standard uneven.

At the close of the 16th century the centre of gravity of Little Poland architecture and sculpture had swung eastwards. The artistic centre in Lvov now assumed a greater importance, use being made of the local stone quarries. Here Poles, the pupils of Cracow Masters, Comoans, Ticinians, Netherlanders and Germans, mainly from Silesia, were active. The connection with Cracow art, still maintained, was more and more strongly coloured by the contribution of the newcomers from distant parts and a certain type of oriental taste encouraged in Lvov by the animated trade with the East and the presence there of many Armenians.

During the first half of the 17th century it became the turn of Lublin to jump into prominence; here Polonized Comoans were dominant. And here, in the field of architecture and decoration, a specialization in stuccowork rather than stone carving was more prevalent than elsewhere. Relations were maintained with the Cracow, Lvov and Kielce ateliers but, simultaneously, bases developing the local versions of the late-Renaissance style with a more native character were established.

And so during this period Little Poland comprised an extensive area with its own centres mainly meeting the local demands. The artistic region of Great Poland, holding a separate position, was bound by certain ties to the Cracow, Lvov and Lublin regions.

The whole of the area of South and Central Poland that we are discussing formed a particular type of artistic commonwealth founded on the integral and consistent development of architecture and sculpture in the Cracow milieu and the successive appearance of new centres, losing neither their genetic ties with Cracow nor with one another. Evident against the background of this artistic landscape is the distinctive work of Bernardo Morando, an eminent Jtalian town-planner and architect, the creator of Zamość.

In the north of Poland the art and influence of Gdańsk began in the 1580s to equal those of Cracow on the south. The Gdańsk late-Renaissance with its Mannerist features was imbued with a brilliant tone by Antonius van Opbergen and Willem and Abraham van den Blocke, Netherlandish architects and sculptors working here at the turn of the century. They produced magnificent municipal buildings and influenced the decoration and architecture of Gdańsk's town houses and sepulchral and alter sculpture. The radiation of this high-quality art varied: lesser in the case architecture, embracing mainly itself; greater in the field of sculpture, where it reached Central and South Poland, its impact mounting during the first half of the 17th century and competing with that of Cracow.

Late-Renaissance architecture and sculpture in Poland has a complex stylistic profile. In the North, the Netherlands version predominated whereas in the South, its passage into the bloodstream of the native style with its, preponderance of genetically Italian elements was more indirect, chiefly via engravings. However the further we move into the first decade of the 17th century, the greater its role becomes.

In this denotation of styles we do not limit the term "Renaissance" to artistic phenomena of the type which had in Italy in the first years of the 16th century shaped themselves into the "classical style" based on the absolute balance of thematic and formal factors as postulated in the theory of Renaissance art. We traditionally apply it to later developments which, while using the same forms, often gave them a different twist leading to the appearance of either a consciously or subconsciously "anti-classical" attitude. This matter comes especially sharply into focus precisely in the particular period of Polish art under discussion when the discipline of the early style, loose enough in the first place, was considerably relaxed in Poland also. This "anti-classical" trend, made familiar for that matter in Poland almost from the first years of the 16th century by the work of the Como ateliers, which in the late Renaissance were chiefly responsible for its consolidation, was forwarded on the one hand by the local tendency to give art a native streak of freedom and decorativeness and, on the other, by the influence of the Mannerist Netherlands and Italian art. These external factors filtered into Poland through the medium of visiting artists and the diffusion of models and treatises.

It was the architecture and sculpture of Santi Gucci (c. 1530—1599 or 1600) whose influence in fact endured right up to the first years of the 17th century which had a basic significance for the first phase of the late-Renaissance in Central and South Poland and the strengthening of the Mannerist trend. This outstanding artist, a Florentine by birth, came to Cracow during the fifties where he worked for a spell before moving and making a base in the Kielce Region, chiefly in Pińczów but also partly in Janowiec. This move to Central Poland was characteristic of the times, for it was an area which had ceased to be a typical artistic backwater, principally thanks to Gucci himself but also to its rich resources of building materials. He worked here mainly for the wealthy Myszkowski and Firlej families. He maintained right up to the end of his life contacts not only with Cracow but also with the royal court, remaining a court artist and building and sculpting for Stephen Báthory and Anna Jagiellonka.

Gucci converted the castles in Pińczów and Janowiec; his most important architectural work in the Kielce region was palatial residence of the Myszkowski family in Książ Wielki (1585—1595). Here the only fortifications were earth works; the main body of this residence, enlivened by projections and with smooth rusticated walls, is formed by the cubic block of a palace with a compact plan, its massiveness counterpointed by small pavilions with light and airy structures on the sides of the courtyard; with extreme sophistication he placed the by now standard arcaded loggias in these all but filigrane pavilions and not in the place itself. This capricious play of the creator's imagination betrays a bemusement with the Mannerist principles with which he became acquainted during his youth in his native Florence. For the first time in modern Polish architecture, Gucci did away with the traditional inner courtyard and designed a palace with a compact plan and a regular interior layout; this, too, established itself in Poland although it co-existed for the time being with the traditional arrangement derived from Wawel Castle. For Stephen Báthory, Gucci erected a no longer existing residence with conventional wings in Łobzów outside Cracow (1585—1587). He was also the author of the conversion of a mansion with a galleried inner courtyard at No 21 Kanonicza Street in Cracow, a characteristic example of an urban dwelling imitating the stately home.

It is also possible that Gucci was the author of the castle in Baranów (1591–1606), the most beautiful late-Renaissance residence in Poland repeating the traditional layout with an interior courtyard and galleries; polished and varied in composition, it has the architect's signature written all over its protecting wing.

Gucci worked more comprehensively as a sculptor. He appears to have been influenced by the Cracow decorative style of the third quarter of the century developed by Michałowicz and the new values independent from it. But even so if this was partly Gucci's inspiration, he transmuted it in an exceedingly individual way creating a campricious and soft style freely employing various decorative elements with a particularly characteristic use of Ionic volutes, concentric bosses, wide and low bands of acanthus leaves and flamboyant vases. Initially for that matter he expressed himself chiefly as a figurative sculptor supplementing the decoration of the Sigismund Chapel with statues of Sigismund Augustus and Anna Jagiellonka (1574—1575). His principal later works, namely the tiered tomb of the Firlej family in Janowiec (1568—1587) and the Báthory tomb in a specially converted chapel in Wawel Cathedral (1594—1595), show the full blossoming of his decorative and figurative style and the suggestiveness which favoured its reception and popularity. Gucci used sandstones and reddish marble in the Báthory tomb, thus creating an original colour contrast, and developed his fantastic ornamental style everywhere. In his treatment of the figure, he displayed a Mannerist stylization of forms. Though following the formulas obligatory in the Polish Renaissance tomb, he surrealized the composition and gesture of the figure bringing in all but dance rhythms. Regardless of the fact that Gucci introduced certain late-Renaissance and Mannerist elements of Florentine art into the development of Polish architecture and, in part, sculpture, he identified himself with local tradition and enriched its trend in an original way; hence his art was above all a manifestation of the native style, especially in the realms of sculpture and ornamentation.

Gucci's style made a forceful impact, less on architecture and more on sepulchral and decorative sculpture. As a result of the long years he spent not only in Cracow but also in the Kielce region during the period when architectural and sculptural ateliers were springing up to serve a wide area, his influence continued to make itself felt after his death, especially during the first quarter of the 17th century. Although it also reached Lublin and Lvov, it was more characteristic of Cracow and Kielce where it often took the form of a direct continuation of his art. Particularly in Pinczów we find during the early years of the 17th century work by stonemasons and sculptors who had presumably been his associates; some were Poles, others no doubt Polonized Italians or Germans; of these the most important was no doubt Tomasz Nikiel (d. before 1605).

Besides the castle in Baranów which shows close connections with Gucci's art, the most important work marked by this author's influence as an architect is the Myszkowski Chapel in the Dominican Church in Cracow (1602—1614). Here, in the contrasting arrangement of the structure's mass with the decorative elements adorning its walls which reveals the artist's fondness for striking effects, we can discern a close relationship with the palace in

Książ Wielki. Similar to it is the somewhat later Tęczyński Chapel in the parish church in Staszów.

In the architectural decoration of tombs, portals and window framings the influence of Gucci's style was superimposed on other currents in the Cracow school of the last quarter of the 16th and the first years of the 17th centuries; these evolved both from the local changes in style and from reference to Italian and Netherlands ornamental models. Here Gucci's influence blended into a complex fabric, but was simultaneously an essential component of this late-Renaissance art enriched by Mannerist elements. Similarly, Gucci's style as a sculptor of tombs with his typically Mannerist treatment of the human figure filtered into the general picture of the Cracow artistic scene at this time. The composition of the figures of Báthory and Anna Jagiellonka and the linear light–and–shadow style of their conception had a wide radius of influence over the Little Poland region and beyond its boundaries.

The tomb of the Kryski family at Drobin near Płock (1572—1576) is close to the Gucci ornamental composition in its decoration, while the figures from Michelangelo's monument for Julius II are echoed in the figurative sculpture, a rare example of the great Italian's influence on Polish art. It is evident that although Gucci left a strong imprint on the Cracow sepulchral monument, it also drew on other sources continually going back to models from Italy itself. This was also due to the existence in Cracow of at least several architectural and sculpture ateliers at this time and the emergence of a number of artists with styles different from Gucci although, unfortunately, we cannot identify them by names. Proof of this is found, for example, in Prospero Prowana's (d. 1584) monument in the Dominican Church in Cracow which adapted to Polish Renaissance sculpture, earlier than Gucci did in the Báthory monument, the scheme of the Roman arch of triumph created in Rome on the threshold of the 16th century by Andrea Sansovino. But, as in the majority of Cracow sepulchral monuments, Gucci's influence is evident in the ornamental parts. Of the burgesses' tombs, those of the Montelupi and Cellari families in the church of St Mary in Cracow have the closest affinities with this artist.

The artistic production at the turn of the 16th to 17th centuries of the Kielce ateliers, especially of those in Pinczów, can be regarded as a continuation of the Cracow decorative style but with a stronger Gucci strain. At times it is difficult to decide whether a work, permeated by this artist's style, was done in Cracow or in the Kielce region. One of the markets for tombs of this kind was Mazovia, especially Płock and its environs, whither the completed monuments could be easily ferried down the Vistula; we have good examples in several smaller tombs in Płock Cathedral and in the monument of Stanisław Kobylnicki and his wife in the church at Kobylniki near Płock (1590). In the tomb of Arnulf and Stanisław Uchański in the church at Uchanie (1594) both the figurative and ornamental parts constitute exuberant and soft-moulded interpretations of Gucci's style but, in character, veer beyond the compass of his personal accomplishments.

Within the Gucci school, especially in the Pinczów ateliers, fantastic animal motifs appeared towards the close of the 16th century in increasing numbers in the decorative trend. Here, the peak achievement is the tomb altar of the Firlej Chapel in Bejsce(1594—1600) whose luxuriant decoration , all but menacing and predatory in expression, is an exceptionally original example of Polish art at the turn of the 16th to 17th centuries; it is probably the work of Tomasz Nikiel. The same conventions were followed in the tomb of Paweł and Anna Uchański which must be considered an import from Pinczów.

Besides the work of Gucci and his circle of influence, much else was happening in the Polish Renaissance architecture of the last quarter of the 16th and first decade of the 17th centuries. There was a continuation of trends more traditional than the architectural art of Italy. More and more sepulchral chapels harked back to the Sigismund Chapel and generally displayed a much simpler layout than Cracow Myszkowski Chapel and less stylistically developed decoration than the Firlej family mausoleum in Bejsce. The Komorowski Chapel in Żywiec (1596—1608) and, the one burgess foundation in the Kielce region, the family chapel of Kasper Fodyga, a Comoan (1614), may serve as examples.

The brick synagogues, being erected from the last quarter of the 16th century mainly in towns east of the Vistula, have a different character; as in municipal building of the previous quarter century, their mass was given a distinctive stylistic expression by a Polish attic. Here it is necessary to mention the synagogues in Szydłów, from the close of the 16th century, and in Szczebrzeszyn from turn of the 16th to 17th centuries.

There was also an enrichment and variation of the exterior and interior design of the brick residences of the gentry; the most representative example is the manor-house in Poddębice (1610—1617) with a tower and a two-tiered loggia. In the residential building of the magnates, the wing layout with an interior courtyard and galleries was continued; apart from the castle in Baranów, belonging to the Gucci circle, it is represented by a score of buildings of more modest dimensions and character (i.e. Gołuchów, c. 1560, extended during the first years of the 17th century); an original position among them is occupied by the converted, originally Gothic, castle in Pieskowa Skała (mainly the fourth quarter of the 16th century) where arcaded loggias were uncovered after the last war. The most magnificent residence is the castle in Krasiczyn, the seat of Marcin Krasiński, one of the mightiest of the borderland nobles; its late Renaissance features, invaded by Mannerism, already intimate the thematic problem proper to the Baroque; its conversion began in 1597 and proceeded by stages for twenty years, with the architect Appiano participating in the first stage. A medley of Polish attics, some of them the most beautiful in Poland, were mounted on the walls and towers; but in contrast to these ostentatiously Renaissance crownings, the galleried courtyard has been reduced to a vestigial first-storey loggia on the staircase. The names of the towers—Divine, Papal, Royal and Gentry—and the sgraffito decoration reflect the ideals of Sarmatianism and the Counter-Reformation and so cross the threshold of the Baroque. To get a clearer understanding of the parallelism of the styles during this turning-point period, it is worth recalling that Krasiczyn and the Warsaw Royal castles were both built at the same time and that the latter is a fully Baroque building.

At the close of the 16th century, the patronage exercised by the nobility on the eastern borders of ethnically Polish soil, which were the central region of a united state, gave rise to a Renaissance town-planning scheme that, both in scale and in the artistic quality of its ideas, exceeded a purely national achievement: the building of the town of Zamość. Jan Zamoyski, one of the most powerful Polish aristocrats of the late-Renaissance period, an educated man in the European mould and a distinguished patron of the arts, entrusted this task in 1578 to Bernardo Morando, an eminent architect from the Venice area who had already been working in Poland for some dozen years (d. 1600), and himself through enlightened counsel contributed to this enterprise.

Zamość was designed as a town with strong modern fortifications for several thousand inhabitants, a vital centre of commerce and crafts situated on important trade routes, a cultural and religious centre and, finally, the magnate's principle residential seat, the capital as it were of the personal kingdom of his vast estates. Morando was given an exceptional opportunity to adapt the concept of the "ideal town," pertinaciously occupying the minds of Italian art theorists during the Renaissance epoch, to specific realities. The architect made skilfull use of their ideas to blend into a harmonious, tuning whole the various factors, tasks and functions inherent in the town's foundation. The town proper was given the shape of a pentagon based on an elongated axis in which there appeared a main transverse axis demarcated by the main and subsidiary market places, a rectangle with the magnate's residence attached to one side of the polygon, and a secondary transverse axis, defined by a collegiate church on one side and the Academy building on the other. The plans for the town were drawn up in 1579 and construction commenced after they had been surveyed in 1581–1583; by the early years of the 17th century the Zamoyski palace, the collegiate church, the Academy, and the first burghers' brick mansions and the Town Hall were completed. Morando was the author of all these buildings. His houses were the model for the remaining dwellings around the marked place, most of them built during the second and third quarters of the 17th century. Despite later alterations, the town preserved its preliminary layout and most of its buildings. In Zamość, Morando proved himself not only a specialist in town-planning on a European scale but also a leading architect. In view of the degree of conversion undergone by most of the buildings that we have mentioned, this can be best judged from the collegiate church (1587—after 1600); although also seriously affected by later alterations, its plan and interior remain virtually unchanged. Here, as in the whole of Zamość, the artist followed mid-century Italian models from before his arrival in Poland and adapted them to local conditions and the wishes of the founder. The structure of the collegiate church, a basilica with rows of chapel opening onto the aisles, was based as to layout on the principles of geometrical relationships, including modules. The main accent of the interior is the bright and extensive nave which Morando contrasted with the harmonious play of light and space in the other parts of the configuration of the church.

The building of Zamość played a certain role in shaping and developing the native trend of architecture and architectural decoration in the latter part of the late-Renaissance phase, to the first forty years of the 17th century. Where in earlier periods the typical Polish Renaissance mainly accounted for itself in various fields of secular building, and decoration deriving from it or from sepulchral sculpture, by now the centre of gravity was shifted towards church architecture in its provincial trend and the burgher's houses. The most typical of these late-Renaissance manifestations occurred in the Lublin region, but they are also encountered in other parts of Poland. This phase is characterized by other stylistic accents than the ealier one, though there exist many points of contact between them. From this aspect the Pinczów ateliers had some influence, as well as the tradition of Gucci's art radiating east of the Vistula, the growing popularity of Netherlands models and the oriental taste coming from Lvov; the Como stonemasons, particularly in the Lublin region, and other provincial architects were able to give individual features to the new stylistic versions that were absorbing, on the one hand, traditional elements and, on the other, folk-art influences. The founders of the buildings generally came among the lesser nobility, gentry or burgesses.

The Zamość collegiate church led this late-Renaissance trend of native church building. In itself it exerted an immediate influence on some of the Lublin or Lvov buildings (i.e. the Bernardine churches, 1600—1617 and 1603—1607); it also played a certain role in the typical church vaulting decoration of the trend under discussion. But in the tide of mid-17th century tate-Renaissance church building stimulated by the victorious Counter-Reformation, it was lhe aisleless church—although there were some imposing basilicas—that predominated with nothing in common either in plan or design with the Zamość collegiate church. The traditional inclinations of the founders and the architects, the indirect and only partial knowledge of architectural "innovations" and the limited building abilities of the ateliers, mainly working in the provinces, caused this aisleless church to become a conglomeration of the old and new. Its layout, towerless, with a narrow elongated presbytery, a corpus supported by buttresses and a high saddleback roof ended by gables were taken from the Gothic; but the presbytery and the windows were now semicircularly closed, the walls plastered the interior covered by cradle vaulting with lunettes and the features Renaissance in character. The many sepulchral chapels which were built during the first part of the 17th century continued the

VII.   KRAKÓW

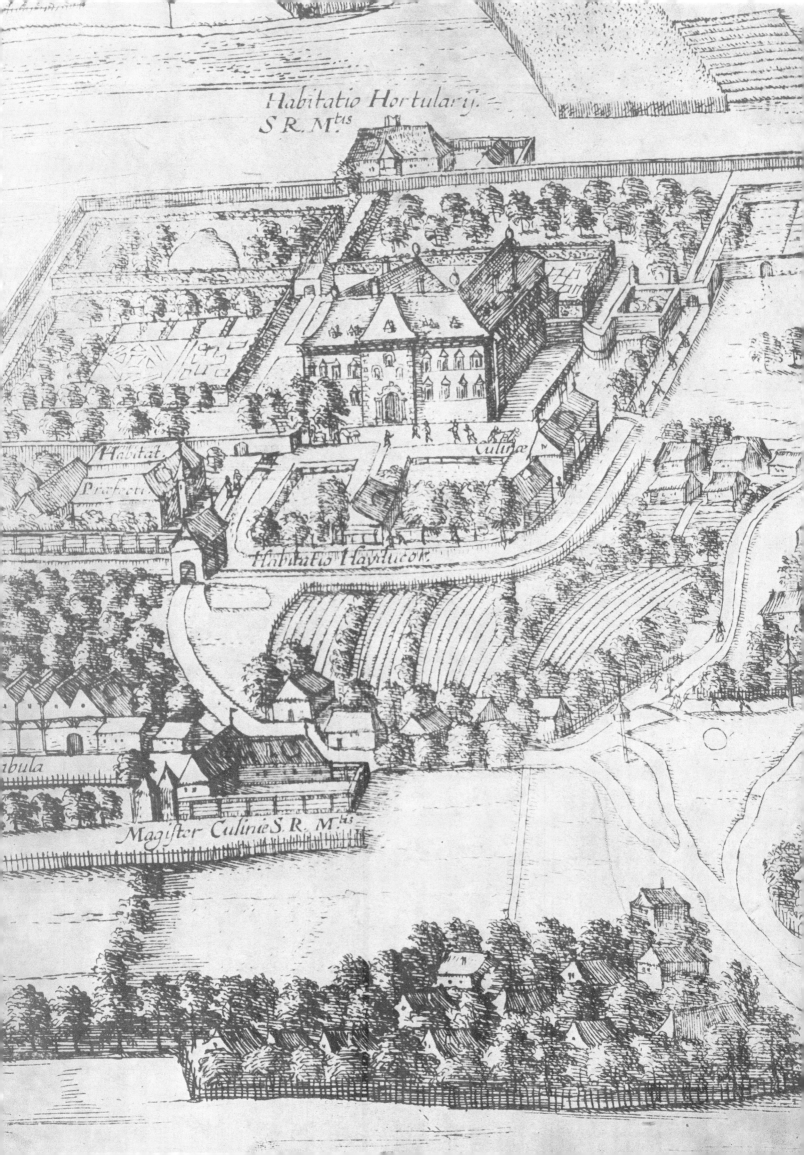

Habitatio Hortularij.
S. R. M.tis

Culinæ

Habitat.
Praefecti

Habitatio Hayductok.

ibula

Magister Culiniæ S. R. M.tis

development line of the Sigismund Chapel but adopted occasionally some of the characteristics that we have mentioned.

The Renaissance features were given an "anti-classical" interpretation with a pronounced folk art flavour. Architectural orders, like the other Renaissance motifs, were treated with a decorative freedom; there were no obligatory theoretical principles, and models from the 16th century Italian treatises were referred to freely or not at all.

In the decorative repertoire, we find the legacy of the post-Gucci Cracow and Pinczów ateliers or even earlier traditions reflected in grotesque and arabesque panels, classical ornamental bands, sequin patterns and rows of orbs or other related motifs; on the other hand, the fantastic animal motifs, once so popular in the above ateliers on the threshold of the 17th century, were abandoned as though out of place in sacral architecture. The stone-carving was inprecise, soft, even a little clumsy; sometimes the decoration was executed in the mortar. Like the whole of the unconstrained interpretation of the Renaissance repertoire of forms, this method of modelling set a folk-art seal on the decoration we are discussing; it was provincial, without a high level of skill and yet, simultaneously, honest, naive and not lacking it own particular kind of originality. These are traits often more valued in art than a routine and cramped adherence to established models which have already become over-traditional.

A decoration of the vaulting using ribs moulded in the mortar with the help of bed moulds was universal and especially characteristic of the Polish late-Renaissance churches of the first forty years of the 17th century; simplifying the question of material, we can call it stucco-work. These ribs, usually arranged in a semicircular pattern, were outlined against the soffito of the vaulting in a network with a geometrical pattern. Square, rectangular, triangular, star or heart-shaped motifs, symmetrical in relation to the axis of the vaulting or scattered more loosely, were linked to one another by additional ribs running in straight lines. Each rib was adorned with a band of bull's eyes (Ionic kymation) and pearls or astragals attached to the side; this set the Renaissance seal on the decoration.

This architecture and decoration of the vaulting, so very native in character, were shaped earlier and separately in Lublin region until, and precisely here, their union took place. Although the genesis of the spatial forms of the church lends itself to a clear explanation, the emergence of this rib decoration is yet unaccounted for. Its forms, fully developed, made their appearance during the first years of the 17th century in the naves and chapels of the Lublin Bernardine church (1603—1607); it contained by now manifold compositional variants and a finally shaped type of rib which became the one in force. The execution of this type of decoration is associated with the architect Giacomo Balin, a Lublin Comoan.

What led to the emergence of this particular type of decorative vaulting? The consecutive stages of its development are not established. Morando's stuccowork, several years anterior to those in the Lublin region, in the Zamość collegiate church had totally different shallow slates and echoed the coffering in the church of S. Maria Miracoli in Venice. Nevertheless, they (and perhaps the ill-planned ribs of the vaulting of the collegiate nave not executed during the architect's lifetime) may have been the starting-point for the later development of stuccowork in which a new method of codifying its forms took place in the Lublin region immediately after 1600. Its antecedents can be found in the Mazovian churches of Giovanni Battista of Venice, with their slat decoration of their vaulting going back even farther, in the late-Gothic cross vaulting. It is also possible that the first church in which the symbiosis of the modernized traditional aisleless type with the new vaulting decoration occurred was the parish church in Kazimierz Dolny during its conversion in 1586—1589 and 1610—1613; Balin was the architect of the second phase. This church may well be regarded as representative of the native trend of the late-Renaissance church architecture. Jan Jaroszewicz (1575—1670) who settled permanently in Zamość and Jan Wolff, temporarily so (d.c. 1650), played an important

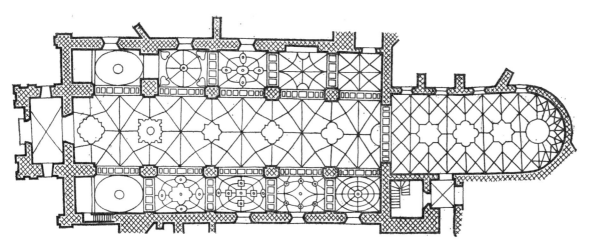

12. Lublin, Bernardine church. Plan, 1:400

role in the further growth of this trend; the former was an architect and responsible for the plans while the latter was generally the builder, though with a certain measure of indepence. Their joint works were the churches in Turobin (1620–1623) and Uchanie (1625), as well as the earlier (c. 1614) stuccowork of the Zamość collegiate church. Wolff also converted the Firlej Chapel in the Dominican Church in Lublin (1630).

The stuccowork style of the Lublin region became popular all over Poland. It appeared in the heart of the area from which, only recently the Lublin region had borrowed so much—in Pinczów, in the vaulting of the church of the Reformed Friars Minor (c. 1640). It is also to be found in the south of Little Poland, in Mazovia, Kuyavya and Great Poland. From the second quarter of the 17th century it began to adopt an increasing number of Baroque motifs without losing that popular art character which distinguishes it, for example, from the contemporary Baroque stuccowork in the vaulting of Giovanni Battista Falconi. This type of native decoration remained in fashion over a long period in the compositions of the canopies of chapel domes, especially sepulchral ones (i.e. the Gostomski Chapel in Środa collegiate church, c. 1640). However, saturated to an increasing degree by Baroque motifs, it survived well into the depths of the second part of the 17th century.

Obviously the intermediate motifs, those between the Renaissance and the Baroque, were also present in the field of sacral architecture during the first part of the 17th century; but in discussing this question we shall limit ourselves to a single example, one close to the group of churches previously mentioned: the church at Gołąb near Puławy (1628—1636). Both in its layout interpretation of architectural features, this building is associated with the late-Renaissance churches of the "Lublin region" type. And yet it deviates from them in that its main façade received two towers, like some of the contemporary Baroque churches, and ar-

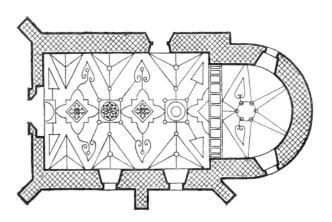

13. Końskowola, church of St Ann. Plan, 1:200

rangements of classical orders were introduced on the elevations, this also being a sign of the new times. Its originality lies in a certain Netherlands touch evident in the contrasts between the stone features, the unplastered walls and the sculpted motifs; on the other hand, Kielce-Pinczów motifs predominate in its decorative repertoire. These characteristics established a bridge-head, as it were, in the Puławy district; Netherlands-like and post-Gucci decoration also appear in the burghers' houses in Kazimierz Dolny. This fact is explained by the town's lively trade with Gdańsk and the neighbouring Kielce region; Janowiec, where Gucci worked for some time, is situated opposite Kazimierz on the other side of the Vistula.

At the other end of the spectrum of the early 17th-century native late-Renaissance style in Lublin region, its chief area of development are the burghers' houses in Zamość, Lublin and Kazimierz Dolny. In Zamość, Morando consolidated with his "model" houses the position of the arcaded mansions, closer in the basic shapes of its elevations to Italian models—those of his native Veneto and of Serlio's treatises—but supplemented with a typical Polish attic and decorative stonework on the lower floors. The Zamość attics were lost during the 19th century but the decoration of many houses, striking in its folk-art sense of form, remains revealing also the orientalising influences coming from Lvov which were to become more pronounced over the course of the first-half of the century. In Lublin there are similar, although less "eastern" houses in which Cracow-Pinczów motifs are blended with Netherlands ones.

Three houses in Kazimierz Dolny are plausibly considered the quintessence of the native style in the late-Renaissance town-house architecture: two adjoining ones belonging to the Przybyło family (1615), the other to the Celejs (before 1635). All are a fascinating artistic phenomenon in which the "European" manner of architectural composition has shrunk almost to vanishing point giving way to bas-relief decoration sown everywhere with a kind of *horror vacui* and modelled and presented with the naivity of popular art. It fills, particularly in the Przybyłos houses, all the surfaces of the elevations. Here we have a comprehensive iconographic programme, half-Renaissance, half-Baroque, in which mythological and other allusions to antiquity are naively mingled with Counter-Reformation ideas. The elements in the decorative repertoire are combined fairly indiscrimately: next to large figures of patron saints of the owners of the houses are a multitude of ornamental motifs—Renaissance, Italian, Cracow and Pinczów, Mannerist, Netherlands and others already with a Baroque flavour. The development of the "Polish attic" reached its zenith in the Kazimierz mansions; they tower like sumptuous battlements over the two Przybyłos houses and the Celej dwelling in which the height of this parapet is almost as great as the basic part of the building. In the granaries, of which there were several score in Kazimierz at this time, ten times the number that have survived, the merchants also made a point of proclaiming their affluence through adornment; limited by the practical function of buildings, they did so chiefly in their attics. Whereas, before the mid-17th century, the Polish attic penetrated ever deeper into the Ukraine and, locally modified, took a new lease of life, in Poland it all disappeared, this being one of the formal signs of the drying-up of the last currents of the Renaissance. During the enlargement of the Morando Town Hall in Zamość by Jaroszewicz and Wolff in 1639–1651, the attic was engulfed by pilasters and cornices suggested by the spreading Baroque fashion which subdued its lively, scalloped shapes and turned it virtually into an ordinary elevational storey.

As we have recalled, Gdańsk constituted during this period the main artistic centre of North Poland, its influences emanating southwards with a lesser range as to architecture and greater one in the fields of sculpture, painting and artistic crafts. Owing to this town's special position in the Polish State, its location, and commercial and cultural relations, it was independent of Cracow but connected with the Netherlands. This association was also emphasized by the stylistic features of the Gdańsk Renaissance for the leading architects and sculptors working in Gdańsk came from the Netherlands.

The Renaissance appeared late in Gdańsk, not until the mid-16th century, and thus at a time when, in South and Central Poland, this style had entered its second development phase. Its stylistic features and sources make the Gdańsk Renaissance belong to the trend known as nothern Mannerism. Three artists gave its its basic identity: Abraham van Opbergen, an architect (1543—1611), Willem van den Blocke, a sculptor (before 1550—1628), and his son Abraham, a sculptor and architect (1572—1628). The latter two came to Gdańsk in 1584, van Opbergen two years later. Although there had been works in the new style prior to the arrival of these eminent artists, the blossoming of the Gdańsk Renaissance is connected with them and gradually faded after the van de Blockes' deaths in 1628.

The most outstanding work of the Gdańsk Mannerist trend in building and architectural decoration is van Opbergen's Arsenal (1602—1605) for which Abraham van den Blocke produced the sculptural decoration. Although a utilitarian military building with a single interior, the architect shaped its exterior like a row of typically burgess gabled houses. In the manner proper to the architecture of the Netherlands and adopted in Gdańsk, the red brick of the unplastered walls contrasts with the architectural features in stone. The decoration is exceedingly rich; the Gdańsk burghers stressed with exaggerated ostentation the military strength of the town by allegorical figures, armed motifs and crests; these are laced with numerous ornaments derived from the popular models of Cornelis Floris and Jan Vredeman de Vries; the latter for that matter stayed for some time in Gdańsk.

An abundance of decoration allied to the clarity of the basic mass of the building was a feature of both Gdańsk Mannerism and the native trend of architecture. But how very different these two styles were, even though the first occasionally influenced the second! A truly "European" standard of design and workmanship reigned in Gdańsk together with scrupulousness and elegance in the carving of the stone or casting of bronze; orientation towards Netherlands sources and only through it, if at all, towards Italian ones was almost total. And yet this in general superb architecture and sculpture lacked precisely that freshness and naivity, that touch of popular art apparent on the building and decoration of the Lublin region which may be less interesting in "standard" but have a fascinating native originality blended with Italianate geometrical forms. This comparison applies only to one trend of art the turn of the 16th-17th centuries because afterwards, in Central and South Poland, the works were by no means inferior in "standard" to those in Gdańsk but still equally different.

Gates and mansions—this was the architectural "programme" in which Gdańsk Mannerism was expressed. An invasion of late-Renaissance Italian influences is evident in van den Blockes' works; in the Hill Gate (1586—1588), Willem succumbed, as did its architect Jan Kramer, to the influence of Sanmichele while Abraham, Willem's son, set through the tiering of the orders and a balustraded parapet with classicist statues a Renaissance stamp on the Steffens' "Gold House" (1609—1617). However, it was the gabled town-house which was dominant in Gdańsk, often with an orderless elevation and characteristic fore-porch; the residence of the Pelplin Abbots, for example, represents a very simple type of mansion (1612). Decorative expression was brought to the Gdańsk mansion by large mullioned windows, which seem to support by ornamental strenght the architectural stone features, contrasted with the deep red background of the walls and particularly in the gable parts. Besides the considerable amount of sculptural work undertaken in Gdańsk itself, the atelier of Willem and Abraham van den Blocke received outside commissions for tombs, sometimes from as far away as from Central Poland, thus competing with the Cracow ateliers. For Stephen Báthory, Willem made the tombstone for Krzysztof, the King's brother, and another in Alba Julia in Transylvania; in Poland, apart from Gdańsk and its environs, we can find this atelier's work, for example, in Barczewo Warmińskie (the monument made in 1598 for Cardinal Andrzej Báthory and Baltazar, his nephew), in Toruń and Łowicz. It was characterized by the propagation of a basically Baroque version of a monument with a kneeling figure, heavily contrasted use of white and black stone, a Netherlandish somewhat cumbersome Mannerist ornamentation and a high standard of craftsmanship. Some of Willem and Abraham van den Blocke's tombs conformed to the traditional Polish Renaissance composition of the deceased's figure recumbent on the sarcophagus.

Gdańsk also established a reputation for the high level of its artistic crafts, particularly metalware; such products were in great demand throughout the whole of Poland.

Silesian architecture and sculpture of the last quarter of the 16th and the first decades of the 17th centuries did not measure up to the originality of expression of the accomplishments of other Polish regions and, with rare exceptions, the standard of workmanship fell short of that of the Gdańsk and leading Cracow ateliers. It is also curious that the decorativeness of feature, although increasing, did not make such a notable appearance as in other districts. The castle in Oleśnica, the most remarkable of the Silesian buildings of its day (remodelling of which was commenced as early as in 1542), is particularly striking for the picturesque arrangement of its clearly defined mass, varied in the upper parts by slender towers and frequently repeated gables, the favourite Silesian Renaissance motifs. Some of the late-Renaissance town houses were more ornamental; the Municipal Assay Office in Nysa (1604) followed the convention of the ornate and palatial mansions. Though to a lesser extent than Gdańsk, Silesia also succumbed to Netherlands influences. The Polish school also made itself felt during this period; some of the burghers' houses adopted the Polish attic and there were tombs of the type with the recumbent figure on the sarcophagus as, for example, in Jan Sitsch's monument in the church of St James in Nysa (c. 1608); under the Cracow influence, this type of tomb had sporadically occurred even earlier in Silesia.

During the 1575—1640 period, easel painting played a much greater role than during the first two phases of the Renaissance. The Gothic tradition, though on its way out, was still apparent right up to the first part of the 17th century but, in general, only in those works from the provincial ateliers of the guilds. The point of departure for the further evolution of the religious scene, which again came to the fore as the Counter-Reformation gained ground, chiefly became Mannerism of a Netherlands origin based on engraved models. This was also encountered in the previous period when it started to take shape; an example is *The Adoration of the Shepherds* from 1572 in Połajewo. Devotional group scenes multiplied, being notably numerous during the first part of the 17th century; expression was given in them to a semi-folk narrative style and they were mainly diffused by monasteries. It was precisely at this time that Tomasso Dolabello, a new arrival from Italy, introduced Venetian elements into Polish religious and historical painting even though at the same time succumbing to the pressure of his new environment. But far more important is the fact that, together with this painting, the modern technique of oil painting became current and was consolidated.

Taking advantage of the attainments of European Renaissance painting, this trend belonged in its entirety to late-Mannerism and Baroque finding its continuation in high Baroque. It is mentioned here only as a characteristic manifestation of late-Renaissance Polish painting, principally in the development of the portrait.

The leading work in this realm is the full–figure likeness of Stephen Báthory (1583), a work by Marcin Kober, a court painter of Silesian birth who was active, chiefly in Cracow, at the turn of the 16th-17th centuries. Even against a more comprehensive European background, it is an original achievement despite its connections with the grand full–figure portrait fashionable during the second–half of the 16th century, felicitously combining a monumental treatment and restrained composition with a decorative play of colours in which the area of red in the costume and emphasis on the decorativeness of the accessories play the main role; on the other hand, the realism in the characterisation of the face is remarkable. Here we have, as in embryo, all the principal traits of the Sarmatian (Old Polish) portrait, so typical of 17th and 18th century Poland. Kober's likeness of Anna Jagiellonka (1586—1596) has a similar but less personal style of formulation and a predominance of reds in the colour play, a procedure that will later be copied in the Baroque paintings of Polish matrons. Our review of Renaissance painting comes to an end with the likeness, full of decorative charm, of Katarzyna (nee Lubomirska) Ostrogska (1597), conceived more plastically and closer to the convention of the grand portrait of the Central European Renaissance epoch.

Commentaries to the Illustrations

157 One of the most important discoveries by restorers after the Second World War were the late-Renaissance courtyard galleries of the main residential part of the castle in Pieskowa Skała. This originally Gothic building, belonging to the wealthy Little Poland Szafraniec family, at least twice underwent conversions during the Renaissance period. The earlier wing layout gave a trapezoid shape to the courtyard; during the alterations in the last quarter of the 16th century, its west wall was diversified with a projection accentuating the entrance gate and a gallery system introduced into the elevation. Two tiers of arcades, corresponding to the second floor of the building, run round the courtyard; the wide openings and the smooth bands of socles, stressed by a line of cordoned cornices, create a horizontal composition and were designed to give the impression that the length of the walls round the fairly small courtyard is greater than it really is; a change in this horizontal rhythm occurs in the projection. The courtyard galleries of the castle in Pieskowa Skała is one of the most picturesque in Poland. The proportioning of the openings, the exclusive use of pillars in the arcades, and the ornamentation of the spandrels between the archivolts with sculpted fantastic mascarons, are stylistically related to the last phase of the Polish Renaissance.

158, 159 Because of its original design and role in the development of architecture in Poland, the residence of Bishop Piotr Myszkowski in Książ Wielki, or Mirów as it is called, is one of the principal relics of the late-Renaissance period in Poland. It was constructed between 1585 and 1595 by Santi Gucci who did a great deal of work for the Myszkowski family and lived for some time in Pińczów which belonged to it. This residence represents the Italian type of *palazzo in fortezza*—a detached palace stripped of its defensive features which have been transferred to the exterior fortifications encircling the building; here they comprise walls with angle towers virtually surrounding the terrace of the knoll on which the palace stands. The Mirów residence is the most outstanding work of architecture in Poland, conceived in the spirit of the Italianate Mannerism represented by Santi Gucci. In it, this distinguished architect and sculptor gave expression not only to the typical intellectual attitude of Mannerism, revealed in the layout, but also the refinement proper to this trend, displayed in the shaping of forms. Symmetrical in relation to both axes, which

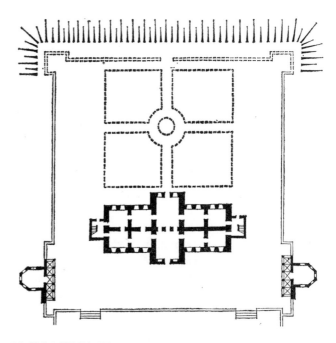

14. Książ Wielki, Mirów residence. Plan, 1:1400

end in projections, the plan of the palace is striking for its crystalline and geometrical purity of division. The compact mass of the palace, enriched by projections, is also clearly defined although, unfortunately, the crowning central part has been disfigured by a Neo-Gothic conversion which removed the Renaissance gables and added battlements endowing the building with the defensive character deliberately excluded from the plans. Gucci sought suprising contrasts by offsetting the mass with lateral pavilions, detached but abutting on the fore-towers, one of which is a chapel and the other, a library. As a foil to the powerful pile of the self-contained palace, he used tiny-looking pavilions whose shape is disguised by openwork arcades merging into the surrounding space. Gucci concentrated in these small buildings the strongest light and shadow contrasts; these one would expect to find in the mass of the central building, whereas here the play of the delicate chiaroscuro of the rustication network is barely discernable on the surface and closely adheres to the face of the wall. The one element used to maintain a certain essential compositional link between the three buildings are the gables with native Renaissance forms which once crowned all the palace projections

213

(only those on the lateral ones have remained), and the fronts of the pavilions.

The Mirów Palace together with, although in a much more mature artistic form, the residences contemporary to it in Zamość and Żółkiew initiated the second development phase of modern residential architecture. The four-winged building with a courtyard galleries and vestigial defensive features was replaced by a palace with a compact plan as one of the elements of a grand axial layout; this design was to be in force during the Baroque epoch.

160, 161 Santi Gucci is associated with the enlargement of the chapter-house, later called the Deanery, at No. 21 Kanonicza Street in Cracow. Converted in 1582—1592 for Canon Stanisław Skarszewski, this originally Gothic building was given the characteristic form of a small palace; it is the most sumptuous 16th-century example in Cracow of the use of the ideas and elements of Renaissance residential architecture for a town house. Once this building had a two-storey frontage (today only vestiges of the upper one remain) and single-storey wings. Four wings enclose an inner courtyard in which the dominant motifs are the galleries on two of the sides supported only by curtain walls. Apart from the other features of the building, the unrestrained and varied composition of the galleries with their alternating rhythms and decorative motifs is well in keeping with Gucci's style, though perhaps he himself only supervised the first stage of the conversion up to 1558. On the ground floor, columns with Ionic capitals were used and on the first storey, pilasters ornamented with perpendicular panels with rosettes. The decoration emphasizes the significance of the *piano nobile*: additionally in the case of the galleries, through the introduction of balustrades and heraldic cartouches in the spaces between the archivolts; in the elevation on the frontage, through a band of sgraffito rustication separating the storeys and larger windows. The portal of the main entrance in this façade is one of the most beautiful in Cracow for here Gucci made good use of his characteristic contrasts; the simplicity of the classical form of the entablature composition on the semi-columns, enlivened towards the bottom by the delicate decoration accompanying it, dominates in the upper part while in the lower one, the rusticated bands encircling the semi-columns establish energetic and harsh accents.

162—165 The castle in Baranów, erected in 1591—1606 for the powerful Leszczyński family, is one of the most magnificent residential structures at the close of the development cycle initiated three quarters of a century earlier by the reconstruction of Wawel Castle. The four-wing type with a galleried courtyard which was binding in 16th-century secular edifices was given a studied architectural version in the spirit of the geometrical principles of the Italian Mannerist and late-Renaissance theorists of the second part of the 16th century but adpated to Polish traditional custom.

This fact, together with the artistic quality of this relic, the details of its design and its features, indicates Santi Gucci as the probable author of the castle which was completed by ateliers associated with the architect's art but already after his death.

The castle has a rectangular plan with side proportions of 1:2. Its block is massive with fairly slender round angle towers whose helmets, underset on the longer sides with decorative gables, impose on the sprawl of the mass a compositional discipline. In the centre of the front façade, energetically thrust forward and crowned with an attic, is a projection with the entrance gate. The attics on the lateral parts of this façade are later ones; the west wing was enlarged in 1695—1700 by Tylman of Gameren when the castle passed into the hands of the Lubomirski family.

The most original features of the castle in Baranów are contained within the wings enclosing the interior; the front wing is only a curtain, while the remaining three with the residential quarters form a horseshoe. Into the thus formed interior rectangle, the architect has as if lowered the elements shaping the courtyard; the level of the floor, raised above the parterre, thereby giving the castle on the courtyard side one storey less than from the outside, and three sets of tiered galleries, along the curtain wall and the elevation of the lateral wings, which are thus the reverse of the residential horseshoe. Hence, the front wing is more massive externally and frailer internally; it is only a supporting wall for the galleries.

Here we are dealing with obvious compositional refinements which give rise to others. We will allow Miłobędzki, a leading authority on architecture, to describe them: "Entering the cavern of the monumental gateway [...] we do not expect to find, instead of a drive stairs leading us onto the courtyard level. Here we immediately are confronted with the scantily-windowed wall of the residential wing which forces us to turn about—and we stand confounded and in wonder at the sight of the magnificent columns of the galleries with a flight of stairs spanning the opening by which we entered". The galleries have elegant

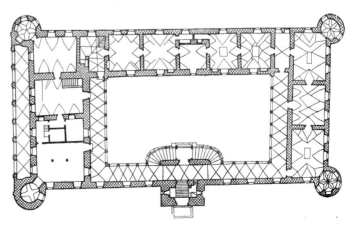

15. Baranów, castle. Plan, 1:800

214

VIII.
WARSZAWA

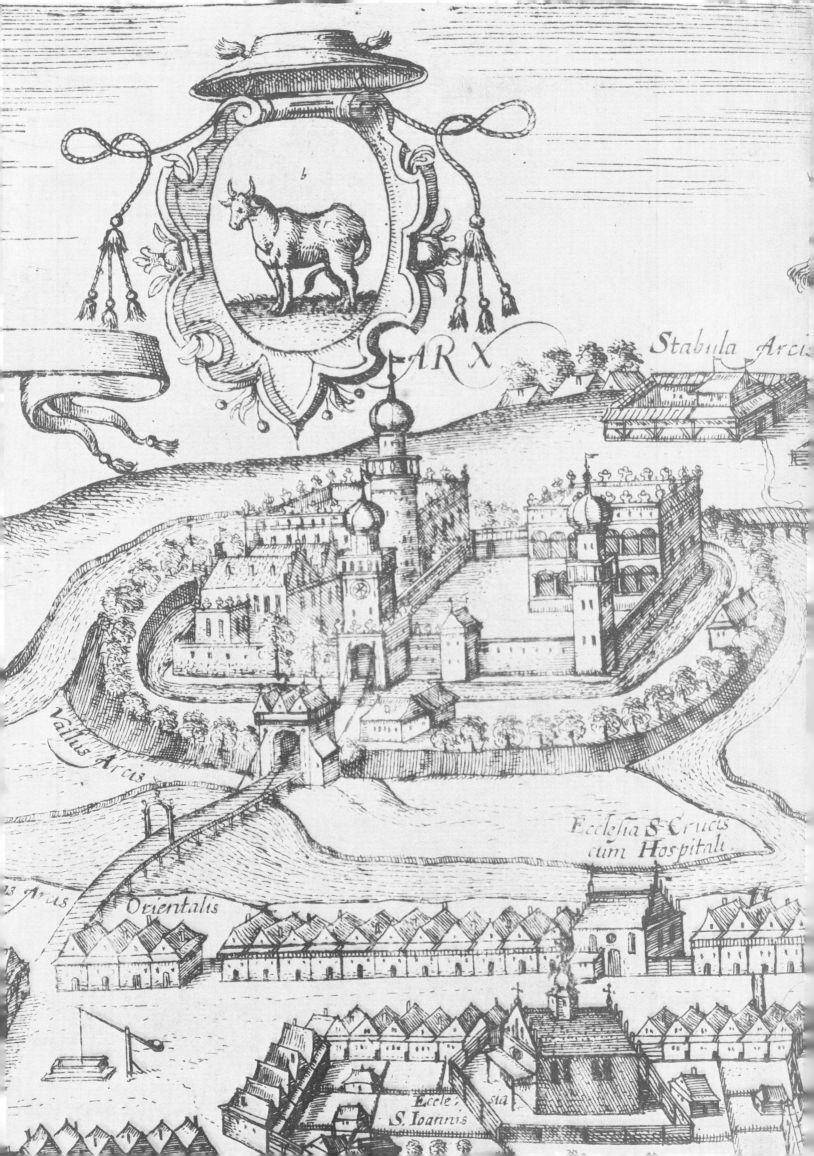

ARX

Stabula Arcis

Vallus Arcis

Ecclesia S. Crucis cum Hospitali

Arus

Orientalis

Ecclesia S. Ioannis

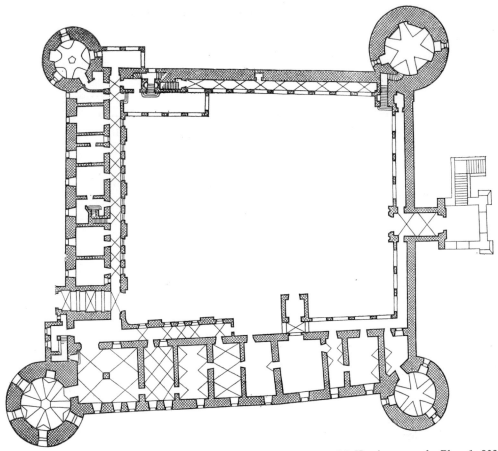

16. Krasiczyn, castle. Plan, 1:800

architecture and sedulous details; on both levels appear the Ionic columns that Gucci favoured, the embossing and rosettes in the spandrels of the archivolts typical of his work, balustrades on the upper tier and socles decorated with mascarons on the lower one.

Here also Gucci's architectural details, popularized by the early 17th-century Cracow-Pinczów ateliers, have very obvious native features. Besides the layout of the building itself, there are more of these, including the gables with their ornamental forms and the attic over the front projection. Because of all these characteristics, this castle is a happy symbiosis of fairly modern (for the times) Italian theoretical principles and Polish ways of shaping, on which the eminent architect has set the seal of his individuality.

In the architectural decoration of the castle in Baranów the portals of the first-floor galleries especially attract attention; they were executed during the first years of the 17th century by one of the ateliers in Pinczów. The production of these ateliers was dominated by the influence of Santi Gucci who, active in Pinczów during the last years of his life, died at the close of the century. The ateliers continued in architectural and sculptural decoration the imaginative motif-rich style of Gucci, the earliest instances of which are found in Cracow. The Baranów portal is a good example. In it there are the characteristic motifs derived from Gucci's art: bosses and rosettes, Ionic column motifs in the level of the panels, and acanthus leaves on the frieze and fantastic animal heads in the upper part; in a lively and fluid way the decorative forms envelop the constructional part of the portal.

166 The fortified manor-house of the Leszczyński family in Gołuchów, built about 1560, was enlarged during the first years of the 17th century into a splendid aristocratic residence by Wacław, Voivode of Kalisz and later Crown Chancellor. Three wings were added on the south side, thus creating an interior galleried courtyard on the lines of the typical Polish Renaissance castle. The Gołuchów residence was converted in 1872—1885 in a French Renaissance style according to the ideas of Viollet-le-Duc; the first-floor arcades of the south wing date back to the early 17th century and give the present building a strong native Polish accent.

167 The artistic production of the Pinczów architectural and sculptural ateliers covered a wide range, from complete buildings with their fittings and decoration to small church utensils. Among the latter is a lavabo (used for washing hands in the sacristy) in the parish church in Chroberz; probably dating back to the third quarter of the 16th century, it is ornamented with popular Renaissance motifs in a semi-folk art stylisation.

217

168 The palace at Poddębice near Łęczyca, erected between 1610 and 1617 by Zygmunt Grudziński, Voivode of Rawa, represents the final phase of the pre-Baroque development of the gentry's residence with a fairly limited layout; it is more of a manor-house than a palace. The partial reconstruction undertaken in the mid-20th century uncovered loggias on two floors of the south façade which once, together with the prominent late-Renaissance gable and adjoining tower, created a picturesque whole in the native late-Renaissance style.

169, 170 At the close of the 16th century the castle in Krasiczyn had the traditional fortress layout of a square plan with a palace on one of the sides and angle towers. Marcin Krasicki, one of the most powerful borderland nobles who inherited the castle in 1597, embarked upon a thorough conversion. This lasted some twenty years but, proceeding in a period of stylistic flux vividly echoed within the orbit of this rich and influential aristocrat's activity, lends itself to a division into definite phases in which various artistic concepts were realized. In the years 1597—1603 Galeazzo Appiano and other architects produced a basically Renaissance-type of building with residential wings enclosing an interior courtyard in which outside staircases placed in a tiered gallery recall cloisters; the walls and towers were crowned with attics and the architectural detail also used Renaissance motifs. On to this traditional design, the owner had a certain thematic programme superimposed which was an expression of the Sarmatianism proper to the Baroque, an ideology espoused by the gentry which was a mixture of self-exaltation and ostentatious Counter-Reformation pietism. One tower was converted into a chapel and called "Divine", the others "Papal", "Royal", and "Gentry", (the Divine and Royal with attics imitating crowns are seen on the reproduction). Baroque ideas were also included in the sgraffito decoration of the walls. The front wing was converted in 1614; the Baroque accent of a gable with a high tower was placed in its centre; an attempt was also made, by painting artificial windows in the courtyard walls, to give a certain uniformity to the spatial conception in the spirit of the new style emanating from the royal court's early Baroque trend. Worthy of notice is the the elegant Renaissance masonry from the first phase of the rebuilding which was supplied by Lvov architectural and sculptural ateliers; the delicate attics of the external elevation of the castle belong to the most beautiful in Poland.

171, 172 King Sigismund Augustus, as his life drew to its close, decided to set up for himself a tomb in his father's chapel. In his will drawn up on 6 May, 1571, he asked to be buried: "In Cracow, in the Castle, in the Great Church, in the Chapel where the body of Our Late Lord and Father [...] lies, in the crypt there below; and above, a monument for Us also [...] to be placed below the marble tombstone of His Majesty [...] with our likeness in the shape of the figure of His Majesty." Approach was made still in 1571 for its execution to the now aged Giovanni Maria Padovano, the sculptor who had made two no longer preserved tombstones for Elizabeth Hapsburg and Barbara Radziwiłłówna, Sigismund Augustus' wives. However, this work was not commenced until 1574—1575, commissioned by and charged to Anna Jagiellonka, the deceased's sister. On 29 April, 1575 the tomb was mounted in the chapel in a new arcaded recess accommodated by elevating the sarcophagus of Sigismund the Old and eliminating the socle beneath it. Thus, both these monuments formed the tiered tomb popular at this time in Poland. The author of the tomb of Sigismund Augustus and the new decorative elements was Santi Gucci, the principal royal architect and sculptor, and not Padovano who had died in the meantime. Like his father's figure, that of the King was executed in red Hungarian marble and, in principle, the composition of Sigismund the Old's figure was repeated although, simultaneously, strictly subordinated to the architectural configuration and even to the decoration. The King's head is modelled as a painstaking portait and yet not devoid of traces of stylization; the same applies to the rich bas-relief armour, deviating in its draughtsmanship from the austere rhythms of the flutings in Sigismund I's armour.

173, 174 The tomb of Anna Jagiellonka in Sigismund Chapel was executed by Santi Gucci in 1574—1575 and so at the same time as the monument for Sigismund Augustus, her brother. Adapted to its allotted place in the parapet of the stall, it consequently does not possess an elaborate architectural setting. The marble slab with the figure of the Queen lies obliquely on the socle completely covered by the inscriptive plaque and is framed in the sides by small socles with spheres and heraldic cartouches and crowned by a narrow cornice. The decoration of the tomb carries the characteristic stylistic motifs of Gucci and his atelier, namely the flat Ionic capitals, amphora, oblated rosettes and embosses. The Queen's figure, carved in high relief, is also typical of the Gucci Manneristic linear stylization of forms with a detailed representation of the jewels and adornments of the robes and, simultaneously, portait-like treatment of the face.

175—177 At Drobin near Płock there is a sepulchral monument executed in 1572—1578 in grey sandstone in memory of Wojciech Kryski and his parents, Paweł and Anna neé Szreńska. Endowed by Stanisław, the deceased's brother, it is the one monument of its particular type in Poland because seated figures in recesses, modelled on and, to a certain extent, copying those in Michelangelo's tombs were introduced for the first time in the design for a tomb for three persons. A logical and organic unity is achieved by linking the vertical recesses with the figures of the parents and the sarcophagus with the son lying at their feet. To a great measure this is also determined by the bonds of feeling uniting the three figures. The parents' heads, bent in their son's direction and the pious gesture of hands touching their hearts, convey an atmosphere of love for their son, while his filial sentiment for them is suggested by the son's recumbent position at their feet. All this creates as it were a Polish type of *sacra conversazione* scene, full of contemplation and intimacy. Further innovations of the composition are the highlighting of painterly and chiaroscuro effects by the placing of light figures in dark recesses and the sparing, but fully plastic, use of decoration in the forms of subtle coils of plants and patera with fruit on the pilasters. The author of this beautiful work should be sought among the Cracow masters; it is likely that there were two of them and that the one executing the decoration was connected with Santi Gucci, but the sculptor of the figures remains unidentified.

Of the two seated figures of the Kryski tomb, that of the woman is more interesting, not only because it is the first fully plastic representation in Polish Renaissance sculpture of a seated female figure, modelled by the sculptor on a compound of the figures of Moses and the Sybil in Michelangelo's tomb for Julius II, but also by reason of the inner life which the maternal figure exudes. Not only are love and solicitude reflected on her face but they are also expressed by both gesture and movement in such a suggestive manner that one gains the impression that the mother is about to rise and step down to the son recumbent at her feet.

Wojciech Kryski, young and elegant, supported in a natural pose on his right arm, lies on the sarcophagus as though reclining on a triclinium. His noble features and the distinction of his figure correspond to Górnicki's description when he made him one of the heroes of his *Courtier*. This astute diplomat, an outstanding figure even by the standards of our Renaissance, who had served on missions to all the European courts, was so heart-broken by the defeat he suffered at the Spanish court of Philip II during negotiations over the Duchy of Bari, Queen Bona's inheritance that, according to the words of Bartosz Paprocki, the author of the armorial, he died of chagrin. Kochanowski commemorated him in his poetry and the nameless sculptor has attempted to present the charm and handsome looks of this young chevalier, a graduate of Padua University and a lover of classical culture by-named "Magnificus" by the English court during his mission in 1555.

178, 179 The sepulchral monument of Andrzej and Barbara Firlej in the parish church in Janowiec was executed by Santi Gucci in 1596—1587. It is chiselled in its entirety in Pinczów stone in the by now traditional composition of a tiered slab with the figures of the deceased. Both the architecture and the figures are treated in an a-plastic manner, a characteristic feature of Gucci's work. The decoration serves to stress the architectural composition of the monument; the most frequently used ornamental elements include flamboyant vases, plant candelabras tipped with three flowers, long and narrow helices, pilasters with Ionic capitals, skulls and cross-bones, bands of leaves and embossed rosettes. Treated to a considerable extent as elements of the composition filling the slab, the figures of the deceased are placed diagonally and, reclining in unnatural positions, give the impression they are sliding from the inclined surface. The artificiality of this arrangement is emphasized by the unnatural twist of the feet, in the man, and the folds of the dress reaching up to the upper corner of the slab, in the woman. Giving Santi Gucci's work its specific character easily distinguishable from other artists', all these decorative and figurative elements were a manifestation of the Mannerist trend, the forms of which, thanks to Gucci, became popular throughout Poland among the gentry and magnate clientele.

180—183 The Gothic chapel of St Mary was chosen by Anna Jagiellonka as a mausoleum for her husband King Stephen Báthory who died in December 1586 and was interred in the Cathedral in May 1588; Santi Gucci was contracted by the Queen and commenced its conversion in May, 1594 which he completed together with the tomb in 1595. This is the one work signed by this artist. The contract made precise specifications as to both the form and content of the monument required with attention drawn to the colour effects that were to be obtained by using white stone and red marble. Santi Gucci followed them to the letter. The monumental architecture of this relic is based on the popular Renaissance design of a Roman arch of triumph and as it were codifies the schemes of a similar type but with a traditional crowning which appeared in Cracow sepulchral sculpture at the close of the 16th century, for example, the monuments of Prospero Prowana (d. 1584) in the Dominican church (ill. 184) and Marcin Leśnowolski (d. 1593) in the church of St Mary. The Báthory monument comprises a high two-tier socle carrying a lofty central arcade separated from the lateral niches with their allegorical figures of Prudence and Fortitude by columns bearing a semicircular arch enclosing a crowning tympanum with heraldic cartouched. A bronze slab with the King's figure carved in high relief forms the centre-piece. The pose of this figure is far from naturalistic, especially because of the almost dancing rhythm in which it is suspended as if in space. In the ingenious crossing of the legs in the lower right corner of the slab, the all but perpendicular positioning of the torso on the left side and the horizontal lines of the folds of the cloak shrouding the royal figure at the top, the artist created one of the most characteristic compositions of the human body, typical of the Mannerist trend in the Polish late-Renaissance. The portraiture of the King's face and hands, although fairly faithfully modelled, was subjected to the stylization characterizing the figure as a whole. In its entirety it constitutes the most outstanding sculptural achievement of Santi Gucci's art.

184 The monument of Prospero Prowana (d. 1584) in the Dominican church in Cracow inaugurated a group of Polish late-Renaissance tombs remarkable for their elaborate architecture with a large central recess topped by a semicircular arch and lateral habitacles; they display a rich decoration enriched with animal motifs, while the figures hark back to the full-sculpted representations of the deceased like that of Sigismund the Old in the Jagiellonian Chapel. Although Jan Michałowicz paved the way for tombs with semicircular niches, their full growth did not take place until the close of the 16th century, parallel to the activities of Santi Gucci's atelier. The author of the monument of Provana, an Italian knighted by Sigismund Augustus in 1557, is an unknown artist who, while drawing on local tradition, also possessed an independent creative perception.

185 The rising demand of the magnates for progressively more magnificent sepulchral monuments at the close of the 16th century increased the production of the Cracow ateliers, drawing on traditional and contemporary sources. The monument of Maciej (d. 1541) and Jadwiga (d. 1559) Opaliński in the parish church at Kościan, set up about 1590 by their son Andrzej, is an eclectic work that ably combines the legacy of the Sigismund tomb in the Jagiellonian Chapel in the form of two recesses closed by a round arch with the painterly and decorative Mannerist style through coloured marble and the introduction of fantastic fauna in the decoration. The fully sculpted execution of the figures and their arrangement on the sarcophagus deviates from the flatness of Santi Gucci's representations; they are conceived more realistically. The wishes of the founder of the tomb may also have had some bearing on this.

186 Within an architectural setting of fine lines and harmonious structure is mounted a bas-relief figure of a girl in an elegant half-seated pose, emphasized by the exquisite moulding of the folds of dress to her body. This tomb was erected in the church in Bejsce by Mikołaj Firlej, at the time Starost of Biecz and, from 1589, Voivode of Cracow, for Elżbieta, his young sister who died in 1580. Executed between 1580 and 1589, this monument can, by reason of its stylistic resemblances, not only as to structure but also as to the composition of the figure, be attributed to the Cracow atelier of Hieronymus Canavesi. Only the plant decoration on the frieze and pilasters recalls the ornamentation of the Pinczów ateliers of the Santi Gucci circle. It is likely that the sepulchral monument of Elżbieta Firlej was designed by Canavesi but built after his death in 1582, and that its executor was an anonymous associate who drew skilfully on ornamental motifs of other ateliers.

187 The sepulchral monument of Andrzej and Elżbieta Modliszewski in the parish church in Łomża, executed in 1589, constitutes a further example of the diffusion of the Gucci type of decoration through North Poland. Its nameless author, possibly from Cracow, has revealed a certain measure of independence in the composition of the lower part of the monument by enlarging it with lateral parts of the same height on which heraldic cartouches are mounted; because of this, the architecture of the tomb gains a greater stability. The figures differ from the Gucci formula, especially the carefully portrayed woman who has been modelled exceptionally meticulously, her dress following the contour of the body and its long, narrow folds emphasizing the shape of the legs which, in other tombs, were carefully hidden under copious drapery.

188 The sepulchral monument of Andrzej (d. 1593) and Katarzyna (d. 1601) Opaliński at Radlin near Jarocin represents the already familiar tripartite scheme with a central semicircularly arched recess with the sculpted figure of the deceased on a sarcophagus and lateral wings embellished with figures, enlarged at the top to accommodate a second recess. A truncation of the lateral wings was made necessary by the shape of the chapel. In that the various elements issuing from the tradition of 16th-century Cracow sculpture are combined in the Radlin tomb, it constitutes to a certain measure a synthesis of the development of Polish monumental art. The dual arch with cartouches over the female figure echoes the art of Michałowicz and offers a vivid reminiscence of the Padniewski tomb in Cracow Cathedral.

189 The diffusion of sculpture from the Cracow ateliers over distant areas had become by the last quarter of the century an everyday matter. The works of Santi Gucci's atelier, in particular, penetrated even the backwaters of Mazovia. In 1590, in the small church at Kobylniki near Płock, Stanisław Kobylnicki set up a tomb for himself and Zofia and Izabela, his successive wives. The knight's figure, architectural setting and decorative motifs are almost identical with those in the Firlej tomb in Janowiec; the difference lies in the fact that the lower part was extended so as to place two slabs side by side. Both the women, clothed in garments with soft and lavish folds seemingly rippling in the wind, became through their stylization more of a decorative element filling out the slabs with a high relief than subjects of portraiture. Even their faces are stereotyped and the accent in its entirety has been transposed to the rendering of their studied poses. This type of conception was to have a considerable impact on Polish sculpture, consolidating its Mannerist trend at the close of the 16th century.

190 The modest burghers' recess tomb with a bas-relief bust of the deceased was transformed in the monument of the Montelupis, a prosperous Cracow family of Italian descent, into a monumental multi-tier wall tomb. It was built on the threshold of the 17th century for the church of St Mary in Cracow by one of the local ateliers and represents a blend of various Italian,

Netherlands and Polish motifs given a characteristic local stamp. The recesses, divided by columns, are adorned top and bottom with a Gucci type of decoration and cartouches with inscriptions encircled by twining ornamentation screening the socles supported by animal paws and human skulls. The lofty finial draws the structure of the monument upwards even though it already has an exalted height because of its position over the stalls. Despite the colour effects and lavish decoration, the heavy architectural construction dominates the whole.

191 The tiered tomb of Arnulf Uchański, Voivode of Bełżec (d. 1576), and his son Stanisław in the church at Uchanie in the Lublin region is to be attributed to one of Santi Gucci's closest associates because of its obvious debts to the Firlej tomb in Janowiec; perhaps it was executed prior to 1590 in the atelier of a Janowiec or Pińczów master. The repertoire of ornamental motifs, identical with that in the Firlej monument, has been enriched by female heads in the finial, Gucci-type bosses decorate the lower pilasters and in the knights figures, the legs crossed even more markedly in a dancing movement, contrast with the subdued upper parts of their trunks. The scalloped crowning, the balusters and gorges on the sides and the flamboyant vases together with the stylized figure give the impression of a great mural decoration rather than three-dimensional sepulchral architecture.

192—195 The tomb of Paweł Uchański (d. 1590 in Constantinople), Voivode of Bełżec, and Anna neé Hubert, his wife (d. 1619), who endowed it, must have sparkled like a jewel on the white wall of the church at Uchanie. Executed in white sandstone, the monument with marble incrustations and alabaster figures of the deceased was originally polychromed; the reds and blues are still preserved on the columns. The architecture of the tomb, emphasized in the central part by columns and allegorical figures, is framed by a sumptuous display of animal and plant ornament dominated by dragons' necks in the crowning, winged griffins on the lateral panels and acanthus leaves in rich patterns in the forms of gorges and pendens The characteristic small figures on the sides of the lower niche recall Indian dancers. The figures of the deceased are carefully executed in alabaster, a soft stone for modelling, and their faces have the precision of chiselling. The Lublin-Pińczów atelier that realized this tomb during the first years of the 17th century drew on the whole Polish and foreign Renaissance inheritance; the polychroming, with all its vividness, has an almost folk-art character.

196 On the summit of the hill overlooking Pińczów stands the chapel of St Ann, erected in 1600. A building with such a site was as unusual in the Polish Renaissance as a detached chapel. Zygmunt Myszkowski, lord of the Pińczów estates, endowed the chapel and almost certainly entrusted it to Santi Gucci who was working for him at this time. This assumption is confirmed by the high standard of this small structure's design and its stylistic character, which tallies with the artistic programmes of this eminent creator. Its lucid and pure layout hinges on the juxtaposing of two cubes—the chapel itself and the galilee—covered by domes. The smoothness of the wall surfaces is accentuated in the first, the architectural decoration with elegantly chiselled features being shifted to the edges of the cube.

197 The tower of the parish church in Żywiec with an arcaded gallery at the top was endowed by Jan Spytek Komorowski, on whose estates the town lay, with the help of Krzysztof, his brother, in 1582—1585. It was constructed in two stages; since the original top of the tower built in 1582—1583 seemed too monotonous, it was altered in 1585 by the addition of an ornamental arcaded gallery. This circular loggia set an obvious Renaissance seal on the tower. On Polish soil it was a fairly isolated architectural motif; on the other hand, similarly crowned towers were more typical of the Bohemian and Moravian Renaissance where by the middle of the 16th century the Comoan builders had accomplished a striking union of the traditional church, town hall or castle tower with the Italian motif of a crowning arcaded gallery which was particularly popular in Lombardy. Giovanni Ricci, who was commissioned to construct the Żywiec tower, was in fact one of the Comoans active in Moravia; he came to Poland by way of Silesia. The late-Renaissance chapel beside the church, one of the many sequels to the Sigismund Chapel, was founded by Krzysztof Komorowski and built in 1596—1608.

198 The Myszkowski chapel in the Dominican Church in Cracow was constructed in 1603—1614. It was intended to be the mausoleum of a family that had only fairly recently amassed power and wealth and wished to display them in a magnificent sepulchral edifice. The principal sponsor of this building, erected on the site of the Gothic chapel of the Carpenter's Guild, was Zygmunt Myszkowski, Castellan of Wojnice and later, Grand Crown Marshal. The Myszkowski chapel is one of the most representative "small" works of sepulchral architecture which, from the close of the 16th up to the mid-17th centuries, were destined to be set up in large numbers reviving the forms, seldom imitated earlier, of the Jagiellonian Chapel. The resemblances in this case are considerable but general; the eighty-year time-lag between the two was bound to affect the appearance of some of the architectural parts and features. The mass is formed by a cuboid completely covered by bands of rustication and enlivened only on the fore-wall by an inscriptive plaque in a cartouche; this simple cubic mass is contrasted with the varied forms of the upper part of the chapel comprising a drum pierced by windows and a dome, ribbed and laminated, bearing the lantern. In view of his close association with the Myszkowski family, this chapel is ascribed to Santi Gucci; certain of the stylistic features as, for example, the exterior application of broad rusticated surfaces similar to those he designed in Książ Wielki, and the originality of the architectural conception also point to this outstanding artist. But the building was erected only after his death, and the hand of post-Gucci Cracow-Pinczów stone-workers is particularly apparent in the upper part of the interior; the sculpted busts of the representatives of the Myszkowski family adorning the foot of the galleried dome and the angels in the coffering on the soffit betray the fact that there were numerous and not always skilled executants. On the lower walls of the interior the use of the motif of arcades with pairs of columns of two-toned marble introduces into the architecture of the chapel a classicist note, one parallel to the stylistic searchings of the royal builders of the early phase of the Vasa Baroque.

199, 200 Like the Myszkowski chapel in the Dominican Church in Cracow (ill. 198), the somewhat later chapel of the Tęczyński family adjoining the parish church in Staszów (pre-1610 -pre-1618) is the work of an architectural and sculptural atelier in the Cracow-Pinczów area. With its strong upwards thrust, this chapel of a noble family rises ostentatiously above the relatively small mass of the Gothic church. Together with the previously mentioned chapel in Cracow, it also represents the early 17th-century post-Gucci trend and, in the same way, reveals the stylistic juncture reached by this type of building, initiated a hundred years earlier by the Sigismund Chapel.

The upper part of the interior of the Tęczyński chapel in the parish church in Staszów is characterized by a maturity of artistic conception which has, not without some sophistication, brought into play all the important factors in architecture: space and the surfaces defining it, light, line, colour and ornament. The arches of the wall beams are a repetition of the semi-circles of the central wall arcades of the lower part of the chapel as they pass into the sphere in which the dominant linear motif is the perfect Renaissance form, the circle. It stresses with an interacting rhythm not only the shapes of the windows and the drum and the foot of the lantern, but also of the bases of the drum and dome (octagonal, on the exterior, in characteristic contrast). The spherical elements are thrown into sharp relief by strips of marble or cornices catching the shadows; thus is created a lucid scheme of boundaries between the surfaces and hence, of the entire spatial composition. These boundary lines are accompanied by small ornamental details without which they would appear too rigid; the heraldic cartouches (of the Tęczyński and Leszczyński families) situated in the spandrels, play a more subdued decorative role. The whole of the upper part is a great reservoir of light which pours abundantly into the high interior through the circular openings, enhancing the alternating formations of flat and spherical surfaces, their linear borders and the contrasts of the white plastered wall

with marble inlays and the play of decorative details. The architect of Staszów chapel is not known. Its interior aptly represents the trend that appeared in the small-scale Polish architecture of the Cracow-Pinczów school where the late-Renaissance and Mannerist current met the early Baroque.

201 The chapel of the powerful Firlej family added to the Gothic parish church in Bejsce in 1594—1600 is, by virtue of both architecture and interior decoration (ill. 202—206) and its state of repair, the most valuable example of small-scale religious building of the Renaissance period in Poland. In the same development line, launched by the Jagiellonian Chapel, it occupies both an outstanding and separate position. It is perhaps the work of Tomasz Nikiel's Pinczów atelier which which was, at the turn of the century, producing architecture and sculpture typical of the Cracow-Pinczów area, for which the starting-point seems to have been the last phase of Santi Gucci's art. The characteristic contrasts of Gucci's art are easily discernable

17. Bejsce, Firlej Chapel in the parish church. Vertical section with view of wall tomb, 1:125

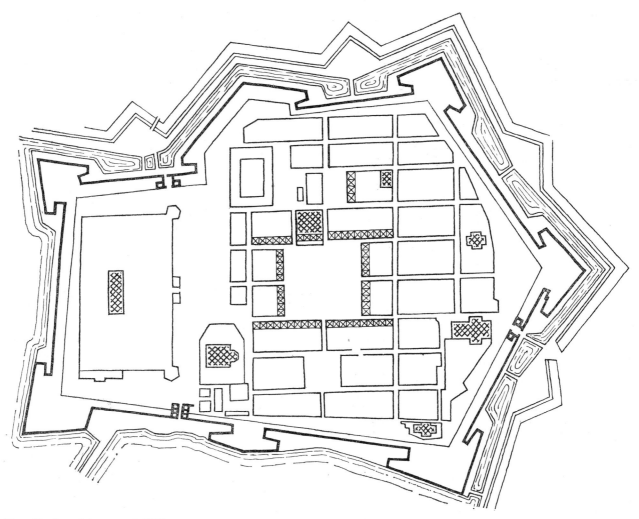

18. Zamość, plan of the town, 1:5000

in the chapel's conception. The staggering wealth of
the interior decoration is offset by the simplicity of
its exterior design which consists of a hexagon with
a dome and lantern. But even in this layout, the architectural and sculptural decoration confined to the upper
part (window frames, Ionic capitals on the corner
pilasters, the friezes with triglyphs and rosettes,
sculptures at the base of the dome, the setting of the
lantern) was opposed to the smooth surfaces of the
lower parts of the walls. Here we have one of the many
versions of the compositions derived from Gucci's
art; furthermore, the motif of large and smooth walls
with circular windows continued to be popular during
the first half of the 17th century and outside the Cracow-
Kielce region as well.

202—206 The tomb of the Firlej family in Bejsce,
executed in about 1600 possibly in Tomasz Nikiel's
Pinczów atelier, attained the ultimate limits of decorative sumptousness in Polish late-Renaissance sculpture.
The deceased, Mikołaj Firlej and his wife, Elżbieta,
are represented kneeling on either side of a crucifix
on the sarcophagus with a multiple, though easily
legible, architectural setting. On the other hand, the
decoration, besides the use of coloured marble,
comprising plant motifs merging into fantastic animal
bodies, wiverns and salamanders flanking the sides,

lithe necks of dragons jutting from the cornice of the
tympanum, bursts disturbingly and explosively
into the chapel interior in which the tomb occupies
a whole wall. The figures of small children in the lateral,
lower niches add yet another splash of colour to this
overwhelming architectural and decorative composition.
The tomb in Bejsce is the apogee of the Mannerist
strivings after visual affects and marks their *nec plus
ultra*. It has the suggestive power with few equals
even in European Renaissance art.

207 Zamość was the first town in Poland and one
of the first of a rare few in Europe which was planned
and laid out not only in terms of function but, as
a work of art. Founded and built wholly anew it gave
shape to the ideas formulated in the Italian Renaissance, among them the theoretical concept of the
"ideal town". Despite later alterations both its basic
design and many of its buildings have survived to this
day, causing it to occupy a permanent place in the
world history of city planning quite apart from its
position among Polish towns.
Zamość was founded by Jan Zamoyski, one of the
powerful nobles of the late-Renaissance period, Chancellor and Hetman of the Crown and a man of great
enterprise, energy and culture as well as a profound
knowledge of the humanities gained in Italy. The town

223

19. Zamość, Lublin Gate, prior to early 19th century. Elevation, 1:200

was to be not only the principal centre of his latifunda, but also, he hoped, the capital of an area that he regarded as his personal kingdom. Hence he assigned it numerous functions: a hub of commerce situated close to major trade routes leading from the west and north-west to the south-east and east; a mighty fortress, since it would lie on an area which had frequently to be defended against invaders; a cultural nucleus spreading its unfluence over a backward region; a religious centre; and finaly, Zamoyski's permanent seat and main residence. All these factors played a role in the planning of the town. The Chancellor's exceptional accomplishments and the knowledge of art he had acquired in Italy, added to the talent and ability of Bernardo Morando, the architect he commissioned to draw up the plans and embark on the building of the town, ensured Zamość the high artistic rank anticipated for it.

Zamoyski signed the contract with Morando in 1578 and the plans were ready by the next year. The surveying was completed and the building commenced in 1581—1583, with the construction of the fortifications beginning in 1587. By the beginning of the 17th century there stood the Chancellor's palace, the collegiate church, the Academy building, the Arsenal, the Town Hall, some non-Catholic shrines and churches, fortifications and the first brick town houses. Until his death in 1600, Morando supervised the project and also designed the model burghers' houses. The unrest in the country slowed down the pace of the building work, so that the major proportion of the buildings planned were not completed till the second or third quarters of the 17th century, when the Town Hall and the Academy were also enlarged and new churches erected.

In the Zamość plan a harmonious unity was made of the outline of a walled and turreted pentagonal and two enclosed rectangles, one in the east quarter comprising the town proper with a checkerboard of streets and the central and subsidiary market places—Solny (Salt) and Wodny (Water)—the other lying against the western side and containing the residential part. Certain irregularities in the plan resulted from the lie of the terrain. The composition accentuated the axial layout. The longtitudinal axis, which also marks the main communication flow, runs from the Chancellor's palace, through the main Market Place and ends in the central eastern tower; on the latitudinal axis, which intersects with the former in the middle of the market places, were located both the subsidiary squares, and on a secondary transverse axis, passing through the centre of the square between the residences and the town proper, were situated the collegiate church and Academy. The fortification embodied the latest achievements of military engineering.

When projecting Zamość, Morando creatively adapted the concepts of the Italian Renaissance theorists of architecture to the task confronting him; one of the principal features characterizing Zamość is the happy union of modern artistic planning with the town's function and programme. For himself, the powerful noble reserved a large site enclosed within the ambits of the fortification and on it ordered a magnificent palace to be built for him expressing the ideas of the Counter-Reformation. But by the very nature of things he overlooked the counterpoising of the palace with the municipal and major part and so the main Market Place was situated all but in the centre and the Town Hall with its tower visualized as the main accent of the height of the whole.

Over the years the Chancellor 's palace and Academy building were fundamentally altered and new churches partly encroached upon the municipal checkerboard where the original mansions also underwent certain conversions and even replacements; the fortifications, repeatedly modernized, were disfigured and, during the 19th century, partly dismantled. And yet so much remains of the Renaissance town that even today we have a complete idea of its original character.

The square Great Market in Zamość is enclosed by houses (one or two storeys), the model for which included Morando's own residence on the south face, later converted; they replaced the original wooden buildings and construction proceeded from the close of

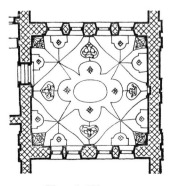

20. Zamość, synagogue. Plan, 1:400

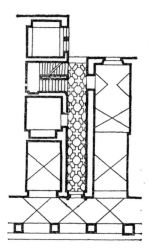

21. Zamość, house at No. 31 Staszic Street.
Ground floor plan, 1:400

the 16th and throughout the 17th centuries. At ground level on the outside arcades ran their whole length, interrupted only by the streets entering the Market Place, this design was to some measure influenced by examples of towns in the Venice region, especially Padua, which both the founder and architect had reason to remember. Originally the houses had valley roofs and attics, which gave their upper parts a certain mobility of form, now lost today.

The chief accent of the Market Place is the Town Hall, thrust forward on the north face. The traditional location of the principal municipal building in the centre of the Market Place was foregone so as not to confuse the optical and communication sequence. The original Town Hall, designed and built by Morando in 1591—1600, was enlarged in the years 1639—1651 by Jan Jaroszewicz, the author of the plans, and Jan Wolff into the magnificent building of today with a tower strongly emphasized as the highest point of the town. The arcades incorporate the Town Hall despite its projection into the covered pedestrian ways of the Market Place and its side streets. The elevations of the building were ordered by cornices and pilasters which also covered the attic and thus partly obscured its separateness; here therefore we have what may be considered one of the ultimate points in the development of this naturalized Renaissance motif, the attic being to a great extend engulfed by a division system of the elevation proper to modern architecture which only took permanent root in Poland under the influence of the early Baroque trend. Consequently, this interesting Zamość stands on the stylistic borderline between the Renaissance and the Baroque. The guardhouse with a staircase was added during the 18th century; later converted, the Town Hall was reconstructed in 1937—1938.

208—212 Most of the houses on the Great Market in Zamość date back to the 17th century, but some of them have even earlier details — from the close of the 16th century; during the 19th century they were reduced to a uniform classicist style and additions made in some cases to their upper parts, removing their attics in the process. Despite these alterations, the initial character of the houses and particularly frontages has been preserved, mainly owing to the arcaded passage running round the square and the large amount of decoration remaining on the elevations. The model houses, designed by Morando, stand on the south face of the square: the Tellani House from 1591—1599, and thus built during Morando's lifetime, and his own dwelling designed before 1599 but erected after 1604. They imposed on the houses on the Market Place a type which remained in force throughout the 17th century: a one-storey with a parterre arcade, a broad frieze running above the arcading, profiled window frames with an inscriptive lintel and a decorative ridged attic. The most original are the Armenian houses on the north face flanking the Town Hall, erected during the second and third quarters of the 17th century, a period in which the architectural decoration of the Zamość houses reached its peak, these Armenian houses being excellent examples: the original attic friezes were preserved as the decoration of the top floor. Initially, as for example in the houses on the south face, the decoration was fairly simple and geometrical in style. At the mid-century came a development of stuccowork with a variety of motifs based on the production of local ateliers, especially that of Jan Wolff; here Pińczów, Lvov, Lublin and oriental motifs were welded into extremely rich and picturesque decorative whole with a semi—folk art character typical of the native late-Renaissance. Besides this exterior decoration on the elevations, to which the portals also belong, the decorative parts in the interiors have also remained: the stuccowork in the arcades, the columns by the windows and the entablatures of the ceilings.

213, 214 The building of Zamość collegiate church was commenced in 1587; by 1598 the basic work was completed though the choir and the appointments were not ready until after 1600 and the consecration took place only in 1637. Bernardo Morando was the architect and also, with the exception of the stucco work in the nave and maybe its old surmounting gables, supplied the models for the decorative details. The church had a varied thematic programme in its conception; it served, together with the first Jesuit churches appearing at this time in Poland, the ideas of the Counter-Reformation, commemorated the military victories of Jan Zamoyski, its founder, and was to be the mausoleum of his family. Obviously too, in a large, newly founded town like Zamość, it was to be the principal church of its citizens. Jan Zamoyski exerted a basic influence on the ideological programme of the church, and also had some suggestions to make on purely architectural matters. He can therefore be regarded as Morando's collaborator. Clergymen from the Chancellor's retinue and the Zamość Academy participated in the framing of the particulars of its iconographic programme.

22. Zamość, collegiate church. Original façade,
early 19th-century view 1:400

The interior of the Zamość church is on the whole
fairly well preserved. On the other hand, its
exterior was much affected by the conversion of
1824—1826 when many of the stonework features were
removed, the façade was recomposed, the roofs lowered
and the gables altered. It is a large basilica with rows
of chapels opening off each of the aisles; the nave is almost
a square in plan abutting on a relatively small polygo-
nal presbytery, flanked by the interior of the Hetman's
sepulchral chapel and the sacristy with the treasury.
The composition of the layout, interior and elevations
derives from Italian late-Renaissance models, mainly
from the architect's native Veneto; he followed principles
elaborated in the theory and practice of Renaissance art,
including the module. Both in the plan and configuration, he displayed a remarkable architectural knowledge
and feeling for light and space. He employed two orders;
the Doric for the exterior elevations, the aisles and
chapels, and the Corinthian for the naves, the latter,
clear and spacious, magnificently sets the tone of the
interior. The general standard of the architecture
is lowered by the workmanship of its features which
were carved to Morando's drawings in the quarries at
Mikołajewo near Lvov and Szczebrzeszyn without
sending the stone to artists from the more specialized
Cracow-Pinczów ateliers.
The stuccowork of the collegiate church dates from
two different stages of its building. Of Morando's
authorship is the reticulation on the presbytery
vaulting, executed in 1594—1600. The stuccowork of
the nave and chapel vaultings in the main body of the
church was executed in 1610—1630 and thus by a later
atelier. Morando's reticulation in the presbytery has
affinities with the listel compositions in the vaulting
decoration of certain Venetian churches, especially of

Santa Maria dei Miracoli; the simplicity of its geometrical arrangement on the suffit of the vaulting directs
our attention to the Giovanni Battista group of
Mazovian churches in which, as in the Zamość collegiate church, decorative ribs form the patterns of
a full cradle vault. The listels of the presbytery of the
Zamość collegiate church are fairly simple yet embellished with a semi-billow motif framed by astragals.
Although differing both in shape and repertoire of
form from the later vaulting decoration that developed
so magnificently from 1600 onwards in the Lublin
region, the stucco reticulation of the presbytery of the
Zamość collegiate church was undoubtedly its portent.

215, 216 The parish church in Kazimierz Dolny is
one of the most typical of the late native current of the
Polish Renaissance but is given a special character by its
picturesque hillside situation. The typicality lies in an
original symbiosis of traditional Gothic elements, in
this particular case even architectural vestiges, with the
new styles of the Polish Renaissance. With its hall-type
layout, elongated presbytery, external buttresses and
high saddle roofs with the gable over the corpus, this
church recalls a Gothic building. But the semicircular
presbytery, the cradle valulting and lunettes of the
interior covered by characteristic ribs, and the rest of
the decorative features are Renaissance, though in
a semi-vernacular version. The Renaissance enlargement was undertaken in two stages, in 1586—1589 and,
more notably, in 1610—1613 when it was given its
final form by Giacomo Balin, one of the Como architects
who had settled in Lublin. The stuccowork of the
presbytery and nave, which date to this second stage,
developed the earlier motifs of the Bernardine Church
in Lublin converted in 1603—1607, possibly also by
Balin. In both these churches the wealth of motifs
outlined against the vaulting by the ribs is staggering—
rectangles, squares with rich forms, triangles, circles,
ovals and hearts, etc. This type of decoration began at
precisely this time its triumphant march through Poland,
reaching far beyond the limits of the Lublin region.

217—219 The two houses of the prosperous burghers Mikołaj and Krzysztof Przybyło, standing on the
Market Place in Kazimierz Dolny, are among the most
interesting and original examples of the native Polish

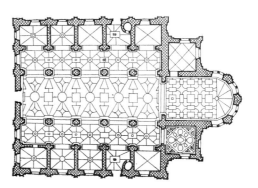

23. Zamość, collegiate church. Plan, 1:800

late-Renaissance. Their building was completed by 1516; the name of their architect, probably a local or Lublin one, is not known. Adjacent and similar, they form a seemingly single mansion, all the more so in that they have a common arcade and two cornices of the parapet walls stretch along the entire breadth of both elevations. However, that these are two distinct triple axial houses with attics is easily confirmed for they differ especially in the ridged crowning and particular divisions and decorations. They are particularly close in type to the Zamość or Lublin houses. Their whole plastic ornament was executed in the plaster.

The unusual character of both these houses is astounding, here they represent a naive, almost folk style of art which is simultaneously full of honesty and fantasy. Everything is treated in a decorative way and constitutes an excellent example of *horror vacui*, as it is termed, in the design of the architectural elevation. The perpendicular elements of division and other classical motifs — pilasters, hermas, frontons and cornices — are grouped on the upper storeys and, above all, in the attic parts, exclusively as decoration. The conception and placing of the bas-reliefs are similar — the large figures of St Nicholas and St Christopher, the patron saints of the owners of the houses, biblical and allegorical figures, religious scenes and fantastic animals are all superimposed on the elevations without observing a common scale. To this is added a freely deployed ornamentation with naively transmuted motifs of Italian or Netherlands origin with which is blended decoration of Lvov-Zamość, Lublin, Pinczów and Gdańsk provenance. This wealth of adornment reflected not only the founders' crude desire to emphasize their worth and standing but also a definite stage of the stylistic development of the native late-Renaissance decoration that attained here one of its peak moments. The choice of scenes and figures, likewise the Latin inscriptions, testify that there was an iconographic programme; it is necessary to seek its author within the circle of the local clergy. In this programme, a delayed provincial humanism is mingled with the Counter-Reformation manifestations almost as naively as in the decoration itself of both these dwellings of the Kazimierz merchants.

220—222 The Celej House in Senatorska Street in Kazimierz Dolny was erected prior to 1635 from the endowment of Bartlomiej Celej, a wealthy townsman. Together with the houses of the Przybyło family on the Market Place, it belongs to the most original native Polish late-Renaissance manifestations. Unlike them, though connected by a general similarity in type and wealth of decoration, it has no arcade and its composition is more studied and the iconographic programme less complicated. Its lofty and richly decorated attic, the most splendid in Poland and almost as high as the house itself, contrasts with the more restrained decorative parts of the parterre and first storey. Over the frieze, ornamented with a row

of niches, rise three fantastically extended dentils on which the decoration is focussed. The niches contain figures of Christ, Mary and Sts Bartholomew and John, the patron saints of the mansion's founder and his son, and of the Kazimierz parish; the contours of the crest are broken by fantastic stylized dragons and basilisks; the variety in the ornamentation is considerable. Both in its motifs and style of decoration, the Celej House is connected with other sources than the Przybyło houses; here we find ourselves within the circle, after Santi Gucci's death, of the Pinczów ateliers, but the Celej attic has its closest analogy in the sculptural decoration of the Bejsce chapel.

223 Of the several dozen granaries erected in Kazimierz Dolny at the height of its splendour as a centre of trade at the turn of the 16th to 17th centuries, only a few have remained on the roads along the Vistula. All of these were restored to their original appearance after the last World War. Dating back to the mid-17th century, the Feierstein Granary gives an idea of the character of the other buildings of this type: one, sometimes, two, storeys with a large attic and an annex on the front carrying the stairs. The forms are simple, the decoration being confined to the main gable and the lateral one on the annex. Vividly contoured with volutes and pinnacles, it represents the native Polish late-Renaissance style in a version characteristic of other municipal buildings, although in this case a simplified one.

224 By the last quarter of the 16th century the fashion for tombstones had spread to the burgher class circles. In general, these were modest monuments with little decoration with the deceased in half-figure placed in a recess enclosed by an arch at the top and a sill at the bottom in which his hands rested; since the eyes were open, the impression of death vanished and the real life effects intensified. The faces were conceived as portraits. Most of these recess tombstones had fairly small dimensions and were easily mounted on church walls or pillars. Jan Przybyło's tombstone, from the turn of the 16th to 17th centuries in the parish church in Kazimierz Dolny, is an example of this type of monument. The pose of the Przybyło image

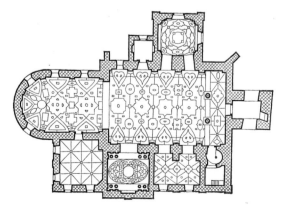

24. Kazimierz Dolny, parish church. Plan, 1:800

is striking and, with the architectural setting almost entirely eliminated, the realistic treatment of the dress is thrown into strong relief.

225,226 In the church at Gołąb, built in 1628— 1636, it is possible to separate the architect's design, probably sent in the form of plans and drawings from outside, from the work of the atelier which realized it on the spot and was also responsible for the architectural decoration of the exterior walls. The resulting symbiosis has an original impress. The architect planned a hall-type church, partly modelled on the native trend of church architecture which had now emerged in the Lublin arrea (nave ending in a semicircular apse, roofs), but gave the façade two towers, introduced a classical arrangement of perpendicular and horizontal divisions on the elevations and crowned some of the openings on lucid lines; all was on the whole a departure from the architectural conventions of this area. The author is unknown, but probably came from outside the Lublin school. The imposition of white features on crude red-brick walls is another original feature of this church. This was a Netherlands habit, as was the repertoire of some of the decorative motifs drawn from patterns (especially the friezes of a furniture character). Most of the features — portals, window frames, the east gable and the capitals of the pilasters — bear the post-"Guccian" stylistic imprint of the Kielce regional ateliers, of which there was one no doubt in this locality; it is these which chiefly give the building the stamp of the native trend of the Polish late-Renaissance.

227,228 A leading role in the dissemination of an original version of the late-Renaissance church in the Lublin region was played by Jan Jaroszewicz (c. 1575—1670) and his associate Jan Wolff (d. 1649—1653). The former, who was burgrave of Zamość, held the official post of the Demesne Architect and designed most of the buildings erected by the Zamoyskis; the latter, a contracting architect, also lived in Zamość during the most active years of his life. It is very likely that Jaroszewicz designed and certain that Wolff executed the enlargement of the church at Uchanie (outside the Zamoyski estates), commissioned by the Daniłowicz family and completed in 1625. It is a simple hall-type church in whose pilastered and arcaded composition and façade can be seen the influence of the Zamość collegiate church; its modest mass animated by the hexagonal chapels built onto the south and north sides of the presbytery. Inside, the interesting decoration of the nave and presbytery cradles and especially the rich and imaginative stucco ornamentation of the soffit of the dome of the south Lady Chapel can be attributed to Wolff, the propagator of the "Lublin School" of stucco reticulation of the vaulting. Two interesting tombstones (ill. 191, 192) supplement the interior decoration of this rural church.

229 The triangular end of the late-Gothic presbytery of the Bernardine church in Przeworsk received during the first half of the 17th century a crowning finish in the native late-Renaissance style. It consists of three protruding gables set at an angle to one another and decorated with rows of blind arcading. Another sign of the survival of the Gothic tradition in the native Renaissance trend in church architecture of the first half of the 17th century is a typical late-medieval gable with characteristic blende decoration travested in Renaissance forms with a softening of the curves and a repertoire of motifs in the new style. Nevertheless, the composition is by now far removed from the harmonious Italianate formula proper to the first phase of the Renaissance in Poland: here the accent is not on studied proportions and orthodox features but on decorative effect.

230 The stuccowork in the native style, initiated in the church of the Bernardine Order in Lublin during the first years of the 17th century, was extremely popular in the interior decoration of chapels far into the depths of the second part of the century. Up to about 1640, Renaissance motifs predominated. Jan Wolff of Turobin and Zamość, the architect responsible for the stuccowork in the Uchanie church, may also be credited with that in the Firlej Chapel in the Dominican Church in Lublin (early 1630s). Plaquettes, both trapezoid and circular, with embellishments and heraldic motifs linked by strings of ribs, ring in a concentric composition the lantern on the soffit of the domes. Together with the listel decoration of the cradled vaultings of naves and presbyteries, the rich ornamental arrangements on the soffits of domes constitute, with their soft forms, a basic element of the native late-Renaissance style.

231 The vaulting of the late-Renaissance nave of the church of the Reformati in Pinczów (the construction of which was commenced before 1615 and completed after 1619) is covered with stuccowork with a geometrical composition of the type propagated by the native trend in church decoration and architecture of the first half of the 17th century. Executed about 1640, the Pinczów stuccowork represents the late developmental phase of this decoration for, in parts, it already bears Baroque features. Here the rolls shaping the motifs have become soft and hence, the stuccoed lines run more pliably; the intertwining spiral motifs appearing in the rectangles and ovals of the central axis of the vaulting are now shaped in the new style.

232 The chapel of the Holy Trinity in the collegiate church in Środa, endowed as a mausoleum by Hieronim Gostomski, Voivode of Poznań, possesses superb stuccowork on the soffit of ist dome. This type of dome decoration constitutes an extremely interesting though somewhat overlooked domain of late-Renaissance art in Poland. In Środa, the ornamental scheme of the dome is radial and comprises eight narrowish segments with trapezoid shapes. The repertoire of ornamental motifs is extensive consisting of aedicules circular and oval medallions, cartouches, putti, linen patterns (rollwork) and bunches of fruit. The interrupted fronts of the two aedicules indicate that a Baroque motif intervened in this Renaissance decoration and so we are obliged to date it to a later period than the completion of the building itself.

233 The portal of the House of the Mazovian Princes, as it is called, on the Market Place of Old Town in Warsaw dates back to the 1630s and represents the final development phase of late-Renaissance stonework in Poland. The Warsaw portal in simpler than its contemporaries in the Kielce and Lublin regions and reveals a debt primarily to decorative motifs of Cracow-Pinczów origin propagated by the late-Renaissance tombs in the Warsaw churches and accepted by local stonemasons. Above all these are angels' heads, Ionic pilasters, socles with cones and Gucci's fovourite rosette motif.

234, 235 The Hill Gate in Gdańsk, built in 1586—1588 was the joint work of the architect Jan Kramer, who fitted it into the town's earth works, and the sculptor Willem van den Blocke, who carved the decoration on its front. It was reconstructed and partly altered during the second part of the 19th century. The Hill Gate belongs to those works of the Gdańsk architecture of the late-Renaissance period in which genetically Italian features are dominant but in the modified version of the Netherlands artists who crystallized the shape of Gdańsk art at this time. The Sanmichele's Gates in the fortifications of Verona exerted an influence on the architecture of this building which followed the scheme of a triumphal arch. The lower part of the Gdańsk gate, covered with lovely rustication, supported a lofty attic ornamented on the entrance side with magnificent heraldic high-relief decoration. Two angels in its centre, holding a crown, flank a cartouche with an eagle, the emblem of the Polish State; beside the lateral cartouches with coats of arms of the city of Gdańsk and Prussia stand lions and unicorns.

236 The house known as "Lion Castle" at No. 33 Długa Street in Gdańsk owes its name to the sculpted lions ornamenting the finial of its portal. Almost completely destroyed in 1945, this mansion was rebuilt after the war and restored to its original appearance, authentic parts of the decoration being preserved in the parterre elevation. "Lion Castle" was erected in 1569 as one of the first burgher houses in the new style. Like the majority of the Mannerist buildings in the town, this mansion was based on Netherlands models which its anonymous author followed with the help of architectural patterns, among them those of Vredeman de Vries. An accumulation of architectural orders was used in the elevation to create a decorative framework, and this was destined to become a feature of many of the later "order" façades of Gdańsk mansions; the principal accent was placed on the portal part of the parterre and the crowning gable. The entrance to "Lion Castle" was once a magnificent hall with exceptionally rich architectural and sculptural decoration; sumptuously adorned interiors in fact were a general characteristic of the municipal and private buildings of the late Renaissance Gdańsk.

237—240 One of the most representative buildings from the late-Renaissance period in Gdańsk is the Grand Armoury, put up mainly in 1602—1605, though the finishing work went on for several ensuing years. It was designed by Antonius van Opbergen, while also involved in the projects were Abraham van den Blocke, an architect and sculptor, and Jan Strakowski, a builder, both of whom followed his plans. Razed during the military operations in 1945, the Grand Armoury was rebuilt and returned to its former splendour. The ground floor, rectangular in layout and comprising a large 15-pillared hall, was originally used to store guns and cannon balls, the first floor, divided into smaller rooms, for

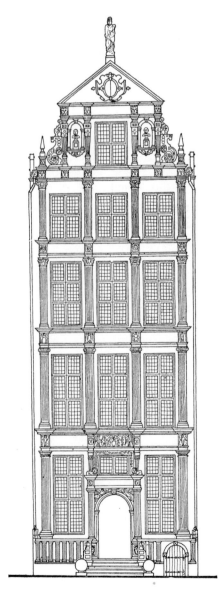

25. Gdańsk, "Lion Castle" House. Elevation, 1:200

229

lighter weapons. This utilitarian character of the interior is belied by the exterior appearance of the building in which the main accents are the urbanistically more important shorter elevations: the east, flanked by small towers, and the west. The east elevation, in particular, gives us some information on the mass of the edifice which, despite its interior layout, feigns the appearance of four concisely attached gabled houses with distinct and parallel ridge roofs. This obvious accentuation of the residential character of this building is also repeated in the more ostentatious east elevation where two segments are similar to the façades of small mansions and the two on the ends are replaced by small slender towers. The building has the typical Netherlands seal of the Gdańsk architecture of the late-Renaissance period but reveals here a special purity of forms. The characteristic feature is the union of the brick background of the wall segments with the masonry inlays: the large rectangular windows have the cross divisioning in stone and are bounded by perpendicular dentilled belts with limestone plaques which also embellish the corners of the elevations. The decorative elements, executed in stone, principally appear on the parterre (the portals) and the gables (a rich showing of ornaments: both linen patterns and furniture, cobochons, pinnacles in the form of vases or obelisques, and sculpture in the round). This repertoire was based on the popular models of Vredeman de Vries who, for that matter, himself worked in Gdańsk for some time. Especially on the east side, there are segmented walls which give the gables of the Grand Armoury the character of attics; serving here to conceal the four rows of tall roofs, they do not seem to have been inspired by the attics in other parts of Poland. The iconographic programme of the decoration was modified to the practical purpose of this building: all the figurative sculptures are knights or allegorical figures associated with war and there are many panoplies and weapons among the ornamental motifs. This programme is especially apparent in the four lovely portals with their sides rusticated at the bottom and an ostentatious exposition of military motifs wreathing the Gdańsk coat of arms held by the lions at the top.

241 The House of the Abbots of Pelplin on Elżbietańska Street in Gdańsk makes a better showing, thanks to the detachment of its front and its slender, simple and all but cubic mass. It is varied only by the lively contours of the gable. The white framing of the rectangular windows with their dense network of leads contrasted with the red brick walls is particularly noticeable here while the relatively modest architectural decoration takes a second place. The ornamental motifs, including the furniture bands decorating the gable, belong to the Mannerist repertoire of early 17th-century Gdańsk architecture. Dating back to 1612, this house was partly reconstructed in 1912.

It is exceptionally representative of the stylistic affinities between the Gdańsk and Netherlands art during the late-Renaissance period.

242, 243 One of the most splendid treasures of Gdańsk architecture of the first years of the 17th century is the Steffens' House, also called the "Golden House" because of its polychromed decoration. It stands on the Long Market Place and was erected in 1609—1617 by Abraham van den Blocke with Johann Voigt as the author of its sculptural decoration. The building was partly rebuilt after its destruction during the Second World War. Unlike most of the burghers' houses in Gdańsk of the Renaissance epoch, this slender and elegant mansion, polished not only as to its architecture but also as to its decoration, was closed at the top of the attic level by balustrading with statues partly concealing the roof and a non-traditional gable. The Steffens' House, by reason of this crowning, the accumulation of ancient orders on three storeys and other motifs, has a more Classicist character than the major proportion of the late-Renaissance building of the Gdańsk townsmen. The rich sculptural decoration in which, besides bas-relief ornamentation, appear decorative figures and busts, is a deliberate echo of classical antiquity and a thematic manifestation of the late Humanism enlightening the Gdańsk patricians by the early years of the 17th century.

244, 245 The leading Silesian residence of the second half of 16th century is the castle in Oleśnica. It gained its characteristic profile when the earlier Gothic castle of the Oleśnica princes was converted along Renaissance lines from the middle part of the 16th up to the beginning of the 17th centuries. In 1542 Prince Jan of Ziembice, the lord of the castle and the husband of Krystyna, the daughter of Chancellor Szydłowiecki, a propagator of Renaissance art, initiated alterations to the west wing together with the construction of a round

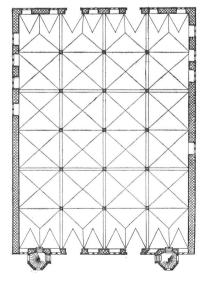

26. Gdańsk, Grand Armoury. Ground floor plan, 1:800

tower on the south-east corner. The main residential seat, the palace, located within the ambit of the Gothic courtyard, was erected from 1559—1563 by Gasparo Cuneo, a Comoan who was also active in Brzeg. It was at this time that the fortified foregate was set up on the east side. During the years that followed, the east (arch. Bernard Niuron), south and north wings were added. By the early years of the 17th century the whole was encircled by earthen and bastioned fortifications according to the new Italian system; the entrance on the east side led through a barbican. Thus, after the reconstruction, round the irregular four-sided courtyard emerged a complex of buildings consisting of particular wings, covered with ridge roofs, and lofty triangular gables that, transversed by cornices and held on the sides by the counter-flow of the volutes, have given this castle its specific appearance recalling the Renaissance building of North Poland.

In the years 1589—1600, the internal south wall and tower were encircled by porches supported by arches which were suspended on corbels and reinforced with volute buttresses, ornamented with fittings. The upper floor to support the eaves was given columns, which in effect created a gallery, a far echo of the Wawel galleries.

246 The tombs with kneeling figures, found in all parts of Poland but especially in Great Poland and Pomerania, are one of the distinctive features of the late-Renaissance period in its Mannerist trend in Poland. A representative type of this kind of sepulchral monument is to be found in Barczewo in Warmia; its author was Willem van den Blocke, a Netherlander who modelled his work on the art of Cornelis Floris. This tomb was executed in 1598 for Cardinal Andrzej Báthory nad Baltazar, his brother. It is a tiered monument possessing Netherlandish characteristics, the Cardinal's massive form in the upper recess dominating the traditional sleeping knight's figure recumbent in the lower one. The dark marble background serves as a contrast to the white figures while the ornamentation, heavy but rich, comprising armour, fruit and female heads fluently chiselled in white marble and also set against a dark background, characterize the Netherlands Mannerist atelier of this master who had settled in Gdańsk.

247 One of the most beautiful and picturesque relics of the Silesian Renaissance is the Municipal Assay House on the Market Place in Nysa. Built in 1604, it was almost totally destroyed during the Second World War. Reconstruction in 1947—1948 returned it to its original state. It constitutes a Renaissance gabled house, as popularly developed in Silesia, for the specific purpose of trade, in this case for weighing goods in the porch and parterre accommodation. Standing detached, the frontage and decorativeness of form and detail stress its representative character as one of the principal municipal buildings. The decorativeness of this building increases from the parterre upwards; the porch is modestly rusticated, the main floor adorned with sculpture and sgraffito and, finally, the gable with its animated contour combines a wealth of architectural and sculptural elements.

248, 249 The window cage, wrought in iron, on the first floor of the edifice of the Collegium Maius in Cracow comes from the 16th century. The lower part of this cage still retains the Gothic decorative composition with the network of diagonally set squares; however, the circle motifs intermingle here and the grille crowning is composed entirely of spiral motifs; characteristic of the Renaissance; it possibly dates from the close of the 16th century.

250 The Polish late-Renaissance helmet from the second half of the 16th century in the Wawel Armoury is a superb example of a high standard of craftsmanship combined with artistic taste. Etched with acid in elaborate plant and geometrical patterns as though of an oriental carpet, this helmet is gilded throughout, has encrusted ornamental rosettes and rivetted embosses. Helmets of this type, with a characteristic elongated and articulated neck piece, round crown with a visor and lengthened cheek pieces, were destined to become an indispensable part of the hussar's armour.

251 The principal product of Renaissance artistic ironware was the grille, used to close entrances and openings not only in the secular but also in sacral architecture; its manufacture was the concern of the locksmith's guilds. One of the loveliest specimens is the church grille, dating back to the second part of the 16th century, belonging to the Suffragan Chapel in Włocławek Cathedral. Here the typical Renaissance motifs of spirals and rosettes — placed in the open spaces — are set in the traditional network of rhomboids.

VII p. 205. Marcin Kober (confirmed activity 1579—1609), an artist of Silesian descent and the court painter of Stephen Báthory and Sigismund III, in his formal en pied likenesses gave the start to a new stage in the development of portrait painting on Poland. The portrait of Stephen Báthory, painted in 1583 and now in the monastery of Missionaries in Cracow, has a particular significance. For here are found as if in embryo those traits that in the future will characterize the typical Baroque "Sarmatian portrait": acute realism far from any possible kind of idealization in the characterization of the face, a scrupulous rendering of the accessories of dress and, simultaneously, an accentuation of superficial decorative veins and of colour and linear values in the depiction of costume. The large area of red — in this portrait, the *kopeniak* (head covering), balanced in colour by a crimson tunic and yellow morocco shoes in time became the principal tone of many Sarmatian portraits. The comparatively slight variation in the dark background is characteristic of Kober's work. Not lacking an original monumentalism, his portrait of Báthory was, as a type of likeness, to be frequently repeated and that also abroad.

252 There can be little doubt that Marcin Kober was the author of the portrait of Queen Anna Jagiellonka in the Wawel collections. The Queen is represented in mourning after the death of Stephen Báthory, her husband, which places the date of the painting between 1586 and 1596. Replicas of this portrait are known to us in the palaces in Wilanów and Schleissheim in Bavaria. As in the portrait of Báthory, in these three likenesses forceful characterization of the aged and tired face of the woman is combined with a flat, decorative treatment of costume and accessories; this conception was to exert some influence in 17th-century Polish portraits of women.

VIII p. 215. The large likeness of Katarzyna neé Lubomirska Ostrogska, a noblewoman from a powerful family, was painted about 1597; it constitutes a true adornment of the Polish Portrait Gallery in Wilanów Museum. Although the dating from the same time as Kober's portraits, it represents to a certain measure a different style strongly reflecting the general trend of European late-Renaissance court portraiture. The author of this likeness, though not over-sensitive to the values of the play of light in his rendering of the hands and face, has on the other hand an inherent and immense feeling for decorativeness, the lady's magnificent dress being virtually the main subject of the painting and of great interest to the viewer for its wealth of motifs — plant coils, human and animal figures and entire miniature scenes symbolizing aspects of the wedding. This portrait was painted in connection with Katarzyna's marriage to Janusz Ostrogski, Castellan of Cracow, in 1597.

PIESKOWA SKAŁA ▶

159

KSIĄŻ WIELKI

160

162

BARANÓW

GOŁUCHÓW

CHROBERZ

168

PODDĘBICE

169

KRAKÓW

175

D. O. M.
Illustr. Stanislaus TARŁO Capit. Sochaczo: qui Ecclesiam Ianovecen=
sem ab Arianis profanatam, spoliatam, ac perplures annos detentam Ecclesiæ Cat
Romanæ restituendam; et in ea corpus suum tumulandum Tabulis supremis
it. Sibi ac caræ Uxori hoc monumentum posuit Anno D. 1599 D. 14 Mens. Iunii

JANOWIEC

182

183

KRAKÓW

184

KOŚCIAN

186

BEJSCE

187

ŁOMŻA

KOBYLNIKI

KRAKÓW

UCHANIE

192

193

194

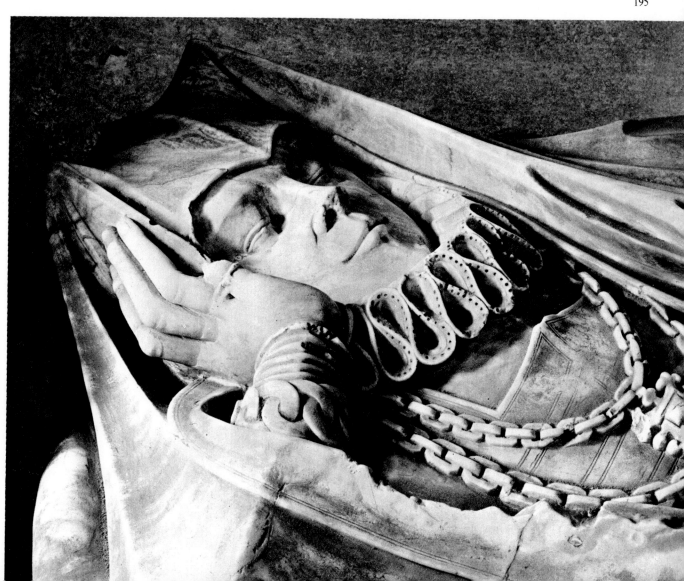

195

196

ŻYWIEC

KRAKÓW

199

STASZÓW

200

STASZÓW

202

203

204

205

BEJSCE

206

ZAMOŚĆ

208

ZAMOŚĆ

209

211

213

215

217

KAZIMIERZ DOLNY

218

KAZIMIERZ DOLNY

224

KAZIMIERZ DOLNY

GOŁĄB

227

UCHANIE

PRZEWORSK

230

LUBLIN

231

232

ŚRODA

233

234

235

GDAŃSK

239

GDAŃSK

240

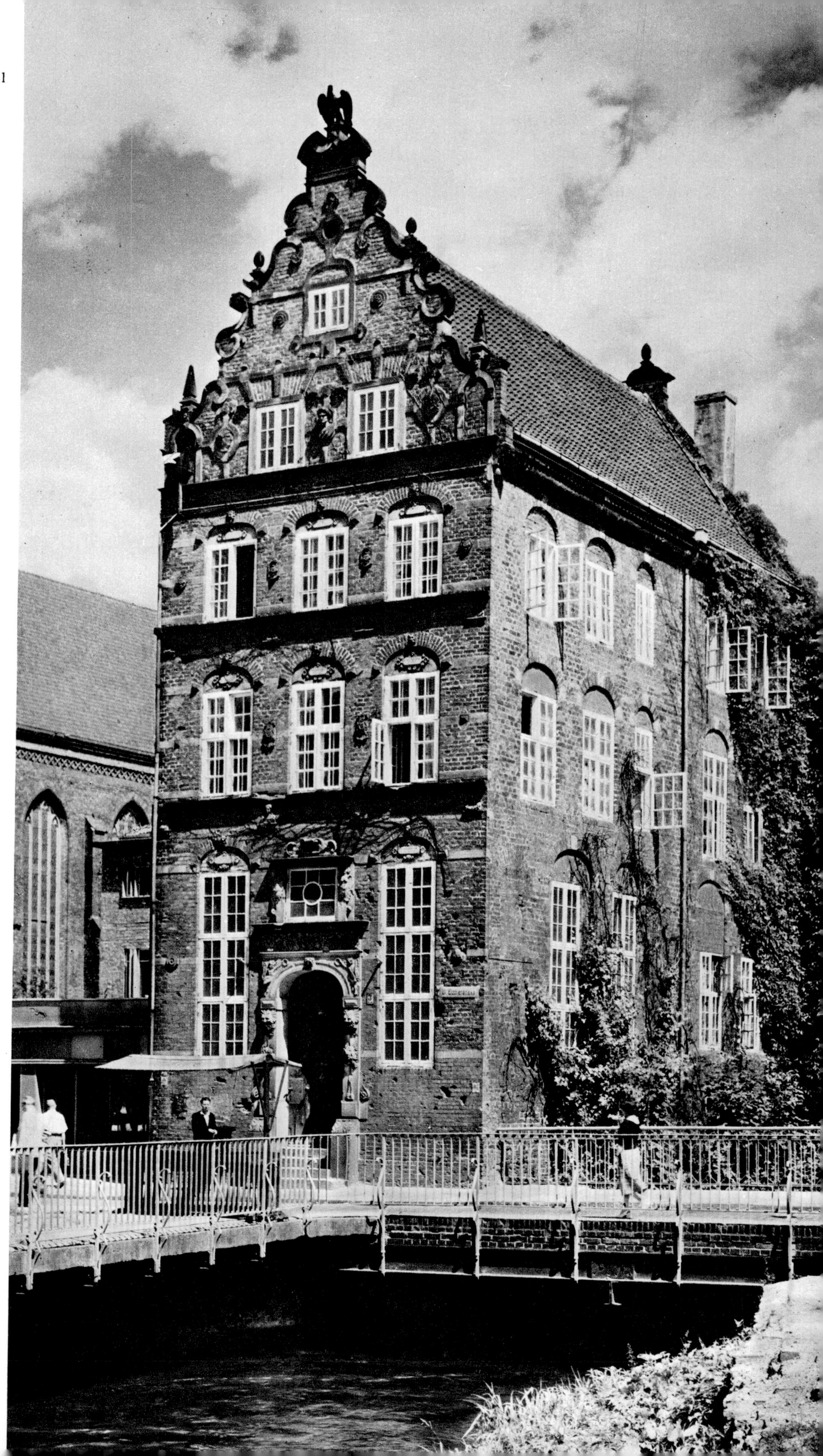

242

GDAŃSK

LAVR MEDICES · · MACCABEVS · · SIGISMVND · · HORATIVS · COCLES · · HENRICVS · IMP

243

OLEŚNICA

245

246

BARCZEWO

247

NYSA

KRAKÓW

251

WŁOCŁAWEK

ANNA REGINA POLONIÆ.
IAGELONIDAR. QVI CC. PROPE ANNOS REGNAVERVNT. SOBOLES VLTIMA.
REGVM. SIGISM. PRIMI. EX BONA SFORTIA. FILIA.
SIGISM. AVGVSTI SOROR. ET STEPH. BATORII COIVX.
CVM ESSET PVBLICO ORDINVM CONSENSV CVM REGE MARITO
CORON AVREA. QVOD EST INSIGNE REGALIS IMPERII TEMPORA REDIMITA
ET SCEPTRO REGIO DEXTRAM IMPLICITA.
SCAPVLASQ. SACR OLEO DELIBVTA. TALIS APARVIT.
ANNO. CHRISTI DOMINI M. D. LXXVI KAL. MAII. HORA. XVII.

KRAKÓW

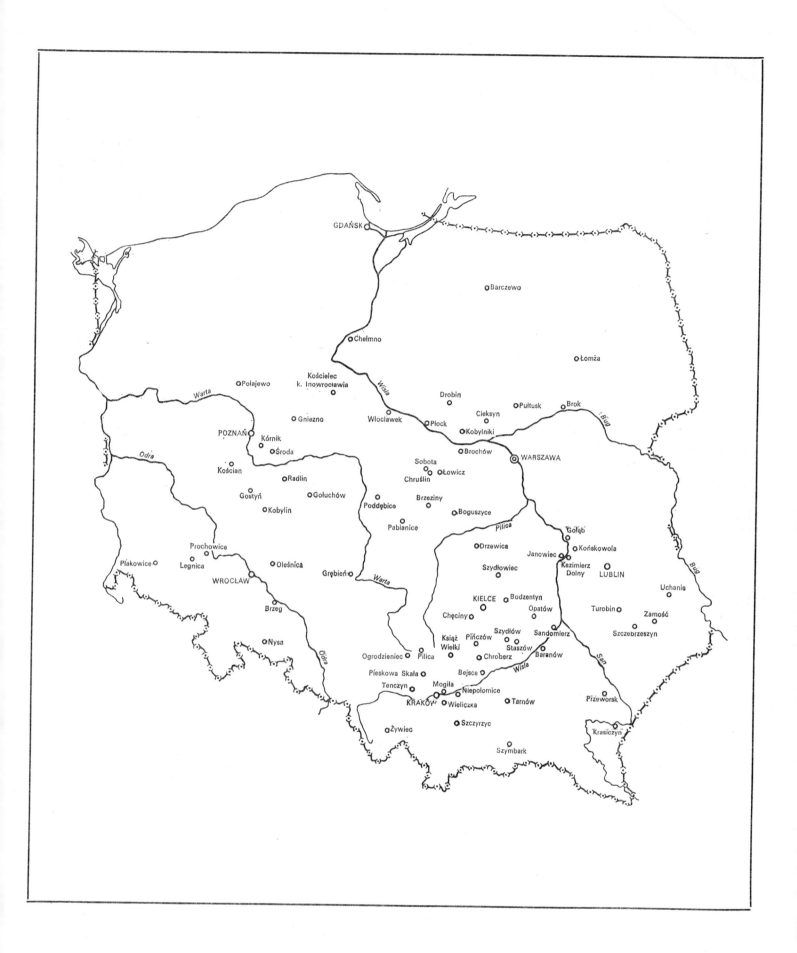

Localities with Renaissance historical monuments mentioned in the book

List of Illustrations

53. Bas-relief with St Peter commending Tomicki to Mary
54--56 Tarnów, Cathedral. Tomb of Barbara Tarnowska of Tęczyn, Bartolomeo Berrecci with the help of his atelier, c. 1527—1530; 54. Tondo with Madonna and Child; 55. Recess with the deceased's figure on a sarcophagus; 56. Barbara's head
57, 58 Gniezno, Cathedral. Tomb of Primate Andrzej Krzycki, Bartolomeo Berrecci's atelier; 57. Tomb without the later crowning; 58. Primate's head
59 Gniezno, Cathedral, tombstone of Jan Łaski, Joannes Florentinus, working in Hungary c. 1516
60 Brzeziny, parish church. Tombstone of Stanisław Lasocki, Bernardino De Gianotis, c. 1535
61 Opatów, collegiate church. Tomb of Anna Szydłowiecka, Bernardino De Gianotis, after 1536
62—66 Opatów, collegiate church. Tomb of Chancellor Krzysztof Szydłowiecki, 1533—1536, main part executed by Giovanni Cini and Bernardino De Gianotis; the *Lamentation* bas-relief—unknown author; 62. Bust of Chancellor from his tombstone; 63.
Putto; 64. Tombstone and the *Lamentation*: 65. Detail from the *Lamentation*; 66. Panoply
67--70 Bodzentyn, Parish church. Previous altar of the Wawel Cathedral, Giovani Cini, 1545—1548; 67. Altar; 68, 69. Detail of the decoration; 70. St Stanislaus' figure
71 Wrocław, Cathedral. Portal leading from the presbytery to the sacristy, 1517
72 Legnica, castle gateway, Georg of Amberg, c. 1533
73, 74 Wrocław, Cathedral. Tomb of Jan V Turzon, 1537; 73. Bishop's head; 74. Deceased's figure
75. Kórnik, Library of the Polish Academy of Sciences. Portrait of Anna Szydłowiecka, miniature from the family *Liber geneseos*, Stanisław Samostrzelnik, c. 1530
76 Cracow, Franciscan Monastery. Portrait of Bishop Piotr Tomicki, second quarter of the 16th century, Stanisław Samostrzelnik(?)
77, 78 Warsaw, National Museum, Triptych from Pławno, Cracow sculptor, 1514—1518; 77. Triptych as a whole; 78. Compartment with the purchase of the village of Piotrawin by St Stanislaus' Szczepanowski
79—81 Szczyrzyc near Limanowa, Monastery Museum. Man of Sorrows attended by the Virgin Mary and the Saints, c. 1515; 79. The whole; 80. Detail: Mary and St John the Baptist; 81. Detail: Sts Andrew and John the Evangelist
82, 83 Warsaw, National Museum. *The Battle of Orsza*, unknown painter, c. 1515—1520. Details of the painting
84 Kobylin near Krotoszyn. Compartment of the triptych with the legend of St Stanislaus Szczepanowski: purchase of the village, a Cracow atelier (?), c. 1518
85 Kórnik, Library of the Polish Academy of Sciences. Central panel of the triptych from the church at Mądre near Środa: *Annunciation*, painter from Great Poland, 1529
86, 87 Gostyń, church of the Philippines. Madonna and Child, monogramist SB, 1540; 86. The whole; 87. Detail with a wiew of Gostyń in the background

88 Grębień near Wieluń, church. A village musician — detail of the polychrome on the ceiling, c. 1520--1530
89—95 Cracow, Sigismund Chapel. Part of the decoration and fittings Nuremberg ateliers; 89. Grille of the chapel entrance, Hans Vischer's atelier, 1530—1532; 90. Silver altar, 1535—1538, the whole with open wings bas-reliefs by Peter Flötner and Melchior Baier; 91. Compartment from *The Adoration of the Magi*; 92. Frieze with the coat of arms of Poland of the Jagiellons, detail of the decoration of a recess for keeping liturgical vessels; 93. Altar with closed wings, compartments painted by Georg Pencz; 94. Bust of Sigismund I, detail of the predella of the silver altar; 95. Silver candlestick, probably by Peter Flötner and Melchior Baier, 1536
96—99 Warsaw, National Museum. Medals of the Jagiellons, Giovanni Maria Padovano, 1532; 96. Sigismund the Old; 97. Queen Bona; 98. Reverse of Sigismund the Old's medal; 99. Reverse of Queen Bona's medal
100 Wieliczka, Salt-Mine Museum. Drinking horn belonging to the miners' guild, Cracow or Nuremburg atelier, 1534
101, 102 Niepołomice, castle, 1550—1571; 101. Courtyard gallery, c. 1637; 102. Detail of the entrance gate arch, Cracow atelier, third quarter of the 16th century
103 Poznań, portal of the Górka's palace, 1548
104 Cracow, portal of the house at No 18 Kanonicza Street. Jambs, first part of the 16th century, lintel by Jan Michałowicz, 1560—1563 (heraldic cartouche from the 18th century)
105 Szymbark, defensive manor-house, third quarter of the 16th century
106 Pabianice, manor-house, Wawrzyniec Lorek, 1566—1571
107,108 Poznań, Town Hall, Giovanni Battista Quadro, 1550—1560; partly destroyed during the Second World War, restored by 1954; 107. Town Hall; 108. Great Hall on the first floor
109—111 Cracow, Cloth Hall. Renaissance conversion 1556—1560, remodelled in the 19th century; 109. Cloth Hall; 110. Detail of the parapet wall; 111. Lateral stairs with loggia, 1558—1560
112 Tarnów, Town Hall. Renaissance conversion, third quarter of the 16th century
113 Chełmno, Town Hall, 1567—1570
114 Pułtusk, interior of collegiate church, Giovanni Battista of Venice, c. 1560
115, 116 Brochów, church of St Roch, Giovanni Battista of Venice, c. 1551—1561; destroyed during the First World War, restored 1924—1929; 115. Interior; 116. View from the front
117 Brok, gable of the façade of the parish church, Giovanni Battista of Venice, 1560
118 Prochowice, castle. Corbels of the second-storey gallery, before 1550
119, 120 Płakowice, palace, mid-16th century; 119. Section of the courtyard, 120. Gateway

121—123 Brzeg, gatehouse, Parios' (Parros') atelier; probably designed by Francesco Pario, sculpture by, among others, Andrea Walter I; architectural parts c. 1550, the sculptural — 1551—1553; 121. Statue of George II; 122. Gatehouse; 123. Section with the busts of the Polish Piast monarchs

124 Brzeg, Town Hall, Giacomo Pario (Parr), 1570—1572

125, 126 Sobota near Łowicz, tomb of Tomasz Sobocki in the parish church, Cracow atelier, c. 1550; 125. Bust of the deceased; 126. tombstone as a whole

127—130 Cracow, tabernacle in the church of St Mary, Giovanni Maria Padovano, 1530s and mid-16th century, 17th- and 18th- century supplements; 127. Tabernacle; 128. Ciborium, 1552; 129. Tondo with the Madonna, 1533—1536 (?); 130. Adoring angel, 1533—1536

131—135 Tarnów, tomb of Hetman Jan Tarnowski and his son Jan Krzysztof in the Cathedral, Giovanni Maria Padovano, 1561—1570; 131. Hetman's head; 132. Jan Krzysztof's head; 133. Tomb as a whole; 134. Pilica, Kasia Pilecka's tomb in the parish church, Giovanni Maria Padovano's atelier, third quarter of the 16th century; 135. Kościelec near Inowrocław, tomb of Jan and Janusz Kościelecki in the parish church, Cracow atelier, 1559

136—138 Tarnów, tomb of the three Jan Tarnowskis in the Cathedral, Cracow atelier, c. 1560; 136. Tomb as a whole; 137. Jan Aleksander's figure, Jan Michałowicz, c. 1557; 138. Head of Jan, Voivode of Sandomierz

139 Poznań, tomb of Bishop Benedykt Izdbieński in the Cathedral, Jan Michałowicz, c. 1557

140 Brzeziny, detail of Urszula Leżeńska's figure from her tomb in the parish church in Brzeziny, Jan Michałowicz, 1563—1568

141—143 Cracow, Bishop Andrzej Zebrzydowski's tomb in the Cathedral on Wawel Hill, Jan Michałowicz, 1562—1563; 141. Detail of the upper part; 142. Bishop's head; 143. Tomb as a whole

144, 145 Cracow, tomb of Bishop Filip Padniewski in the Cathedral on Wawel Hill, Jan Michałowicz, after 1572; remodelled in the 19th century; 144. Tomb as a whole; 145. Detail of the Bishop's figure

146, 147 Poznań, tomb of Andrzej and Barbara Górka in the Cathedral, Hieronymus Canavesi, 1574; 146. Recess with the figures of the deceased; 147. Detail of Andrzej's figure

148 Kielce, tomb of Elżbieta Zebrzydowska in the Cathedral, Giovanni Maria Padovano, after 1553

149 Szamotuły, tomb of Jakub Rokossowski in the parish church, Hieronymus Canavesi, 1580

150 Boguszyce near Rawa Mazowiecka, detail of the polychrome on the wooden ceiling of the parish church, 1558

151 Cracow, Jagiellonian University Museum. Portrait of Benedykt of Koźmin, 1540s

152 Połajewo near Czarnków, central painting of the triptych in the parish church: *The Adoration of the Shepherds*, Mateusz Kossior, 1572

153 Cracow, State Art Collections in Wawel Castle. Arras with a landscape with animals, from the Sigismund Series, Brussels atelier, third quarter of the 16th century, after Willem Tons's cartoon

154 Cracow, State Art Collections in Wawel Castle. Helmet of the armour once in the possession of Mikołaj Radziwiłł the Black, Polish production, 1561

155 Cracow, City of Cracow Historical Museum. "Hen" of the Archers' Company in Cracow, a Cracow product, c. 1565

156 Cracow, Cathedral on Wawel Hill. Relief on Sigismund Augustus's tin coffin, *Allegory of Touch*, Gdańsk atelier 1572

157 Pieskowa Skała, castle courtyard. Arcaded courtyard from the close of the 16th century

158, 159 Książ Wielki, palace, Santi Gucci, 1585—1895; 158. Main building and chapel; 159. Chapel

160, 161 Cracow, chapter-house at No 21 Kanonicza Street, with Santi Gucci's participation, 1581—1592; 160. Courtyard; 161. Portal of the main entrance

162—165 Baranów, castle, Santi Gucci and his atelier, 1591—1606; 162. View from the outside, attic from the second quarter of the 17th century; 163. Courtyard; 164. Portal in the gallery of the first floor; 165. Section of the gallery

166 Gołuchów, castle, c. 1560 and first years of the 17th century, conversion 1872—1885. Courtyard and original gallery of the first floor, the first years of the 17th century — in the wing seen opposite

167 Chroberz near Busko, lavabo in the parish church, third quarter of the 16th century

168 Poddębice near Łęczyca, palace, 1610—1617

169, 170 Krasiczyn, castle, 1597—1618, initially with the architect Geleazzo Appiano's participation; 169. Courtyard; 170. The Papal and, nearby, the Royal Towers

171, 172 Cracow, tomb of Sigismund Augustus in the Sigismund Chapel, Santi Gucci, 1574—1575; 171. King's figure; 172. His bust

173, 174 Cracow, tomb of Anna Jagiellonka in the Sigismund Chapel, Santi Gucci, 1574—1575; 173. Tomb as a whole; 174. Detail of the figure

175—177 Drobin near Płock, tomb of Wojciech Kryski's and his parents' in the parish church, Cracow atelier, 1572—1578; 175. Tomb as a whole; 176. The Mother's figure; 177. Wojciech's figure

178, 179 Janowiec near Kazimierz Dolny, tomb of Andrzej and Barbara Firlej in the parish church, Santi Gucci, 1586—1587; 178. Tomb as a whole; 179. Detail of Andrzej's figure

180—183 Cracow, tomb of Stephen Báthory in the Cathedral on Wawel Hill, Santi Gucci, 1594—1595; 180. Tomb as a whole; 181. King's head; 182. Tombstone with the King's figure; 183. Heraldic cartouche on the socle

184 Cracow, tomb of Prospero Provana in the Domican church, Cracow atelier, fourth quarter of the 16th c.

aged during the Second World War, reconstruction 1947—1948

248, 249 Cracow, window cage wrought in iron in the Collegium Maius, 16th century; 248. Window cage; 249. Detail of the crowning

250 Cracow, State Art Collections in Wawel Castle. Polish helmet, second half of the 16th century

251 Włocławek, grille of the Suffragan Chapel in the Cathedral, second half of the 16th century

252 Cracow, State Art Collections in Wawel Castle. Portrait of Anna Jagiellonka, Marcin Kober, 1586—1596

Colour Illustrations

PL. I Cracow, Jagiellonian Library. *The Bell Foundry,* a miniature from the *Codex of Baltazar Behem,* Cracow atelier, before 1505, p. 9

PL. II Cracow, National Museum, Czartoryski Section. *Building a Church,* a miniature from *Pontifical of Erazm Ciolek,* Cracow atelier, c. 1510, p. 19

PL. III Warsaw, National Library. *St Stanislaus,* a miniature from the codex *The Lives of the Gniezno Archbishops,* Stanisław Samostrzelnik, c. 1530, p. 29

PL. IV Grębień near Wieluń, an affiliated church. A court musician, detail of the polychrome on the ceiling of the nave, c. 1520—1530, p. 39

PL. V Cracow, State Art Collections in Wawel Castle. Arras with the coat of arms of Poland and Lithuania, from the Sigismund Series, Brussels atelier, third quarter of the 16th century, p. 133

PL. VI Cracow. State Art Collections in Wawel Castle. Detail from "The Building of the Tower of Babel", arras from the Sigismund Series, Brussels atelier, after Michiel Coxcie's cartoon, third quarter of the 16th century, p. 143

PL. VII Cracow, Monastery of the Missionaries, Stephen Báthory's portrait, Marcin Kober, 1583, p. 205

PL. VIII Warsaw, National Museum, Branch in Wilanów. Portrait of Katarzyna Ostrogska, painter active in Poland about 1597, p. 215

At the back of the plates are details of Polish Renaissance prints

Selected Literature

General Studies

S. KOMORNICKI, *Kultura artystyczna w Polsce czasów Odrodzenia* [Artistic Culture in Poland in the Times of Renaissance], in: *Kultura staropolska*, Kraków 1932, pp. 533—605.
Historia sztuki polskiej [History of Polish Art], vol. 2 Kraków 1962, Part 5, pp. 5—240 (authors: A. Bochniak, C. Ciołek, T. Dobrowolski, T. Mańkowski, S. Sawicka, J. Szablowski, T. Tołwiński).
S. LORENTZ, *Odrodzenie w Polsce* [Renaissance in Poland], Warszawa 1954.
Studia renesansowe [Studies in Renaissance], edited by M. Walicki, vol. 1, Wrocław 1956; vol. 2, Wrocław 1957; vol. 3 Wrocław 1963; vol. 4, Wrocław 1964.
Odrodzenie w Polsce. Historia sztuki [Renaissance in Poland. History of Art], *Odrodzenie w Polsce* [Renaissance in Poland]. Materials from the session of the Polish Academy of Sciences, 29—30 October, 1953, Polish Academy of Sciences, vol. 5, Warszawa 1958, pp. 131—381.
S. KOZAKIEWICZ, *Początek działalności Komasków, Tessyńczyków i Gryzończyków w Polsce. Okres renesansu (1520—1580)*, [Beginning of Activities of the Comoans, Ticinians and Grisonsians in Poland. The Period of Renaissance (1520—1580)], "Biuletyn Historii Sztuki," vol. 21, 1959, pp. 3—29.
J. BIAŁOSTOCKI, *Pojęcie manieryzmu i sztuka polska* [The Concept of Manierism and Polish Art], in: *Pięć wieków myśli o sztuce*, Warszawa 1959, pp. 192—214.
M. GĘBAROWICZ, *Studia nad dziejami kultury artystycznej późnego renesansu w Polsce* [Studies on the History of Artistic Culture in the Late Renaissance in Poland], Toruń 1962.
T. DOBROWOLSKI, *Sztuka Krakowa* [Cracow Art], 4th edition, Kraków 1971, pp. 209—343.
Pomniki Krakowa Maksymiliana i Stanisława Cerchów [Monuments of Cracow by Maksymilian and Stanisław Cerche], with text by Dr F. Kopera, vol. 2, Kraków-Warszawa 1904.
H. KOZAKIEWICZOWA, *Relazioni artistiche tra Roma e Cracovia nella prima metà del'500*, Wrocław 1972.
Dziesięć wieków Poznania. III. Sztuki plastyczne [Ten Centuries of Poznań. III. Plastic Art], Poznań 1956, pp. 28—38, 94—100, 134—137, 159—164, 196—205, 213—217, 224—226, (authors: A. Dobrzycka, J. Eckhard, P. Michałowski, J. Orańska, T. Ruszczyńska, A. Sławska).
Studia nad renesansem w Wielkopolsce [Studies on Renaissance in Great Poland], edited by T. Rudkowski, Poznań 1970.
W. KALINOWSKI, *Miasta polskie w XVI i pierwszej połowie XVII wieku* [Polish Towns in the 16th and the First Half of the 17th Centuries], "Kwartalnik Architektury i Urbanistyki," vol. 8, 1963, pp.167—225.
A. MIŁOBĘDZKI, *Zarys dziejów architektury w Polsce* [An Outline of the History of Architecture in Poland], 2nd edition, Warszawa 1968, pp. 119—168.
Z. DMOCHOWSKI, *Dzieła architektury w Polsce* [Works of Architecture in Poland], Londyn 1956, pp. 169—244.
W. HUSARSKI, *Attyka polska i jej wpływ na kraje sąsiednie* [Polish Attic and Its Influence on the Neighbouring Countries], Warszawa 1936.
S. KOMORNICKI, *Dwory murowane w Małopolsce z czasów Odrodzenia* [Brick Manor Houses in Little Poland from the Period of Renaissance], "Prace Komisji Historii Sztuki," vol. 5, pp. 62—116.
J.Z. ŁOZIŃSKI, *Grobowe kaplice kopułowe w Polsce, 1520—1620* [Sepulchral Dome Chapels in Poland, 1520—1620], Warszawa 1973.
M. ZLAT, *Brzeg* [Brzeg], Wrocław 1960.
B. GUERQUIN, *Zamki śląskie* [Silesian Castles], Warszawa 1957, pp. 27—30 and passim.
H. and S. KOZAKIEWICZOWIE, *Polskie nagrobki renesansowe. Stan, problemy i postulaty badań* [Polish Renaissance Tombstones. State, Problems and Research Propositions], "Biuletyn Historii Sztuki", vol. 14, 1952, pp. 62—132; *ibid.*, vol. 15, 1953, pp. 3—57.
J. KŁĘBOWSKI, *Renesansowa rzeźba na Śląsku, 1500—1560* [Renaissance Sculpture in Silesia, 1500—1560], Poznań 1967.
H. KOZAKIEWICZOWA, *Renesansowe nagrobki piętrowe w Polsce* [Renaissance Storeyed Tombstones in Poland], "Biuletyn Historii Sztuki," vol. 17, 1955, pp. 3—47.
M. KOŁAKOWSKA, *Renesansowe nagrobki dziecięce w Polsce XVI i pierwszej połowy XVII wieku* [Renaissance Children Tombstones in Poland in the 16th and the First Half of the 17th Century], in: *Studia renesansowe, op. cit.*, vol. 1, pp. 231—256.
J. DUTKIEWICZ, *Grobowce rodziny Tarnowskich w kościele katedralnym w Tarnowie* [The Tarnowski Family Vault in the Cathedral Church in Tarnów], Tarnów 1932.
M. WALICKI, *Malarstwo polskie. Gotyk-renesans-wczesny manieryzm* [Polish Painting. Gothic-Renaissance-Early Mannerism], Warszawa 1961, pp. 31—51, 322—346 and Pl. pp. 128—220.

B. Wolff-Łozińska, *Malowidła stropów polskich I połowy XVI w. Dekoracje roślinne i kasetonowe* [Polish Ceiling Painting of the First Half of the 16th Century. Plant and Coffer Decorations], Warszawa 1971.

T. Dobrowolski, *Polskie malarstwo portretowe. Ze studiów nad sztuką epoki sarmatyzmu* [Polish Portrait Painting. Studies on the Art of the Old-Polish Epoch], Kraków 1948, Part 1, passim; Part II, pp. 57 ff.

Detailed Studies.

Beginnings and Early Development of the Renaissance in Poland

Katalog zabytków w Polsce, t. IV. *Miasto Kraków*, cz.I: *Wawel* [Catalogue of Monuments in Poland, vol. 4: City of Cracow, Part I: Wawel], collective work edited by J. Szablowski, Warszawa 1965.

S. Komornicki, *Franciszek Florentczyk i pałac wawelski* [Francis the Florentine and Wawel Castle], "Przegląd Historii Sztuki," vol. 1, 1929, pp. 57—69.

T. Dobrowolski, *Zamek na Wawelu, dzieło architektury polskiej* [Castle on Wawel Hill, Work of Polish Architecture], in: *Studia renesansowe, op. cit.,* vol. 1, pp. 140—185.

T. Mańkowski, *Dzieje wnętrz wawelskich* [History of the Wawel Interiors], 2nd edition, Warszawa 1957.

A. Misiąg-Bocheńska, *Głowy wawelskie* [Wawel Heads], Warszawa 1953.

K. Sinko-Popielowa, *Hans Dürer i Cebes wawelski* [Hans Dürer and Wawel Cebes], "Biuletyn Historii Sztuki i Kultury," vol. 5, 1937, pp. 141—163.

H. Kozakiewiczowa, *Z badań nad Bartłomiejem Berreccim* [Studies on Bartolomeo Berrecci], "Biuletyn Historii Sztuki," vol. 23, 1961, pp. 311—327.

S. Komornicki, *Kaplica Zygmuntowska w Katedrze na Wawelu,* 1517—1533 [Sigismund Chapel in the Wawel Cathedral], "Rocznik Krakowski," vol. 23, 1932, pp. 47—120.

A. Bochniak, *Kaplica Zygmuntowska* [Sigismund Chapel], Warszawa 1960.

L. Kalinowski, *Treści artystyczne i ideowe Kaplicy Zygmuntowskiej* [Artistic and Ideological Contents in the Sigismund Chapel], in: *Studia do dziejów Wawelu,* vol. 2, 1960, pp. 1—129.

S. Lorentz, *Nagrobek Zygmunta I w mauzoleum wawelskim* [Tombstone of Sigismund I in the Wawel Mausoleum], "Biuletyn Historii Sztuki," vol. 15, 1953, No. 3/4, pp. 25—33.

H. Kozakiewiczowa, *Mecenat Jana Łaskiego. Z zagadnień sztuki renesansowej w Polsce* [Jan Łaski's Patronage. Problems of Renaissance Art in Poland], "Biuletyn Historii Sztuki,", vol. 23, 1961, pp. 3—17.

H. Kozakiewiczowa, *Spółka architektoniczno-rzeźbiarska Bernardina De Gianotis i Jana Cini* [Architectural and Sculptural Cooperation of Bernardino De Gianotis and Giovanni Cini], "Biuletyn Historii Sztuki," vol. 21, 1959, pp. 151—174.

T. Dobrzeniecki, *Tryptyk z Pławna* [Triptych from Pławno], Warszawa 1954.

W. Tomkiewicz, *"Lament Opatowski" (Próba interpretacji treści)* [Opatów "Lament." An Attempt at the Content Interpretation], "Biuletyn Historii Sztuki," vol. 22, 1960, pp. 351—364.

Z. Ameisenowa, *Kodeks Baltazara Behema* [Codex of Baltazar Behem], Warszawa 1961.

S. Herbst, M. Walicki, *Obraz bitwy pod Orszą. Dokument Historii sztuki i wojskowości XVI w.* [Painting of the Battle of Orsha. Document of the History of Art and the Army of the 16th Century], "Rozprawy Komisji Historii Kultury i Sztuki Tow. Naukowego Warszawskiego, " vol. 1, 1949, pp. 33—68.

B. Przybyszewski, *Stanisław Samostrzelnik* [Stanisław Samostrzelnik], "Biuletyn Historii Sztuki," vol. 13, 1951, No. 2/3, pp. 47—87.

A. Bochniak, *Mecenat Zygmunta Starego w zakresie rzemiosła artystycznego* [Sigismund the Old's Patronage of the Artistic Crafts], in: *Studia do dziejów Wawelu,* vol. 2, 1960, pp. 131—301.

Consolidation and Self-Assertion of the Renaissance Style

S. Świszczowski, *Sukiennice na rynku krakowskim w epoce gotyku i renesansu* [The Cloth Hall in the Cracow Market Place in the Epoch of Gothic and Renaissance], "Biuletyn Historii Sztuki i Kultury," vol. 10, 1948, No. 3/4, pp. 285—309.

J. Kowalczyk, *Fasada ratusza poznańskiego. Recepcja form z traktatu Serlia i artystyczny program* [Façade of the Poznań Town Hall. Reception of Forms from Serlio's Treatise and Artistic Programme], "Rocznik Historii Sztuki," vol. 8, 1970, pp. 141—176.

E. Gąsiorowski, *Rynek i ratusz chełmiński* [The Market Place and Town Hall in Chełmno], "Kwartalnik Architektury i Urbanistyki," vol. 10, 1965, pp. 3—29.

J.Z. Łoziński, *Renesansowy dwór obronny w Pabianicach i jego budowniczy Wawrzyniec Lorek* [The Renaissance Defensive Manor in Pabianice and its Builder Wawrzyniec Lorek], "Biuletyn Historii Sztuki," vol. 17, 1955, pp. 99—125.

J. Chyczewski, *Kolegiata pułtuska na tle kościelnego budownictwa mazowieckiego XV i XVI wieku* [The Collegiate Church in Pułtusk as against the Mazovian Church Building of the 15th and 16th Centuries], Warszawa 1936.

M. Zlat, *Brama zamkowa w Brzegu* [Gatehouse in Brzeg], "Biuletyn Historii Sztuki," vol. 24, 1962, pp. 284—322.

K. Sinko, *Hieronim Canavesi* [Hieronymus Canavesi], "Rocznik Krakowski," vol. 27, 1936, pp. 129—176.

J. Pagaczewski, *Jan Michałowicz z Urzędowa* [Jan Michałowicz of Urzędów], "Rocznik Krakowski," vol. 28, 1937, pp. 1—84.

E. Kozłowska-Tomczyk, *Jan Michałowicz z Urzędowa* [Jan Michałowicz of Urzędów], Warszawa 1967.

J. Przeworska, M. Walicki, *Strop z XVI w. kościoła w Boguszycach* [The 16th-Century Ceiling in the Church at Boguszyce], "Studia do dziejów sztuki w Polsce," vol. 1. 1929, pp. 105—115.

M. Gębarowicz, T. Mańkowski, *Arrasy Zygmunta Augusta* [Arrasses of Sigismund Augustus], "Rocznik Krakowski," vol. 29, 1937, pp. 1—220.

Heyday and Decline of the Late Style

J. Szablowski, *Ze studiów nad związkami artystycznymi polsko-czeskimi w epoce renesansu i nad renesansem zachodnio-słowiańskim* [Studies on Polish-Bohemian Artistic Connections in the Period of Renaissance and on the West-Slavonic Renaissance], "Prace Komisji Historii Sztuki," vol. 9. 1948, pp 27—64.

A. Fischinger, *Santi Gucci, architekt i rzeźbiarz królewski XVI wieku* [Santi Gucci—King's Architect and Sculptor], Kraków 1969.

M. Zlat, *Zamek w Krasiczynie* [Castle in Krasiczyn], in: *Studia renesansowe, op. cit.,* vol. 3, pp. 5—149.

S. Herbst, *Zamość* [Zamość], Warszawa 1954.

J.A. Miłobędzki, *Ze studiów nad urbanistyką Zamościa* [Studies on the Town–Planning of Zamość], "Biuletyn Historii Sztuki," vol. 15, 1953, pp. 68—87.

W. Husarski, *Kazimierz Dolny* [Kazimierz Dolny], Warszawa 1953.

W. Tatarkiewicz, *Typ lubelski i typ kaliski w architekturze kościelnej XVII wieku* [Lublin Type and Kalisz Type in the Church Architecture of the 17th Century], "Prace Komisji Historii Sztuki," vol. 7. 1939—38, pp. 23—60.

J. Kowalczyk, *Kolegiata w Zamościu* [Collegiate Church in Zamość] Warszawa 1968.

J. Kowalczyk, *Kościół pobernardyński w Lublinie i jego stanowisko w renesansowej architekturze Lubelszczyzny* [Former Bernardine Church in Lublin and Its Position in the Renaissance Architecture in the Lublin Region], "Kwartalnik Architektury i Urbanistyki, " vol. 2, 1957, pp. 137—145.

H. Kozakiewiczowa, *Nagrobki Kryskich w Drobinie k. Płocka* [Tombstones of the Kryskis' at Drobin near Płock], "Biuletyn Historii Sztuki", vol. 28, 1956, pp. 3—23.

L. Krzyżanowski, *Plastyka nagrobna Wilhelma van den Blocke* [Willem van den Blocke's Sepulchral Art], "Biuletyn Historii Sztuki," vol. 20, 1958, pp. 270—298.

M. Walicki, W. Tomkiewicz, A. Ryszkiewicz, *Malarstwo polskie. Manieryzm—barok* [Polish Painting. Mannerism—Baroque], Warszawa 1971, passim.

Index of Places and Antiquities

Index of Artists

Phothographs by:

Zbigniew Kamykowski 1—3, 13, 14, 16, 17, 20, 22, 23,
26, 28, 30—42, 45—70, 73—100, 105, 125—156, 167,
171—195, 202, 204—206, 224, 230, 246, 248—252;
Renaissance prints on p. 10, 20, 30, 40, 134, 144, 206, 216
colour plates I—VIII and jacket;
Edmund Kupiecki 4—12, 15, 18, 19, 21, 24, 25, 27,
29, 43, 44, 71, 72, 101—104, 106—124, 157—166, 168—170,
196—199, 207—212, 214—223, 225—229, 231—245, 247;
Mirosław Raczkowski 201; Jerzy Szandomirski 213;
Witalis Wolny 200, 203.

Figures drawn by Zbigniew Dolatowski

Editor of Polish version: Stefan Hołówko
Editor of English version: Izabela Rodzik
Layout editor: Andrzej Matysiak

Arkady Publishers, Warsaw 1976. First edition
796/R.S. Price zł 420.—